DATE DUE		
NOV 1 8 1997		
DEC 2 3 1997		

LACHLAN McINTOSH
and the Politics of Revolutionary Georgia

Courtesy of the Independence National Historical Park Collection

LACHLAN McINTOSH
and the Politics
of Revolutionary Georgia

HARVEY H. JACKSON

THE UNIVERSITY OF GEORGIA PRESS
Athens

Copyright © 1979 by the University of Georgia Press
Athens 30602

Set in 10 on 12 point Mergenthaler Janson type
Printed in the United States of America

Library of Congress Cataloging in Publication Data

Jackson, Harvey H
   Lachlan McIntosh and the politics of Revolutionary Georgia.
   Bibliography
   Includes index.
      1. McIntosh, Lachlan. 1725–1806.   2. General—United
   States—Biography.   3. Politicians—Georgia—Biography.
   4. Georgia—Politics and government—1775–1865.   5. Uni-
   ted States—History—Revolution, 1775–1783—Campaigns
   and battles.   I. Title.

E207.M13J32   975.8′03′0924 [B]   78–8995
                  ISBN 0–8203–0459–X

TO MARCIA AND KELLY

Contents

Preface

I have spent my whole Life ever paying the highest Respect to the
Good Man and despising those who Sacrifice the good of the community for their own private interested Views & if this is a Crime I
confess myself Guilty.

Lachlan McIntosh to John Wereat, January 8, 1780

In 1735 the Georgia Trustees acknowledged the growing tension
between England and Spain by sending agents to the north of
Scotland and recruiting some 170 Highlanders to guard the colony's
Florida frontier. Well known for their Jacobite sympathies, these
experienced soldiers, their clan system disintegrating under English
pressure, willingly agreed to serve Oglethorpe and the Trust as they
had served their Highland "lairds." [1] Led by Captain John McIntosh
Mohr, the expedition set out for the northern bank of the Altamaha
River; there they built their town and named it Darien. [2]

Lachlan McIntosh, second son of the captain, was only eight years
old when he and his family crossed the Atlantic. [3] From that time
until his death in 1806 he was party to, or witnessed, most of the
events that transformed Georgia and her sister colonies into independent states, and those states into a nation. The important body
of records he left, though widely scattered, has long been a rich
trove for historians, yet while these collections, and many others
containing material relating to him, have established McIntosh's
significance, no effort has heretofore been made to bring them all
together, to reveal the man and, through him, the era. What follows
is an attempt to do just that.

Although it is unfortunate that few of McIntosh's personal family
letters remain (which makes it difficult to present the intimate
analysis usually associated with a biography), more than enough
material survives to allow an assessment of his character and to show
how it affected his development as a planter, politician, and military
leader. More importantly, however, these papers shed considerable

light on the inter-Whig struggle for power that shaped the coming and conduct of the Revolution in Georgia, and on the political realignment that marked the state's efforts to deal with changes wrought by the war. When seen in this context, the career of Lachlan McIntosh, a central figure in the conflict to determine "who would rule at home," offers new, important insights into the genesis of Georgia and, to a somewhat lesser degree, the United States. His is a story that needs to be told.

Words are inadequate to express my gratitude to the many who aided in this study. To Professor G. Melvin Herndon, who introduced me to Lachlan McIntosh, guided the project through its initial stages, and continued as a source of advice and inspiration, I owe a particular debt. Professors Kenneth Coleman, Phinizy Spalding, and Edward Cashin have also encouraged my efforts, as have Edwin Bridges and George Lamplugh. To these scholars and friends I offer my sincere thanks. Mrs. Lilla M. Hawes of the Georgia Historical Society, whose knowledge of the McIntoshes is encyclopedic, has been most gracious and helpful, as have Mrs. John D. Lane, Miss Bessie M. Lewis, and Mr. Edward G. Williams. I gratefully acknowledge my debt to them, and to the National Society of the Colonial Dames of America in the State of Georgia for the generous award which enabled me to spend an uninterrupted summer in research.

Because material relating to McIntosh is so scattered, the services of the staffs of those libraries and institutions mentioned in the bibliography were essential. The courtesies extended by these often anonymous individuals made my task far easier. Among them, however, are some whose efforts on my behalf deserve special thanks: Mr. Marion R. Hemperley and Mrs. Pat Bryant of the Georgia Surveyor-General Department, Miss Ann Pederson of the Georgia Department of Archives and History, Dr. David R. Chesnutt of the Henry Laurens Papers, and Mrs. Gwen Bell of the Clayton Junior College Library. I must also acknowledge the contribution made by the late Dr. Len Cleveland of the Georgia Archives. In every way he exemplified the best in our profession, and he is sorely missed.

I further thank Mr. Malcolm M. MacDonald of the University of Georgia Press, whose encouragement has been essential to the completion of this project, and Professors Harold Davis and W. W. Abbot, whose insightful criticisms and suggestions were most helpful.

To Carolyn Howell and Deborah Jolley, who typed most of the manuscript, goes my appreciation for their willingness to work long and often odd hours on my behalf, and to the members of the Social Science Division of Clayton Junior College my thanks for listening, often patiently, to what must have seemed like endless McIntosh stories.

Finally, I wish to thank my parents, Harvey and Elizabeth Jackson, for early exposing me to history; my in-laws, Bernie and Bobbie Flood, for their enthusiasm; and my daughter, Kelly, for keeping this whole thing in perspective. But my deepest thanks are reserved for my wife, Marcia, who typed, read, suggested, criticized, and comforted. Without her, nothing could have been done.

CHAPTER ONE
The Altamaha Frontier

That Captain McIntosh has the chief command over them . . . That
they first cultivated their lands and then built their houses, which it
were to be wish'd the people of Savannah had done.

Journal of the Earl of Egmont, December 11, 1736

After nearly three months on the winter Atlantic, the rubber-legged
cargo of the *Prince of Wales* lurched ashore, crossed the muddy road
that paralleled the river, then struggled up the steep bluff that
commanded the gateway to Georgia. At the top, Savannah waited in
weatherbeaten splendor, full of the promise of permanence but
hardly its realization. Sandy streets delineated Oglethorpe's dream,
but half the lots lay vacant and weeds grew in the squares. Surrounded on three sides by dense forest that was ready to reclaim the
bluff if Savannahians dared lay down their axes, the town revealed
what nearly three years of toil in America might produce. It was not
an encouraging sight.

But the Scots, with admirable if unrealistic confidence, ignored
the example set by Savannah, turned their attention to the task
before them, and within a month were ready for the final phase of
their journey. Then, loading into *piraguas*, they rode the cold February winds down the coast and in less than a week entered the
Altamaha's brackish mouth. Through low marshy islands that divided the broad river into narrow channels the small flotilla sailed,
until it landed at the foot of the first high ground. There, within sight
of the ruins of England's previous attempt to guard her empire's
southern flank, the immigrants chose to make their stand.

Rumors that a Spanish garrison already occupied the area fortunately proved untrue, for while Captain McIntosh's men were
confident that they could "beat them out of their Fort & have Houses
ready built to live in," the Scots' rather fearsome image was decep-
tive. Though initially they presented "a most manly appearance

with their Plads, broad Swords, Targets, & Fire Arms," close inspection would have revealed weapons of poor quality and doubtful effectiveness.[1] There was no doubting the Scots' courage, but if their landing had been opposed, courage alone might not have been sufficient. Still, with the military efficiency for which they were chosen, they secured the site and, as the sun sank red across swamps and pine barrens, built their fires and planned their future.

A cold mist still hung close to the river when they awoke, and had hardly dissipated when work began. As days stretched into weeks, the palmetto brush and scrub pine fell before axes, swords, and fire, and by month's end Darien was taking shape. Soon, nestled among the giant moss-hung oaks that had survived the Scots' assault, there was "a battery of 4 pieces of Cannon . . . a Guard house, a Store house, a Chappel & several Hutts for particular People," among them was the widow of a comrade who had not survived the rigorous journey.[2]

Houses for the rest were postponed until more land was cleared and crops were planted, a sacrifice that was rewarded when the first harvest produced enough corn to meet local needs, plus a surplus to sell. Initial reports to the Trustees painted a glowing picture of the "extraordinary industrious" people of Darien, but one good corn crop did not make a self-sufficient settlement. Meat still had to be supplied from Savannah and other ports north, and during that first year the provisions were often late. The result was many anxious and hungry days, but through the efforts of Captain McIntosh and the cooperation of the people, the settlement survived.[3]

Young muscles and minds toughened on the frontier, clan loyalties became community loyalties, and family ties, especially among the McIntosh children, grew stronger. It was a time for observing, learning, and doing; a time for exploring the limits of individuality, secure in the knowledge that if a crisis arose, many were willing to help. And at the center was John McIntosh Mohr, teaching his children the advantages and responsibilities of leading, setting examples with care, for in Darien, as in Scotland, sons were expected to assume the duties of their father. It was not a matter to be taken lightly, and the McIntosh children learned their lessons well.

The formative years for Darien were also the formative years for

Lachlan McIntosh. Shaped by the same forces as the community, his early life is all but indistinguishable as a separate entity. Like his friends and relatives, his existence was a blend of Highland traditions and frontier practicality, from which evolved, though not immediately, ideas and institutions similar to those evolving in other colonies. Yet the frontier, which gave so much, also took its toll, and in time the McIntoshes felt its harsh, indiscriminate hand. The sluggish, black water of the Altamaha was a major source of recreation for the colonists, especially the children. They fished its canebrakes, swam along its weed-hung banks, and came to know it as a friend. Then the friend turned against them. In the summer of 1737, while swimming with his brothers, Lewis, the youngest McIntosh, was attacked by an alligator, dragged away, and killed.[4] The shock of his death bound the surviving children together in a union which, in time, came to transcend all other loyalties. As they grew older, it became increasingly evident that, in all matters, "family" considerations took precedence.

During those early years Darien fought to survive, and its success was due in no small part to John McIntosh. In 1739 he supported the beleaguered Trustees in their efforts to keep slavery out of Georgia, and in return Oglethorpe advanced the community £200 to enable it to raise cattle, which were sold to a regiment recently stationed at Fort Frederica on nearby St. Simon's Island. This new economic venture, which had been more the captain's concern than the inhumanity of slavery, relieved the Scots of dependence on the nearly exhausted soil and gave Darien a new lease on life. The Trustees also authorized that a store be set up in the town to dispense supplies and serve as a factor for goods produced locally. As one might expect, John McIntosh was placed in charge.[5]

Toward the end of its fourth year, Darien was still a military-oriented settlement. The fort, which now boasted ten cannon, dominated the bluff, while the Scots contented themselves with "Tight and Warm" huts built on small town lots close to the stockade. Some nearby fields were cultivated, lumber was sawed, and the income from the sale of cattle gave the community an air of frontier prosperity. Captain McIntosh, his reputation enhanced by the economic security he helped to bring, used his position and his knowledge of English and the Highland dialects to become Oglethorpe's spokesman to the Scots.[6] It seemed the McIntosh family had the situation well in hand.

Security on the frontier, however, was the exception rather than the rule, and in the fall of 1739, when the men of Darien finally were called to serve the function for which they were sent to Georgia, the McIntoshes learned just how tenuous their existence had been. Anglo–Spanish relations had deteriorated to the point where negotiations were useless, and that year, with Mr. Jenkins's severed ear as an excuse, war was declared. Oglethorpe, elated at the decision, quickly organized an expedition against the Spanish stronghold at St. Augustine and placed Captain McIntosh's Scots in the front ranks. The invasion was a fiasco. In the only direct engagement, the Highlanders were caught in an exposed position and over half were killed. John McIntosh and some ten of his men were taken prisoner and lodged in a Spanish jail.[7]

The disaster at Fort Mosa had a crushing effect on the people of Darien. Losses were so heavy that the entire community was disrupted and the few families which remained intact lacked the resources to see after their less fortunate neighbors. The captain's family was among the destitute. William, the eldest, who fought at Mosa but escaped, stayed with Oglethorpe and later served with distinction at the battle of Bloody Marsh. Lachlan, then thirteen, and his younger sister Anne were sent to Bethesda orphanage, outside Savannah, while the other children remained with their mother, who decided to leave Darien and seek refuge at Fort Palachacola on the Savannah River. There, with aid from William Stephens, the Trustees' secretary, they were protected and sustained. Mrs. McIntosh stayed at the fort for nearly two years, and when the Spanish threat in the south had eased, returned to Darien to await her husband's release.[8]

While his mother was at Palachacola, Lachlan McIntosh remained at Bethesda, where his limited education received some improvement, though his spiritual needs seemed more the concern of his instructors. He left the orphanage when his mother returned home, but rather than join her and give the impoverished family one more mouth to feed, he enlisted in the regiment at Frederica.[9] The war was almost over, however, and his duties on St. Simon's were probably limited to herding cattle and standing guard. This was to be his only formal military experience prior to the Revolution, but it hardly mattered, for the sons of Captain John McIntosh Mohr knew well what it took to be a soldier.

Sometime between 1744 and 1748 John McIntosh was released and the family reunited. But the captain's imprisonment had taken its toll. During his absence his authority had been assumed by others, and though he later served as a justice of the peace, and held lesser offices in what after 1758 became St. Andrew's Parish, he never regained his former status.[10] Even his duties as family leader soon devolved on his sons, as the ill and aging captain began to spend most of his energy on his farming operations. It was a far cry from his life as a military chieftain.

During the next four years Lachlan McIntosh remained with his family at Darien. Little is known of his activities, but it may be assumed that most of his time was spent working on the family farm or perhaps in the store. On December 27, 1748, he took his first step toward economic independence. That day the Georgia President and his Assistants received his petition for a grant of 500 acres on the Newport River, opposite St. Catherine's Island. The Board, expressing satisfaction with "the Capacity and Industry of the Family in general," granted the request.[11] But he did not take up the grant at that time. After the Treaty of Aix-la-Chapelle in 1748, British wartime aid to Georgia ended. A recession resulted which caused such an exodus that it seemed the colony "became almost entirely depopulated." Twenty-one-year-old Lachlan McIntosh took his eleven-year-old brother George and joined other immigrants who went to Charleston.[12]

South Carolina's capital made a lasting impression on the young McIntoshes. The major trading center of the southern colonies, its businesslike bustle and crowded commercial district showed them just how provincial Georgia was. In addition, the charm and grace of Charleston society set a standard which few American cities were able to match. Its example was not lost on the young men from Darien. George was put in a grammar school and later apprenticed to an architect. Lachlan found employment in a counting house, and though he did not "make his fortune," he at least prospered and was soon able to supply his brother with £100 in Carolina currency as "pocket money" and buy a young Negro to assist him.[13] The brothers were close and the elder always felt protective toward his younger charge, a feeling which characterized their relationship the rest of their lives.

Nearly six feet tall, athletic, described by one friend as the "handsomest man he had ever seen," and possessing a ready wit that in later, more reserved years would be seen only by close associates, young Lachlan McIntosh began to make friends and slowly wind his way through the labyrinth of Charleston society. His efforts found an influential ally when, during his third year in the city, he met Henry Laurens. A rising member of the merchant elite and a man of considerable political promise, Laurens took a genuine liking to the Georgian, invited him into his home, and, though only three years McIntosh's senior, became a guiding force in his career.[14] It was a relationship which grew into a long business association, produced a political alliance, and, most importantly, gave Lachlan McIntosh one of the most loyal friendships he was to experience outside his family.

For nearly eight years Charleston was the center of McIntosh's life. He served Laurens well, made the most of the connections he developed, and generally seemed to impress those with whom he dealt. There was one, however, upon whom the impression was extraordinary. Sarah Threadcraft, who lived with her mother and stepfather, John and Esther Cuthbert, in Williamsburg, South Carolina, became the object of his attentions, and after a proper courtship they were married, on New Year's Day 1756.[15]

The marriage was to be a long and happy one, but relations with his new relatives were strained from the start. Prior to the marriage, he lent Cuthbert nearly £700 (an indication of the young Georgian's success) and when, shortly after the wedding, the note came due, his father-in-law bluntly refused to pay. Laurens and John Hordren, another Charlestonian, were called on to arbitrate and they awarded the money to McIntosh, but Cuthbert remained unmoved. As tempers flared, the creditor apparently realized that to force payment would place his wife's family in uncomfortable financial straits, and so, swearing never again to deal with "so troublesome a man," he dropped the case on the promise of a future settlement.[16]

No doubt his decision not to press the issue rose from a genuine sensitivity to the needs and feelings of others, but it was also the product of a desire to wrap up his business quickly and return to Darien. Since he had left his father's health had declined and family affairs demanded his attention. In addition, the Trustee experiment had ended and Georgia was rapidly becoming the land of opportunity for those with ability and resources to exploit the situation. By 1754 royalization was a reality, and with changes in government came economic changes which promised the aggressive and well-connected a prosperous future.

Royalization brought with it the "headright" system of granting land, under which the head of a household could petition the Governor and obtain 100 acres for himself and 50 acres for each member of his family. Slaves, whose presence had finally been legalized, were counted as family. If a man were judged able to cultivate them, he could buy up to 1,000 additional acres at one shilling for every 10 acres. Under these regulations a plantation economy was emerging in Georgia, and its staple crop was rice. Between 1754 and 1769 Georgia rice production increased from 3,000 barrels per year to 15,000. Export values grew in proportion and the colony began to experience an economic stability unknown during the Trustee era. It was during the first decade of royal rule that Georgia's planter "aristocracy" was born.[17]

Apart from land, two other ingredients were necessary for the making of a rice planter—labor and credit. It has been estimated that to cultivate 130 acres of riceland a planter needed about forty working slaves, which, with his other expenses, would increase his initial investment to nearly £2,500, capital or credit, just to begin operations. Under favorable circumstances, however, the investment could be paid off within a decade. After that the costs were low and the profits high. But in the mid-1750s, few Georgians had the capital to begin. South Carolina was the most obvious source of credit and slaves, and the man who was able to obtain them enjoyed a significant advantage over his competitors. With Laurens to aid him, Lachlan McIntosh found himself in that enviable position and quickly seized the advantage.[18]

By late 1756, McIntosh, his wife, and brother were back on the Altamaha. He used his and his family's influence to get George appointed commissary of supplies for Fort Frederica, then turned to his own affairs. The government allowed him to take up his earlier grant, adjacent to which his father and older brother, William, had also obtained land. It would not be the last time that the family's grants adjoined each other, and in the next decade the McIntosh holdings became a prominent feature of southern Georgia. Land was not the only addition. Shortly after the new year began, Sarah McIntosh gave birth to her first child, a healthy son. The boy was named John after his grandfather; an ancient name for a new and promising generation. Now a man with new family responsibilities, Lachlan McIntosh's activities took on an added sense of purpose.[19]

Soon the advantages gained from the years in South Carolina began to show. On February 3, 1758, McIntosh received headright grants totaling 500 acres for his wife, son, and the sixteen slaves he had acquired.[20] The land, ideal for rice planting, was on a swampy, muck-rich island in the Altamaha across from Darien, with easy access to the means for shipping the staple to market. In such a remote area of a province where slavery had been legal less than a decade, Lachlan McIntosh had put together the ingredients to make him a leader in the region's economic growth—good land and the labor to work it. His potential was quickly recognized in Savannah, and only four days after that grant was signed the Governor and his Council allowed him to purchase 500 additional acres on the same island.[21] Thus, in less than a week, Lachlan McIntosh, thirty years of age, obtained the land upon which was to rest his status as a member of Georgia's small but powerful planter elite.

Few planters were ever content with their holdings. Land was security, and though a man might not be able to cultivate what he had, he still wanted more. In this respect Lachlan McIntosh followed the norm. Rice quickly became his primary source of income, and as his plantation flourished he set about to expand and consolidate his holdings. Enlisting the aid of his brother William, the two exchanged their 1,000 acres on the Newport River for equal acreage on two nearby islands, Broughton and Doboy, belonging to Jonathan Bryan.[22] This gave Lachlan McIntosh access to nearly 2,000 acres of rich riceland, only a small part of which he could cultivate.

But it was not enough, and as the years passed McIntosh holdings increased. As the 1750s drew to a close, the family, with its interests interlocked to secure and protect social and economic status, was well on its way to becoming preeminent in the region. Yet, at the same time, the McIntoshes were so integral a part of the life of St. Andrew's Parish that those things which benefited the family tended to benefit the local majority as well.[23] Thus it was easy for the new generation to look to the successful McIntosh sons for guidance, just as the previous generation had looked to John McIntosh Mohr. And all the while, moving forward as the leader of the family, was Lachlan McIntosh.

CHAPTER TWO
The Family Dynasty

Certainly the want of Liberality & a generous freedom in dealing hath
restrained you from making a great deal of Money—and I wonder at
it the more, because in every thing else you discover superior sense &
understanding—Do for God's sake get the better of that foible.

Henry Laurens to Lachlan McIntosh, September 28, 1768

The McIntoshes were hardly alone in taking advantage of opportunities offered by royalization. Throughout the colony, aggressive
and talented men made similar advances, and what emerged, with
halting, fitful steps, was Georgia's colonial aristocracy. Freed from
the shackles of Trustee dreams, these individuals, at the outset little
more than middle-class merchants and farmers on the make, forged
alliances which moved to dominate the newly created Assembly and
through it to control the colony. Having chafed too long under the
Trustees' absentee rule, they were determined to master their own
future. Royalization was a blessing only if it allowed them this.

That attitude set the stage for executive–legislative clashes which
punctuated politics in colonial Georgia, but in most of these Lachlan
McIntosh was a spectator rather than a participant.[1] To him, politics
was a means to an end, and that end was economic security. His
years of poverty and dislocation had a marked effect and he was
determined that his family would never go hungry again. Aware that
governmental policies, local and provincial, influenced economic
growth, he saw the occasional need for active participation in politics, but controversy was not good for commerce. For that reason it
was only when issues threatened his valued security that he became
involved.

The strategy that was employed to secure and preserve economic
independence was soon obvious. One brother would stand for election to the Commons House of Assembly, where he could see after
family interests on the provincial level. Meanwhile the others would

hold local offices and manage family plantations. The problem, of course, was making the plan work, and the scope of their success is a clear indication of McIntosh power and prestige. Most of the burden of directing family financial affairs fell to Lachlan McIntosh, for with his connections in Charleston and among coastal merchants he seemed the natural choice to manage its diverse and growing interests. But in assuming these responsibilities he also, in effect, assumed the leadership of the family. Captain McIntosh, weak and infirm, was still titular head, but it was obvious to all that the real decisions were made by his second son.

Parish offices soon came their way. Some, such as tax assessor and collector, offered the advantages they sought, while others, such as commissioner for repairing forts, were simply part of the civic duties expected of community leaders.[2] By 1760 this attention to local responsibilities paid off when neighboring St. James Parish, where Lachlan McIntosh owned land, selected him to represent it in the Commons House. But though it was the right office, he was the wrong man. On October 13 McIntosh took his seat, but his interests clearly lay elsewhere. After only three days he asked for four weeks' leave to "go into the country upon extraordinary occasions." He never returned, and St. James sent another representative in his place to the next session.[3]

McIntosh's decision to give up his seat was indicative of an attitude he exhibited throughout his life. He was a man of strong views and action. Debate and compromise, essential tools of government, were arts he willingly left to others, so long as he remained free to pursue his interests. Also, there was another reason for his action: the rapid decline of his father's health. Never a well man after his years in prison, John McIntosh nonetheless refused to withdraw from family and community affairs. Though his sons relieved many of his burdens, he remained as active as his health would permit. Finally, the old captain lost the fight. In 1761 he died at his plantation on the Sapelo River.[4]

The same month that Lachlan McIntosh took his seat in the Commons House, Georgia received her last and most outstanding colonial Governor, James Wright. An experienced administrator and dedicated servant of the King, he gave the colony a stable government under which its people prospered. As long as local interests coincided with those of the crown, Wright was a popular leader; when the two interests were at odds, the Governor stood firm as the representative of royal authority. Nevertheless, colonial leaders in the Assembly generally favored Wright's programs and, by cooperating with him, were able to expand their role in policymaking—up to a point. But when the legislature tried to make good its claims to powers and privileges the Governor felt were not its due, Wright blocked the efforts, causing frustrations which seethed below the surface throughout his administration.[5]

The arrival of Wright had little immediate effect on Lachlan McIntosh. With his legislative career behind him, he returned to the duties of à St. Andrew's squire. His father's death placed even more family responsibilities on his shoulders. William, increasingly preoccupied with his own affairs, was not named an executor of his father's estate, and John had departed for Jamaica, where he became a successful planter-merchant and the family's link to West Indies markets.[6] This left the youngest brother, George, to aid Lachlan in managing the increasingly complex McIntosh affairs.

The source of this increasing complexity, as well as a principal reason for his elevation to family leadership, was McIntosh's relationship with Henry Laurens. By early 1763 the two had made joint investments in land, slaves, and commerce which served as the foundation for their informal yet active partnership. Laurens was the financial adviser, factor, and source of credit, in one instance advancing some £2,000 in merchandise to establish McIntosh as a merchant in Darien. The venture was never as successful as Laurens had hoped, but it added diversity and profit to the McIntosh operations. Thus aided, Lachlan McIntosh and his family became an economic force with which Georgians had to reckon.[7]

For his part, McIntosh was Laurens' link to opportunities on the Georgia frontier, and he served that purpose well. With the Peace of Paris of 1763, land south of the Altamaha was safe for settlement. This territory was claimed by both Georgia and South Carolina, however, and controversy erupted when Governor Thomas Boone of South Carolina announced that he would accept requests for grants in the area.[8] Laurens quickly seized the initiative, obtained a warrant of survey for 3,000 acres in the disputed territory, and sent his surveyor, Edmund Egan, to lay it off. His action was challenged by another South Carolinian, Colonel Thomas Middleton, who sought the same land and had sent his surveyor, John B. Girardeau, to claim it. It was a close race, until McIntosh intervened. He intercepted Girardeau, entertained him, and while the surveyor was recovering from the effects of too much McIntosh rum, Egan claimed the property for Laurens. Middleton protested, but in vain. The land went to his competitor and a new element was added to Darien's economic growth.[9]

After this initial acquisition Laurens tried to expand his south Georgia interests, and McIntosh was involved. The usually slow process of obtaining land was hastened somewhat by the fact that McIntosh was a competent surveyor and well versed in Georgia land laws. A number of transactions resulted, but none so important as when the South Carolinian purchased 900 acres that McIntosh owned on Broughton Island,[10] where Laurens developed a rice plantation. And though McIntosh never managed it for him, he kept a close check on its operation. With their plantations side by side, the interests of the two became ever more tightly linked.

McIntosh's activities during the years between the Great War for the Empire and the American Revolution were many and varied, but his plantations remained the focus of his attention. And like most planters, he had a nearly insatiable desire for land. Between 1763 and 1776, through royal grants and purchases, McIntosh amassed over 14,000 acres, primarily in St. Andrew's Parish adjacent to previous grants. But since his labor force seldom numbered over sixty slaves, he was never able to put more than a fraction of his land into cultivation. Thus some of the richest riceland on the Altamaha lay idle. Yet the land was not obtained with speculation in mind, for during that period he sold only one 150-acre block.[11] As quality riceland was scarce, the mere knowledge that he owned some of the best gave McIntosh at least part of the security he sought.

By the eve of the Revolution, McIntosh's acquisitions had taken a well-defined pattern. His most valuable property was on a series of islands in the Altamaha, close to Darien. His major planting operation (still known as General's Island) was directly across from the town. It was an ideal location, with sufficient water to flood the fields, rich soil, and easy access to transportation. In addition he operated a sawmill and produced lumber and shingles which were usually sold to Laurens and shipped to the West Indies. Like so many of his contemporaries, McIntosh expanded his interests to compensate for weaknesses in the single-crop plantation system, and so long as Laurens helped with the commercial aspects of their relationship, his ventures were generally profitable.[12] By 1776 he had combined his talents for exploiting land and labor with the mercantile expertise of Henry Laurens, to become one of the wealthiest planters in southern Georgia.

As one McIntosh prospered, so did the others—though to different degrees. William's property was over 7,000 acres by 1774, but much of it was scattered throughout the parishes adjacent to St. Andrew's.[13] He never established a plantation on the scale of his brothers', and of the three who remained in Georgia, he was the least active in local politics. On the other hand, the star of George McIntosh was on the rise. Though George was fourteen years William's junior, George's land holdings were more extensive and most were near Lachlan's in St. Andrew's. He also owned a work force of over forty slaves, something William lacked.[14] The similarity of economic interests reinforced the bonds between Lachlan and George, and though they always showed affection and respect for their older brother, it was clear that he was the lesser member of the three.

In 1764 the McIntoshes decided to make George their candidate for the Commons House, and with little apparent difficulty he took his seat as a delegate from St. Andrew's Parish. Selected with him was Robert Baillie, husband of the McIntoshes' only sister, Anne. This meant, for all practical purposes, that until the Assembly was dissolved, four years hence, the McIntosh family was the parish's link with the royal government. While George served in Savannah, Lachlan served contentedly at home, surveying roads, supervising the rebuilding of Fort Frederica, and holding the offices of tax collector and justice of the peace. The positions the three men held made it possible for the family coalition to dominate the affairs of the parish.[15]

During those years, others were appointed to public offices in the area, but they posed little threat to the hold the McIntoshes and their kinsmen exerted over Altamaha politics. Yet in one instance an appointment outside the family bore future significance for them. In February of 1768 the list of justices of the peace contained the two McIntoshes, Baillie, and a new name—that of a man whose career was to change the lives of Lachlan and his brother dramatically. It was the first time the name of Lachlan McIntosh was linked with that of Button Gwinnett; it would not be the last.[16]

In late 1768, after four years of unbroken power, the McIntosh coalition's domination of St. Andrew's politics was interrupted. In April the Assembly had been dissolved, and when the new Commons House convened in the fall, and George McIntosh and Robert Baillie appeared to take their accustomed seats, their election was challenged. Before the matter could be settled, Governor Wright dissolved the Assembly for violating his instructions by considering the Massachusetts circular letter's protest of the Townshend Acts. When new elections were held, neither McIntosh nor Baillie was returned.[17]

What caused the challenge is unknown. Perhaps Baillie, a Loyalist a decade later, had revealed enough of this ideological bent during earlier clashes between Governor and legislature, to turn the electorate against himself and his brother-in-law. Perhaps the general antiauthoritarian drift of the colonists had caused them to "turn the rascals out" simply because they had been in office long enough. Or perhaps the McIntosh coalition, unsure of itself, had attempted to manipulate the election in its favor and was caught. All must remain conjecture, however, for the records are silent. Nevertheless, it was the end of Baillie's career in the legislature and a major setback for his counterpart. But as was to be the case so often in years to come, Lachlan McIntosh came to his brother's aid.[18]

For two years the McIntoshes watched others dominate the St. Andrew's delegation, while they waited for the moment when they could reestablish their political arrangement. Meanwhile a controversy erupted over taxing the four parishes south of the Altamaha—an area within the McIntosh sphere of influence but not represented in the Commons House. Though these "lower" parishes had been taxed before, times and ideologies had changed, making arguments over "no taxation without representation" hard to ignore. For his part, Governor Wright was sympathetic, but felt he lacked the authority to extend representation without royal permission. Lachlan McIntosh watched events unfold with growing interest, until, late in 1770, a seat in St. Andrew's fell vacant; then he stood for the post and won. Despite George's political problems, it was clear that Lachlan's power and prestige were intact.[19]

Shortly after McIntosh's election the Commons House, with an independence that had been growing since the Stamp Act controversy, refused to pass a tax bill unless the Governor issued writs of election for the disputed parishes. Wright, who had written London for leave to do just that, refused to act until his instructions were changed. Far from happy with its inability to carry the day, the legislature continued to press the executive on other matters, determined to have him acknowledge its authority. But the Governor was in control and he knew it; thus when the House refused to retreat from positions he found objectionable, Wright dissolved the Assembly.[20]

To many the dissolution simply bore out what was already known, and resented: Georgia's legislature had far to go before it could match the accomplishments of assemblies to the north. But for the moment, McIntosh may have had other things on his mind. Once Wright received authority to issue the writs he acted, and when the votes were counted it was revealed that one of the four parishes, St. Mary's, had chosen George McIntosh to represent it.[21] Whether this was the McIntosh plan all along will never be known, though it should be noted that George did not own property in that parish until just before his brother took his seat in the Commons House. With the Governor and most of the colony supporting an extension of representation, it is not difficult to believe that when McIntosh saw his chance to help matters along he took it. George's election reestablished the family's link with the central government and Lachlan McIntosh never served in the Commons House again. Still, this venture into politics must have left a mark, for it would have been difficult to have served in that Assembly and not wonder what Georgians would have to do before they could govern themselves.[22]

Other events also were aiding the restoration of the McIntosh dynasty. Early in 1772 George married Ann Priscilla Houstoun, a member of one of the colony's most respected families.[23] This union, laced with political and economic overtones, greatly enhanced the McIntoshes' considerable prestige and placed them squarely among Georgia's social elite. Soon afterward, George, his reputation apparently restored, joined Sir Patrick Houstoun, his wife's brother, as St. Andrew's representative, and once again the McIntoshes and their relations dominated the parish's political life.[24] For the remaining years before the Revolution, George, Sir Patrick, or both served St. Andrew's in the Commons House of Assembly. The family interests were well cared for.

Though his status seemed such that he could be elected almost at will, Lachlan McIntosh continued to avoid politics, content to look after affairs on the Altamaha. Working closely with Laurens, whose schooner, the *Broughton Island Packet*, plied a regular route between Darien and Charleston, McIntosh was able to get his rice, corn, lumber, and shingles to the best markets. In most cases Laurens directed the final sale and McIntosh enjoyed the advantage of having one of America's shrewdest businessmen handle his affairs, which, as much as anything else, accounted for his business successes.[25] Laurens provided credit, slaves, and advice. All McIntosh needed to do was manage his affairs wisely; but outside of planting, he seldom did. To succeed in business, one had to be willing to take risks, and he was not willing. Time and again he was berated for lacking the "Liberality & . . . generous freedom in dealing" that was necessary to make one's fortune as a merchant, but the point continued to elude the Georgian.[26]

Baffled by his friend's inability to seize the offered opportunities, Laurens nonetheless continued to give advice, which more often than not was ignored. McIntosh's only excuse for his lack of action was that his "circumstances" confined him, but Laurens saw the real reason. It was not, he wrote McIntosh, that "circumstances" confined the man but that the man had "confined [his] cir-

cumstances."[27] Still, McIntosh was unmoved. He had taken prudent risks to establish his planting and auxiliary enterprises; they
brought him a comfortable living, and he was generally satisfied. If
more risks were to be taken, they would be taken within the context
of ventures already established; and even then, they were not to be
rushed into.

In the end, Laurens was forced to recognize that he was dealing
with a man whose ambition was limited by his vision, a man who
lacked the ability to see those things on the rim of possibility and the
daring to try to achieve them. Moderate prosperity had made
Lachlan McIntosh cautious. He would rather preserve what he had
than risk it to gain more. Nevertheless, the two saw in each other
qualities they needed and respected. They drew on each other's
particular talents and advantages, but did not exploit them.[28] Provincial and restrained, McIntosh complemented his cosmopolitan
and aggressive counterpart and the two pulled well in tandem,
alternating the lead as circumstances demanded.

In essence, the mature Lachlan McIntosh was a cautious, conservative man, noted for his "superior sense & understanding" in public
matters, serious, conscious of status and procedure, and often striking contemporaries as cold and abrupt. Yet in private, to the small
circle he drew around him, he was a hospitable, loyal friend and an
affectionate, loving husband and father.[29] But lurking beneath his
restrained exterior was an emotional side, a quick temper that led at
times to ill-conceived actions, causing no small amount of trouble.
Nevertheless, if his methods were questionable his motives were
generally sound, for he was an honest, forthright man and he drew
comfort from that fact.[30] He was, in the classic eighteenth-century
sense, an American country gentleman, a bit rough around the
edges, but a man with whom others had to reckon.

As the 1760s drew to a close Lachlan McIntosh could feel a sense
of accomplishment that few were able to boast. Within limits set
largely by himself, he was a successful planter and leader. For the
time, life was good. Economic troubles came and went, but none
was serious enough to disrupt the stability of his Altamaha existence. The pattern seemed set. He would plant and harvest with the

seasons, serve his parish and colony in affairs that pertained to him, and live out his days in the imposing house on Darien Bluff. But the times were "out of joint," and soon events would shatter the peace of the Altamaha planter beyond repair.

CHAPTER THREE
The Cloud Gathers Thick

I think this province is remarkable for a number of parties, and I am afraid we shall find it too true that a house divided against itself can never stand.

Joseph Habersham to William Henry Drayton, February 1776

In Darien, the opening of the new decade gave little indication of the turmoil its years would bring. The town basked lazily under the south Georgia sun, her people moving about their tasks with a steady, unhurried pace, perfected during nearly twenty years of peace and relative prosperity. Like the ruins of Fort King George, rotting on the weed-covered knoll about a mile downstream from the main square, the military origins of the settlement seemed all but forgotten. Entering the deep waters of the Altamaha, vessels docked at wharfs where plantation produce lay stacked alongside the fruits of the Indian trade. In all, it was scarcely the breeding ground for rebellion.

Like so many of his contemporaries, Lachlan McIntosh seemed hardly the stuff from which revolutionaries are made. The royal government had done well by him: given him land, political power, and the security he valued so much. But it was there that the problem lay. The royal government which sustained him was, as he saw it, in Savannah, not in London, and it was, or should be, run by Georgians, not Englishmen—a distinction he keenly felt. So long as the government's policy reflected the wishes of men like himself, he was a loyal citizen, but when other interests threatened to dominate and alter that system, he was ready to rise in opposition.

McIntosh had become increasingly uneasy over Britain's policies toward the colonies. It was not that they affected him directly, but what they seemed to indicate for the future. Vice Admiralty courts, British troops in Boston, and the change in attitude which accompanied England's "new colonial system" were topics of complaint in correspondence with Laurens, and the South Carolinian, who was directly affected, wasted no words in declaring the need for his state and Georgia to "be keen in asserting their liberty & sullenly & stubbornly resist against all unrestricted Mandates and admonitions tending to enslave them." [1] Such uncompromising sentiments did not fall on deaf ears.

But concern was one thing, action another; and Lachlan McIntosh remained his cautious self. Between 1770 and 1773 he watched storm clouds gather in the north, lent a sympathetic ear to Georgians grappling with royal authority, raised rice on the Altamaha, and kept his own counsel. Even in the summer of 1774, when outraged Georgians met in Savannah to voice opposition to the "Intolerable Acts," he stayed home. He was not, however, oblivious to events taking place in the capital, for brother George, as was customary, attended the meetings and saw to the family interests. But what George McIntosh reported to his brother was hardly the united opposition to arbitrary rule that the protesters' chosen designation, Whig, implied. Indeed, what resulted from a tavern meeting one muggy August night was the splintering of the movement into factions which threatened to destroy the "common cause." To Lachlan McIntosh, long an observer of Georgia politics, it must have seemed strangely familiar. [2]

The roots of this conflict were deeply embedded in Georgia's past. Soon after royalization, prominent citizens of Savannah and the surrounding area (designated Christ Church Parish in 1758) gained control of the lower house of the Assembly and, though challenged from time to time, never relinquished it. Apparently, most Georgians accepted this with little protest, for what was good for Savannah generally benefited them as well. As a result, by 1760 the colony's older areas, particularly along the coast and a short distance up the Savannah River, had fashioned a political coalition based on family ties, economic connections, and social compatability, which those who were not included had little hope of overcoming. Initially at least, few seemed anxious to try, for not only did the leaders of this coalition emerge as protectors of property and status, they emerged popular heroes as well. During the clashes with Wright and his predecessors over the policies and privileges of the lower house, these men stood firm as champions of legislative superiority, home rule, and liberty.[3] That, during the 1760s, was an enviable and meaningful position to hold.

From all indications, the Christ Church coalition knew what it wanted: to control Georgia the way it controlled the Commons House. To accomplish this, it seemed they needed only to follow the example in other colonies. Over the past years, legislatures to the north had gained control of finances and appointments, and served as forums for discussing (and denouncing) British policies.[4] Georgia's legislative leaders wanted to do the same, but could not. The relative youth of Georgia's system was surely one factor, but the main obstacles had been the Governors, and James Wright in particular. More independent and determined than his counterparts, Wright had prevented the Commons House from expanding its power at his expense, but the coalition, equally determined, had refused to give up. If, they reasoned, an issue was found on which the Governor could be forced to compromise, erosion would begin. Ultimately, they would wear away his authority, leaving in its place a system of legislative superiority that they could control.[5]

This approach to reform—to alter the system at the top but leave the rest all but untouched—has given Christ Church and its supporters the designation "conservative."[6] It is an appropriate title, for throughout the conflict they worked to preserve as much of the prerevolutionary socio-economic-political structure as evolving issues and ideologies permitted. Thus they moved with caution, knowing that their status, whatever its limitations, was protected by the very system they attacked. Having many within their ranks who remembered Trustee rule, the coalition was well aware of the advantages brought by royalization; meanwhile, the fact that some were related to Wright's supporters tempered their stand.[7] The protests against Britain were to be used to undermine the Governor's position, but that was all. Their goal was reform, not revolution.

Resistance from Wright was expected, but what made the coalition's task more difficult was a group led by citizens of St. John's Parish, men with little reason for caution. These descendants of New England Puritans had arrived almost simultaneously with royalization, bringing with them a tradition of hard work and accomplishment, and (according to Governor Wright) "a strong tincture of Republican or Oliverian principles."[8] Settling midway between Savannah and Darien, they cleared their land and soon had formed a plantation economy to rival that of older, more established areas. Unwilling to see the fruits of their labors pass through the hands of Savannah middlemen, the people of St. John's built their own port, Sunbury, which in 1761 became Georgia's second port of entry.[9] As its population and economy expanded, St. John's seemed well on its way to becoming a creditable rival to Christ Church.

Not surprisingly, the social and economic attitudes of St. John's leadership differed little from those of the Christ Church coalition. These Puritans were as much a part of the colonial elite as any—or at least thought themselves to be. But despite their accomplishments, they were unable to translate economic status into political power. In the Commons House, where men of republican principles would seek an outlet for political ambitions, Christ Church led and St. John's reluctantly, followed. The events of 1774, however, forced the men of St. John's to face their situation squarely, if they had not done so already. Should conservatives dominate these new protests, as they had those in the past, little would change. True, the Governor might give in if pressure became great enough, but fundamental as that was for Georgians' struggle to control their destinies, a lessening of Wright's authority would do little for St. John's. Before its position could be improved, Christ Church's hold on the legislature had to be broken.[10]

What the leadership of St. John's sought, therefore, was a total redistribution of power—which earned them the animosity of conservatives and the epithet "radicals."[11] But to accomplish this they needed an issue, upon which they could challenge Christ Church's long-held position as popular spokesman and, in so doing entice the conservatives into an arena outside the security of the Commons House. The Intolerable Acts and a subsequent call for a Continental Congress provided that issue. On August 10, 1774, Georgia Whigs met in Savannah to determine a course of action. Eight resolutions, defending American rights and denouncing the acts, were passed unanimously, at which point representatives from St. John's proposed that delegates be sent to the Congress. Immediately, conservatives rose in opposition, for to do what the radicals demanded meant to go outside the system, creating new mechanisms of government which could threaten the old. Fearing this might unleash uncontrollable forces, conservatives closed ranks and held firm; the resolution failed.[12]

With that the meeting broke up and the combatants retired to plot strategy, hoping to convince the uncommited (there were many) that their factions could best protect American rights.[13] McIntosh, for his part, watched all this with considerable interest. He knew both factions and their leaders well. He and Laurens had dealt with them in business, respected their talents in government, and sympathized with the desire of each to direct its own affairs. Of the two factions, however, his closest associates, in business and in private affairs, were conservatives—especially John Wereat, Joseph Clay, and the Habersham brothers, James Jr., John, and Joseph. He understood their reluctance to commit themselves fully to the cause, and very probably agreed that, for the time, it was prudent not to send representatives to the First Continental Congress or to boycott British goods under the Continental Association. Nevertheless, McIntosh did not openly ally himself with them. While representatives from St. Andrew's attended meetings held by both factions, giving that parish the aura of impartiality, the leading member of its leading family watched and waited.

Then, on January 12, 1775, in the town whose streets and squares he had surveyed for the royal government only eight years before, Lachlan McIntosh took the step which ultimately broke his ties with that government forever. On that day, in the meetinghouse at Darien, he headed a committee which voted to "acquiece & Join in all the Resolutions passed by the Grand American Congress in Philadelphia . . . and [to] most Heartily and Cheerfully Accede to the Association." Limitations on land grants, the raising of quitrents, crown-controlled offices, and excessive executive authority were the subjects of reproach that winter day, but what was clearest in their protests was the unwavering belief that American rights could be best protected by officials responsible to Georgia, not Britain. It was a bold statement of principles, and one which, in a colony so badly divided, would be difficult to uphold.[14]

Because of his well-known reluctance to intervene in colonial politics, McIntosh's role as leader of the Darien committee comes as something of a shock. A recent letter from Laurens, warning that Parliament was set on a course to bring "the Bostonians & in *them*, all America at [its] feet," no doubt deepened his concern, but that same letter cautioned that only through "firmness and Moderation" could the colonists hope to alter the course events seemed to be taking.[15] The latter sentiment better suited the Georgian's nature, but he disregarded his friend's advice. For Lachlan McIntosh, the stand he took that day was hardly moderate.

Still, it would have been difficult for him to have done otherwise. The McIntoshes had come to Georgia, as refugees from English-dominated Scotland, to serve the Trustees, not the crown. After royalization, that allegiance was transferred to the colony, Georgia; and there is nothing to indicate that, in the process, they developed a similar attachment to George III. Thus, equating present "oppressions" with those "our Fathers were not able to bear & [which] drove [them] into this Wilderness," Lachlan McIntosh took his stand.[16] The timing of his action, however, was dictated by other considerations. There is no doubt his sympathies lay with the Whigs, but if the movement could have continued without his active participation he would gladly have let it. That seemed impossible. With the Whigs splintering into factions determined to dominate or damn the cause, McIntosh felt compelled to intervene, and the Darien petition was his means. Coming from one of the most prominent "neutral" Whigs in the colony, the petition enunciated principles upon which, he hoped, all could unite—a statement of purpose for Whigs who seemed to have lost their purpose.

As a means of carrying the resolutions into effect, the committee declared support for the Provincial Congress, which was called by conservatives to meet in Savannah six days hence. To the sponsoring faction, the meeting was designed to wrest initiative from the radicals, who saw the strategy and refused to attend. But McIntosh saw it as a logical step toward building a consensus, and threw his support behind it. He did not, however, see fit to add his presence. Having taken his stand, he withdrew—hoping, it seems, that the movement would regain its momentum and carry on without him. Once again, therefore, George McIntosh made the journey to Savannah while Lachlan McIntosh stayed home.[17]

The Provincial Congress assembled on January 18, but most parishes either sided with the radicals or (more probably) had no desire to take part in a factional struggle which seemed to have little to do with the cause of American rights. Finding only five parishes in attendance, the conservatives decided that whatever action they took would lack real force. Therefore, after adopting the Association with some reservations and selecting Archibald Bulloch, Noble W. Jones, and John Houstoun (all from Christ Church) as delegates to Philadelphia, they adjourned on January 25.[18] Still hoping to give its work the appearance of popular support, the Provincial Congress sent the resolutions to the conservative-dominated Commons House, which was sitting at the same time and had several members who attended both meetings. Approval by that body, a foregone conclusion, would go far toward establishing conservative control over the Whig movement. But before the legislature could act, Governor Wright prorogued it.[19]

Conservative Whigs were in a state of confusion. Wright's action was a serious setback for their hope to alter the system in their favor, and pressed by the radicals, they could not afford to lick their wounds and wait for a better day. Significantly, although their delegates to the Continental Congress declined to attend because they lacked authorization from the colony, St. John's, showing no such reluctance, attempted to seize the initiative by selecting Lyman Hall as its representative.[20] In the meantime, many previously uncommitted Georgians, outraged by what Wright had done and excited at news of fighting in the north, joined the "cause." The result was a movement in search of a leader, yet at first neither faction was able to fill the need. Finally, realizing that their struggle for control was hindering rather than helping the cause (as well as their own particular goals), radicals and conservatives decided to work together; but it was a marriage of convenience. Both agreed that the Governor's power had to be reduced before anything could be accomplished; otherwise, divisions ran as deep as before. However, to implement that one common principle, a Second Provincial Congress was called and Georgia moved one step closer to revolution.[21]

On June 29, 1775, the Darien committee, with Lachlan McIntosh still in charge, met to select its delegates to the new Congress. Of those chosen, the majority were either members of the McIntosh family or close friends. George and William McIntosh were selected, and—no doubt to the surprise of many—Lachlan McIntosh was included in the list of representatives.[22] If the factions were willing to unite in the common cause, so was he, and thus his days of neutrality were numbered.

The Second Provincial Congress met on July 4, 1775, and soon brought Georgia into the mainstream of American opposition to British policies. It delcared that the Continental Association was to go into effect at once and that Georgia would support all policies of the Continental Congress. Five delegates were chosen to attend the Congress in Philadelphia, a boldly worded petition to George III was approved, and the colonists' general dissatisfaction with the system which governed them was expressed through a series of resolutions. A number of committees were set up, the most important of which was a Council of Safety, designed to keep the government functioning while Congress was not in session, and on July 17 the Provincial Congress adjourned.[23]

The Second Provincial Congress was "Georgia's first revolutionary government," though most of its members did not see it as such. To all Whigs, however, it was an instrument of change, although conservatives were determined that changes should be less than the radicals demanded. In the last half of 1775, Georgia's royal government was slowly and deliberately stripped of its power, and by the new year it appeared that most colonists were either Whigs or had declared themselves Loyalists, and in some cases had left the state. The line between Georgian and Englishman, so ill defined in years past, was fast being drawn.[24]

In this crucial interim the Council of Safety was the most powerful force in the Whig movement. Endowed with the authority to act as an executive and, like the Provincial Congress, unencumbered by royal instructions, the Council called for elections, handled money, appointed committees, saw to enforcement of Congress's resolutions, and directed military affairs. There was little check on its powers, which sometimes extended even into the legislative and judicial areas. It was this influential body, on which George McIntosh sometimes served, that guided much of Georgia's revolutionary activity.[25]

Lachlan McIntosh's role in this usurpation of royal authority is unknown, but St. Andrew's Parish was as active as any in enforcing Whig directives, and there is no doubt that he led those efforts. By January 1776, success seemed assured. Attempts by Governor Wright and his supporters to carry out official functions were either opposed or simply ignored, and it was clear that the Whigs ruled Georgia. There was, as yet, little open talk of separation from Britain, but men as politically aware as the colony's new leaders realized that the situation was intolerable to the crown. Some type of confrontation could not be avoided for long.[26]

With the Continental Congress promising material aid, Georgians prepared to oppose any British attempt to restore either the royal government or normal trade relations. Word had reached the state that two British warships and a transport were en route to Georgia, either to plunder the sea islands for livestock or to attempt to obtain supplies through normal channels. Little could be done to prevent the former, but if the British tried to buy supplies at Savannah in violation of the Continental Association, the Whigs would be forced to prove their dedication to the cause. "Fearing for [the] public safety," the Council of Safety called the militia to Savannah and placed Samuel Elbert in command. Ships were prevented from sailing, coastal watches were alerted, houses of potentially dangerous individuals were searched, and in some cases arrest orders were issued. On January 13, the expected news was received. The British warship *Tarmar*, with several auxiliary vessels, was sighted off Tybee Light. The Whigs waited for the next move.[27]

Needless to say, Wright was heartened at the appearance of the *Tarmar*, and five days later, when she was joined by three more warships and their supporting vessels, his spirits soared. But though the Governor insisted that the ships were peaceably disposed and wanted only to buy supplies, his opponents knew the implications of what he asked. If the Association were allowed to be violated openly, Whig credibility would be damaged beyond repair; and Wright would regain power by default. The choice for the new government was no choice at all. Wright was arrested and most who had not agreed to support the Association were disarmed.[28] To preserve any semblance of their authority, Whigs knew they had to resist.

The day after his arrest, Wright was put on parole of honor and forbidden to leave town or to contact the ships.[29] Meanwhile, militiamen converged on Savannah and tensions ran high. Untrained and poorly supplied, these troops seemed hardly a match for those on the warships, but if the Whig cause was to survive, something resembling an army would have to be created. Some three months earlier, the Continental Congress had authorized a Continental battalion for Georgia, with officers chosen by the Whig government. When the Provincial Congress was called to order on January 20, 1776, this was one of the first matters of business and with it the consensus disintegrated.[30]

Conservatives nominated the militia's Colonel Samuel Elbert, one of the few Whigs with military experience, to command the new battalion. The radicals countered with Button Gwinnett, a St. John's planter who had served one term in the legislature. Clearly, Elbert, the best qualified, and having the conservatives' endorsement, seemed assured of the victory, for up to this point the Christ Church faction had dominated the Provincial Congress as it had the Commons House. But in the previous session concessions were made to weld others to the united front—concessions which expanded the electorate and gave additional representation to rural and western areas. This, in effect, diluted the traditional sources of conservative strength and introduced a new element into the factional struggle, which could swing the balance either way. Which way it would swing was the crucial question, and the answer came quickly. The vote was taken and the winner was Button Gwinnett.[31]

"Lofty and commanding" in appearance, "mild and persuasive" in speech, Button Gwinnett strode onto the scene like a man who knew what he wanted and was determined to have it. Though his career as a revolutionary would last less than two years, during that time he was to alter Georgia politics as few have done before or since. Yet, in spite of his contributions, he remains something of an enigma. Modern Georgians know him as the signer of the Declaration of Independence whose signature is the most valuable of the lot, but beyond the borders of Georgia his name is seldom mentioned. How he became "a Whig to Excess" and what he meant to the future of the Revolution have been lost in a sea of contradictory interpretations and patriotic pride.[32] But he was not an enigma to his contemporaries. They knew what he had been, what he was, and many—especially the conservatives—feared what he might become.

Like many of his radical associates, Gwinnett came late to Georgia. Raised on the fringes of gentility as the younger son of a Gloucestershire vicar, he decided that rather than serve that class he would be part of it, but his first attempt, in a Bristol mercantile firm, ended in failure. So he cut his losses and in 1765, at the age of thirty, arrived in Savannah. Renting a store and advertising himself as a merchant, he soon found that the unsettled state of the economy, concern over the Stamp Act, and his lack of capital and connections made a rapid rise in the colony's small and well-established commercial community all but impossible. With the versatility that marked much of his career, Gwinnett abruptly changed course. Less than two months after arriving, he left Savannah, obtained a loan, and bought St. Catherine's Island in St. John's Parish. Button Gwinnett, merchant, was about to become Button Gwinnett, planter.[33]

Shortly after settling in St. John's, Gwinnett moved into the fluid politics of the parish. Appointed justice of the peace in 1767, he served his "apprenticeship" in various local offices, until in 1769 he was selected to serve in the Commons House. It was the same Assembly in which Lachlan McIntosh later served, the one that challenged Wright on the taxing of unrepresented parishes. The whole experience must have made a profound impression on Gwinnett, for despite his inexperience, the day after he was sworn in he was placed on the committee which led the assault on the Governor's position. It seemed that Button Gwinnett's moment had arrived. But just as everything appeared to point to a long and illustrious political career, matters that had been left unattended asserted themselves with a vengeance.[34]

Apparently Gwinnett's talents for planting were no greater than those he displayed in business, for the new legislator found himself so deeply in debt that all other pursuits, including politics, had to give way to the struggle for financial solvency. Hounded by creditors, he borrowed from one to pay another. The years between his service in the Assembly and the outbreak of the Revolution revealed him to be a man of limited commercial skill, prone to questionable, almost desperate, financial dealings, who realized few of the goals he initially sought. The greatest blow came when his personal property was seized and sold, and St. Catherine's Island went on the block. By 1774, Button Gwinnett's once promising future seemed dismal indeed.[35]

But revolutionaries seldom rise from the ranks of the contented, and the most volatile are the ambitious whose ambitions are thwarted. Gwinnett came to Georgia seeking what England denied him, prosperity and status. When Savannah, and circumstances, frustrated his efforts, he turned to St. John's, which welcomed him with open arms. There, politically at least, he found success and briefly enjoyed the standing he sought. Then he lost it, not because he was a poor politician but because he was a poor businessman. In Georgia, as in most colonies, few who failed at the latter could hope to succeed in the former. If Gwinnett was to prevail, either his inadequacies would be corrected or the system which made such shortcomings so delimiting would have to be altered significantly.

Button Gwinnett gave little indication that he was one to accept full responsibility for what befell him. Rather, he was inclined to lay part (if not all) of the blame on those lawyers, merchants, and planters with whom he dealt, and on the system which enabled them to control his life. Such an attitude, however, did not develop in a vacuum, for there were many in St. John's who agreed with him, and who may have helped him reach these conclusions. Despite their best efforts, the leaders of St. John's had watched their political power decline in relation to that of Christ Church. Meanwhile, the colony's economy was still dominated by the Savannah-based coalition and its South Carolina associates, the same group with whom Gwinnett struggled. Neither Button Gwinnett nor his friends could see much future in perpetuating the system.

In the final analysis, it all came down to this. Though Georgia's institutions were maturing as the Revolution neared, the quarter century preceding the struggle witnessed a transformation of the colony's political and social structure. Accompanying this were tensions, which usually were revealed when assertive elements confronted entrenched elements. The result was an increased awareness of secondary status by the former and, after 1775, a deep sense of vulnerability in the latter. Gwinnett's situation was linked directly to these tensions, and his response did much to make them dominant forces in shaping Georgia's revolutionary movement. Fully aware of his increasing inability to control the circumstances that ordered his conduct, Gwinnett was able to translate colonial demands for "freedom" and "independence" into personal terms and goals. Once that was done, it was only a matter of finding and seizing the opportunity to exert his considerable energy toward a solution.[36]

That opportunity came in 1775, and Button Gwinnett, a financial failure whose record of political activity since 1770 was nil, made his move. After his close friend Lyman Hall left for Philadelphia, Gwinnett advanced to a position of leadership among the radicals. But instead of operating within the framework of the united front, he set out to destroy the movement's fragile unity and establish in its place a radical-led coalition which would end conservative domination once and for all. That summer Button Gwinnett found his political calling. Working with remarkable effectiveness, he organized a "nocturnal Cabal" among Whigs in the western and southern parishes. Then, displaying a political ability which has generally gone unappreciated, he convinced an already discontented back country that the interests of Christ Church ran contrary to the interests of the state. To guarantee their security, prosperity, and self-government, he insisted, the conservatives had to be removed from power.[37] Button Gwinnett's revolution was against more than the British.

And though he succeeded, his victory was short lived. Though Gwinnett's new following rose to the occasion and elected him to head the battalion, the conservatives, fearing for their future in a state dominated by such a popular movement and the likes of "Colonel" Gwinnett, refused to abide by the decision. It was a critical moment. A mass defection of conservatives might revive the moribund royal government and spell the end for all Whig hopes.

The radicals, hardly political amateurs, saw the dilemma and decided to wait for the time when there would be no place for conservatives to turn. Gwinnett withdrew from consideration, as did Elbert, and a compromise candiate was sought. All agreed that their choice should be a proven leader, possessing strong Whig sentiments but not associated with either faction. Military experience was considered secondary, since gentlemen believed that a natural leader would be able to handle military problems as easily as civilian problems—and one must not forget that, despite their "popular" appeal, the radical leaders still saw themselves as "gentlemanly" as their conservative counterparts. After some deliberation they reached a decision, and the man they selected, for better or worse, was Lachlan McIntosh of Darien.[38]

The other offices were divided between the factions. Conservative candidates Elbert and Joseph Habersham were made lieutenant colonel and major, reinforcing the elitist opinions held by most of that faction. Two of Colonel McIntosh's sons, Lachlan Jr. ("Lackie") and William, were also given positions, but the bulk of commissions below major went to radicals.[39] Though it might seem that once again radicals were relegated to secondary status, such was not the case. Having made considerable progress in welding "the people" to their cause, the lower-position officers, in direct contact with men in the ranks, promised to give the radicals an additional base upon which to build their movement. In the end, they got the best of the bargain.

Another aspect of the compromise sent Gwinnett to Philadelphia to join Georgia's other delegates at the Congress.[40] This meant that the two most capable and influential radicals, Gwinnett and his mentor, Lyman Hall, were out of the state, which gave conservatives an opportunity to undo what the radicals had done. But it also meant that the radicals wielded extraordinary influence in determining Georgia's, and to a much lesser degree America's, stand against British policies. And it was that stand, made in Philadelphia, that ultimately determined how far the radicals would be able to carry their "reforms" at home.

The fact that McIntosh had little military experience hardly bothered those who selected him. His social status, family name, and political posture, plus the fact that at forty-eight he was something of an elder statesman in the Congress, made him an acceptable choice. For his part, he accepted the office with reluctance—a natural attitude, considering the task which lay before him. Once the selections were made, the new colonel and his officers swore an oath to be "subservient to such supreme and civil powers of this Province" as were established—if such powers did not contradict orders of the Continental Congress or Continental officers.[41]

The origins of this oath are obscure. Instructions for it came from the Provincial Congress, but which persons or factions demanded that it be administered has never been fully revealed. In later, more partisan times the radicals insinuated that it was their idea, designed to ensure civilian control of the military. But McIntosh, under the same partisan circumstances, declared that he "insisted on recognizing civil authority and that all the officers do likewise."[42]

It is probable that most Whigs supported the oath. Their English heritage, with its distrust for armies, would have made such a pledge logical and even necessary. For McIntosh, such an "insistence" was good politics. In this way he assured both sides that he planned to pursue a path of moderation, while assuring himself that if problems arose among the factionalized officer corps, he could turn to the state government for help. Since he got along well with the state's leaders, even with Gwinnett, he had little reason to distrust his civilian superiors.[43]

But the oath had a loophole. The state's orders were to be followed only if they did not contradict the orders of the Continental Congress or Continental officers. This left a gray area that bothered McIntosh. In his first report to General Washington he asked for instructions on "how far we are under the control of the Provincial Congress . . . and what rank we hold when acting with militia or Provincial troops."[44] Neither Washington nor any other Continental officers, civil or military, could provide an acceptable answer. Contradictory lines of command hampered the war effort throughout the struggle, and this issue returned to plague McIntosh and Georgia again and again.

CHAPTER FOUR
A Time for War

Tell me how liberty thrives about the swamps of Altamaha?
  Henry Laurens to Lachlan McIntosh, January 27, 1776

Our Cause is just.
  Lachlan McIntosh to John McIntosh Jr., November 28, 1776

The compromise having been struck, Georgia's Whigs turned to the enemy ships off Tybee Light—a bad situation that had just taken a turn for the worse. On the night of February 11, Governor Wright and some of his supporters broke their parole and fled to H.M.S. *Scarborough*, from which he made a last appeal to Georgians to resupply the vessels or face the consequences. The Council of Safety refused and, in anticipation of an attempt to take supplies by force, ordered about twenty boats loaded with rice to be anchored against Hutchinson Island, upriver from the city.[1] This low body of land, directly across from Savannah and extending above and below it, was separated from South Carolina by shallow streams and marshes, which the Whigs believed unnavigable. Thus, it was reasoned, any attempt to secure the supplies would have to pass beneath the city's defenses.

But Savannah's defenses, weakened by "numberless avenues" of invasion, were questionable at best. McIntosh's call for troops to fill the ranks of his Continental battalion brought no more than thirty recruits, while the militia, some 500 strong, was all but leaderless because the new colonel, unsure of his authority, was reluctant to take charge. It may not have been quite the "open, straggling, defenceless and deserted town" that McIntosh described,[2] but he was close to the truth. To complicate matters further, the Continental Association was to expire March 1, and the Council of Safety, unable to decide on its extension, had adjourned in disgust.[3] Fully

aware of the Whigs' internal dissensions, which the selection of
McIntosh had mollified only slightly, the commanders of the British
ships rocked at anchor and waited for the supplies to come to them.
They had every reason to expect that it would be only a matter of
time before the boycott, and perhaps even the Whig movement,
would come to an inglorious end.

After much deliberation, McIntosh felt compelled to act, "least
the Colony should be tamely given up." With genuine reluctance, he
moved to take command of the "disorderly and Raw Militia" and set
about to defend an area with which he was admittedly unfamiliar. It
was hardly the ideal situation for launching a military career, but he
felt, as he had with the Darien petition, that he had no alternative.
Convinced that the British intended to take Savannah and restore
Governor Wright, Colonel McIntosh placed guards at likely landing
sites and set up ambushes on the roads leading to the city.[4] These
preparations, however, reduced the number of troops available to
guard the waterfront and placed a heavy burden on the already
overextended forces.

Then the British made what McIntosh interpreted as the first
move in their plan to capture Savannah. Several vessels and trans-
ports sailed up the river to within three miles of the town, where the
Whigs had sunk a boat in a futile effort to block the channel.
McIntosh sent 150 men under Colonel Archibald Bulloch to prevent
their landing, but the British only "paraded" their ships before the
Georgians, who fired a few harmless shots in defiance, then settled
back to wait.[5] This movement sent the Council of Safety into
emergency session, and on the day the Continental Association was
to expire they finally voted for renewal. Convinced at last of the
gravity of the situation, the Council sanctioned McIntosh's assumption of command by ordering him to see that only authorized vessels
left port and that all others had their rudders and rigging removed.
Without protest, the Continental commander and his militia troops
set out to obey the orders of the state government, and the lines of
authority became even more blurred.[6]

With uncharacteristic swiftness, the Council also ordered the
appraisal of property of "friends of America," indicating that if it

became apparent that Savannah would fall, the city was to be burned rather than surrendered to the enemy. In such a case, the Continental Congress would be called upon to reimburse loyal Whigs. This resolution was approved by a mass meeting of Whig property holders; and McIntosh again moved to carry out the orders of the state.[7] On the evening of March 2 the British made their long-awaited "assault." As darkness fell, the schooner *Hinchinbrook* and the sloop *St. John* sailed up the river, but, instead of attacking the town, entered the shallow passage behind Hutchinson Island. Now sensing that the vessels might be able to move behind the island and land troops above his defenses, McIntosh sent a detachment to Yamacraw, a village about a quarter mile upriver, which seemed the most logical landing site. There the detachment set up a battery of three four-pound cannon and waited for the new day to dawn.[8]

But McIntosh had misjudged the British intent. The riceboats, swaying at the upper end of Hutchinson Island, were the objective—not Savannah. During the night, the British landed some 300 men on the back of the island, and this force, protected by darkness and dense undergrowth, worked its way, undetected, across to the boats. There they found that, though it had been two days since the rudders and rigging were ordered removed, those orders had not been carried out. The riceboats were ready to sail.[9]

As the sun rose the next morning, a group of Whigs rowed slowly across the river to begin the postponed derigging. To their surprise, they found the riceboats and themselves in enemy hands. At almost the same moment, the two British warships attempted to come round the island and cover the vessels' escape. McIntosh, as yet unaware of the riceboats' capture, believed this to be the long-awaited assault on Savannah and ordered the Yamacraw battery into action. This cannonade was aided by the tricky river current, and for nearly three hours the British ships, and the battle itself, remained in a precarious limbo.[10] Finally, in early afternoon the warships rounded the island and rendezvoused with the riceboats. McIntosh and the Whigs, now fully aware of the situation, sent a party under a flag of truce to secure the release of the captured Georgians, and when that delegation was also taken prisoner, the enraged Americans resumed their attack.[11] For the rest of the afternoon black powder smoke drifted across the river as Georgia's army got its baptism of fire.

In Savannah, news of the actions along the river so enraged some citizens that they demanded the British position be assaulted forthwith, which Colonel McIntosh would have gladly done had boats been available to ferry the troops across. Public anger continued unabated and later that afternoon, after seeing citizens attack the property of some Savannahians believed to be sympathetic to the British, McIntosh concluded the time had come to burn the enemy out.[12] The sun was sinking behind the city when a ship, its masts, spars, and rigging coated with pitch, was set ablaze and set on course toward the British. But the fireship, chosen as much for the fact that its owner was a Loyalist as for its suitability, proved too large and grounded before it reached the target. As it burned, immobile against the darkening sky, the Whigs prepared another vessel, a sloop, and sent it into the night.[13]

The second fireship moved across the river, while the frantic British worked to cut the riceboats free, but they were only partially successful. The blazing vessel rammed two of the moored boats and swung around in the current to threaten others. Fire at sea is a sailor's nightmare, and in this case the closeness of land did little to ease the fear. Taking the ten vessels they were able to free, the British moved upstream, abandoning the rest. Also abandoned were a number of British soldiers, who panicked and attempted to retreat across the island. Slogging through the mud and sawgrass, illuminated by burning ships, and urged on by the Whigs' musket fire, their "laughable confusion" entertained the Americans on the Savannah shore.[14]

A short time later, the British warships took their prizes and, using "a channel never known before," moved behind the island, picked up the exhausted troops, and escaped downstream. The battle was over. In all, the Americans counted "two white men and one Indian wounded," while the British acknowledged six casualties, though McIntosh felt there were surely more. In the darkness, Savannahians gathered along the river and watched the burning vessels as they "passed and repassed with the tide." It was a scene

which, under normal circumstances, would have been "truly hor-
rible," but that night it was greeted with "gratitude and applause."[15]

The next morning McIntosh had the few undamaged riceboats
brought across the river and placed under heavy guard. Royal Chief
Justice Anthony Stokes and several members of Wright's council
were imprisoned, to be used in exchange for the Georgians, and
defenses were strengthened in case the British moved against Savannah. But there was no real need; for the time being, the city was safe.
A few days later the British fleet, with the Royal Governor, sailed
away, leaving only two ships behind as a token show of force.[16] But
Lachlan McIntosh knew this lull was only temporary. In other
quarters, the war was beginning in earnest.

Though protected on the north by South Carolina, the islands,
inlets, rivers, and trackless forests which formed Georgia's eastern,
southern, and western flanks were open and inviting. By the most
generous estimates, no more than 2,000 men were available to guard
what seemed to be more frontier than colony, and they were poorly
supplied, unorganized, and untrained. Loyalists in Florida, many of
whom were Georgians who had been driven from their homes by the
excesses of zealous Whigs, knew the posture of the colony. Organized into the Florida Rangers and led by the notorious but
capable Thomas Brown, these exiles raided at will between the
Altamaha and St. Mary's rivers, raising havoc in the land of the
McIntoshes.[17] Georgia seemed ripe for the picking, and many hands
were anxious to help with the harvest.

Britain's desire to restore royal government to Georgia extended
beyond the salving of wounded pride. If rebellions in the north were
to be suppressed, Georgia's role might prove critical, for the colony
was a supply officer's dream. Cattle ranged on her coasts and Sea
Islands, while her farms and plantations were easily accessible
sources of rice, grain, and other foodstuffs. Even if Savannah remained in rebel hands, to control the rest of the colony would
drastically shorten British supply lines. Georgia's fall was also seen
by many, Whigs and Loyalists, as the first step toward the restoration of South Carolina and eventually the other colonies, which was
stressed by Georgians when they asked South Carolina for aid.

Support from that quarter was slow in coming and the new government, aware of its exposed position, cast about for the best means of securing itself. All eyes turned to St. Augustine.

On January 1, 1776, the Continental Congress had recommended that South Carolina, North Carolina, and Georgia make a coordinated effort to take the Florida capital, with the cost of the expedition borne by the "united colonies." [18] To Georgia's Whigs, the resolution seemed the answer to their problems. If St. Augustine fell, pro-British Indians would lose their source of supply and the Rangers would lose their haven. The southern and western frontiers would be secure and the problems of establishing a stable Georgia government could be given full attention. St. Augustine, aware of the mood of its neighbor, had begun to prepare for the expected invasion. Still, the British garrison was weak, and though Governor Patrick Tonyn was determined to hold it at all cost, many civilians had fled the city. [19] Their fear, however, was unjustified, for the Americans were no better prepared than their enemy, a fact of which Lachlan McIntosh was acutely aware.

Colonel McIntosh's first concern was the Continental troops, or rather the lack of them. Recruiting officers worked hard, but the results were poor. An officer's boast, that he signed fifteen men in fifteen days, underscores the point, for at that rate months would pass before the battalion reached full strength. A number of factors contributed to the situation. South Carolina's high enlistment bounty attracted many recruits, and those who remained in Georgia were reluctant to enlist, knowing that the pay was grossly insufficient to support themselves and their families in the face of an estimated 200–300 percent inflation. [20]

There was also the attitude of the people. Reporting to General Washington, McIntosh noted that the province had done quite well in its enlistments, considering "the ease in which the poorest People generally live . . . and the prejudice they have to any regular service, on account of the restraint that anything of a strict discipline requires." However, it was numbers that mattered, and the Georgia battalion had raised only 286 men by the end of April. About eighty more were expected, but even that would bring the force to less than half the strength set by Congress. These Continentals, when added to the approximately 600 state militia, gave the Whigs less than 1,000 men—hardly enough for defense, let alone an invasion.[21]

Apart from men, McIntosh's battalion lacked clothing, arms, equipment, and, above all, training. Officers who were not engaged in searching for recruits spent their time instructing troops as best they could, but the "high compliments" paid the units for their proficiency on the drill field hardly meant that they were prepared to fight. Therefore the immediate security of the southern and western frontiers was placed in the hands of two detachments of horse militia commanded by Colonel McIntosh's brother, William. Each with sixty members, their purpose was to check cattle stealing and Indian raids, which, for the time, was all that could be realistically hoped for.[22] As Georgia continued its preparation, it became increasingly clear that if the province was to be defended, it could not be accomplished by Georgians alone.

Fortunately, others realized the state's predicament. The Continental Congress knew a united effort was needed to defend all the southern colonies, and on February 27, 1776, it organized the provinces from Virginia to Georgia into the Southern Military Department. Major General Charles Lee was placed in command, with John Armstrong of South Carolina, Andrew Lewis and Robert Howe of Virginia, and James Moore of North Carolina to serve as brigadiers. Orders were issued for troops to be raised and a new flurry of activity began. Georgia's concerns were not entirely erased by these events, for word had reached the province that over 2,000 troops were in St. Augustine's fortress, prepared to attack. McIntosh accurately discounted this since East Florida lacked provisions to support so large a force, but the rumor was enough to unsettle many Georgians.[23] Congress's action raised their hopes and the Whigs waited to see the results.

Lee appreciated Georgia's vulnerability and, upon arriving at his Charleston headquarters, requested that the state send a delegation to inform him of its circumstances and needs. McIntosh, Jonathan Bryan, and John Houstoun were chosen and in early July they met with the general. The gist of their argument was that an undefended Georgia meant an undefended South Carolina, an assessment with which Lee agreed, although he felt this security could be handled less elaborately than the Georgians proposed. Lee promised, however, that he would forward their assessment to Congress—with his endorsement. This, and pressure from Georgia's delegation, produced an appropriation of $60,000 for use by McIntosh's Continentals, and to outfit four galleys to guard the coast. It was less than McIntosh had hoped, but it was a beginning.[24]

Lee's positive attitude toward their problems was only partially responsible for the high spirits in which McIntosh and his companions returned home. While in Charleston, they had witnessed Sir Peter Parker's unsuccessful attempt to take the city, a failure which McIntosh felt might well determine the fate of America.[25] However, their spirits declined as soon as they crossed the Savannah. British activity below the Altamaha had increased, and although a raiding party under William McIntosh captured nineteen prisoners, the Georgians had found a strong fort at the St. Mary's plantation of Governor Wright's brother, Jermyn. It was clear from William's report that the British were anticipating an invasion and that the capture of St. Augustine would not be easy.[26]

By this time McIntosh had begun to have doubts about the feasibility of a full-scale attack on the East Florida capital, doubts shared by General Lee, but Georgia's government still clung to the idea. South Carolina, however, refused to send troops to defend Georgia, much less to trek into the Florida swamps. Arguments that it was better to have the enemy at the Altamaha than at the Savannah did not move the South Carolinians.[27] With his family still in Darien, Colonel McIntosh kept a careful eye on the Rangers, and as their raids increased so did his anxiety. His troops were concentrated in and around Savannah to guard the seat of government, leaving the defense of the frontier to his brother William's horse troops. "Jaded & tired out" from chasing Loyalists through the hot and humid countryside, and short of every provision, they were a thin line of defense. Meanwhile the younger children begged for "Spelling Books, or Primers," Lackie set the slaves to building a barn to house their "verry fine Crop of rice," and Colonel Lachlan McIntosh struggled to find a way to protect what remained of the family's normal way of life.[28]

By the end of July McIntosh had made his decision. If all the

Loyalist settlements between the Altamaha and St. Mary's rivers could be destroyed, the frontier, and of course Darien, would be safe for a time. Then forts could be built and the perimeter secured against further attack. Lee liked the idea and, since it seemed to render an expedition against St. Augustine unnecessary, later adopted it as an alternative. Encouraged by his commander, McIntosh spread his plan about and quickly found supporters. On July 30, 1776, the Council of Safety "recommended" that he and his officers "volunteer" to go into East Florida. Nothing could have pleased him more.[29]

If there were doubts about Lachlan McIntosh's ability as a commander, the incursion into East Florida should have dispelled them. Crossing the Altamaha in early August, he divided his force, sending one element against Wright's fort on the St. Mary's and leading the other in a series of lightning raids against settlements in the disputed area. Giving Loyalists a taste of what the Rangers had given Georgians, McIntosh's troops, in what a Floridian described as a "most cruel and wanton manner," systematically destroyed crops, drove off cattle, carried away Negroes, and generally spread terror among the people.[30]

While the British recovered from McIntosh's raids, the other American column struck Wright's fort. Surprise was complete and the entire garrison, apparently including Governor Wright's brother, surrendered. With that, the Loyalist population was thrown into a panic and rapidly filled the roads and trails that wound south to St. Augustine and safety. McIntosh quickly consolidated his forces and returned to the Altamaha. In his wake he left "every settlement to the northward of St. John's River . . . broken up" and the British in a state of confusion, unable to determine if he intended to resupply and return, or if the invasion was over.[31] McIntosh returned to Savannah just in time to take part in the announcement of the Declaration of Independence and to greet General Lee, who, after finally convincing South Carolina of the need to defend Georgia, had marched south to inspect Georgia's situation.[32] Overjoyed at McIntosh's report, the general concluded that the capture of St. Augustine was unnecessary and turned his attention to matters of defense. But the Council of Safety, confident after McIntosh's "victory," protested. Arguing that the security was only temporary, they called for a full invasion to rid Georgia permanently of the British menace. Lee pointed out that the state was hardly prepared for such a complex operation but the Council refused to listen. Supply and transportation problems were glossed over, plunder was expected to be more than adequate to pay the troops, and the result was to be a completely secure Southern Department. It was a rosy picture but one that Lee refused to accept.[33]

Lee's position was plain. He recognized Georgia's value to the cause and was willing to go on record for a vigorous defense of the province, but to him an invasion of Florida was sheer folly. He felt it wisest to set the line of defense at the Altamaha and to abandon the entire area south of it, but Georgians, including McIntosh, would have none of it. As one might expect, the days which followed saw the division between commander and Council grow till agreement was impossible. Accused of a lack of concern for the state, its soldiers, and its people, General Lee became as much the subject of criticism as the enemy and Georgia's adamant leaders prepared to carry on, with or without his support.[34]

Dismayed by the attacks, Lee's patience finally gave out, and in a bitingly sarcastic letter to General John Armstrong he gave what has become the most famous, and perhaps most accurate, description of the Georgians who opposed him.

> The people here are if possible more harum skarum than their sister colony. They will propose anything, and after they have propos'd it, discover that they are incapable of performing the least. They have propos'd securing their Frontiers by constant patrols of horse Rangers, when the scheme is approv'd of they scratch their heads for some days, and at length inform you that there is a small difficulty in the way; that of the impossibility to procure a single horse—their next project is to keep their inland Navigation clear of Tenders by a numerous fleet of Guarda Costa arm's boats, when this is agreed to, they recollect that they have not a single boat—Upon the whole I should not be surpris'd if they were to propose mounting a body of Mermaids on Alligators.[35]

Lee's criticism was not confined to private letters, and as the outspoken general aired his views the breach between himself and the Georgia government widened. Soon the line was drawn, with

Lee calling for a defense perimeter at the Altamaha and the Council of Safety pressing for a full invasion. McIntosh, who liked neither proposal, preferred the latter to having the enemy at Darien's door, and threw in his lot with the state. Lee was forced to give in. Toward the end of August preparations began for an invasion, to be commanded by an officer who gave it little chance for success.

The resulting expedition was everything Lee predicted. Poorly planned and wretchedly executed, it amounted to little more than a clumsy reenactment of McIntosh's earlier venture into the same area. Some troops got as far as the St. John's River but the bulk of the army hardly made it to the St. Mary's. Oppressive heat and swamp fever caused more casualties than the enemy, as the ragged units struggled through sawgrass, scrub brush, and briars which raked their shanks and dragged them to an exhausted halt. And while the men suffered the leaders argued, until, to the relief of all, Lee was called north to assume a new command and the fiasco ended. There is no record of McIntosh's role in the abortive invasion. In fact, there are few records that relate to it at all—those who took part in it apparently preferring to forget.[36]

Yet there were aspects of the expedition that could not be forgotten. The poor supply system forced soliders to live off the land, and since most advanced only a short distance beyond the Altamaha, the land off which they lived was America. McIntosh's plantation was one of the many that was plundered by the hungry troops. His entire rice crop and the corn, peas, and potatoes that were stored for winter were snatched up by marauders. Fences were torn down, cattle run off, and buildings wrecked, despite Lackie's frantic efforts. Surveying the damage, Colonel McIntosh realized what must be done. He had protected his home from his enemies, only to have it destroyed by his friends, and there was no time to rebuild. He gathered his family and what was left of their possessions and moved them to Savannah. Darien and the life he loved would have to wait for better times.[37]

As the Georgia troops straggled back across the Altamaha, Floridians reclaimed the land that had been theirs. Establishing bases along the frontier, Loyalist Rangers, often with Indian support, began a series of raids that threw the countryside into turmoil.

William McIntosh's cavalry was the only active Whig unit in the disputed area, but its horses were worn out and its ranks thin. Efforts to raise more troops produced scant results, even in St. Andrew's Parish, whose defense was the object of most Whig efforts. Reports of a large force moving north from Florida dramatized the need for action, but in Savannah the old factionalism flared again and the situation on the Altamaha seemed forgotten.[38]

It was left to Colonel McIntosh to propose what was to be Georgia's first real plan for defense. Rejecting talk of a new offensive for the purpose of "conq[ues]ts and extending [Georgia's] Teritorys," he turned to a realistic evaluation of the situation. Aware that he had a pitifully small force to protect a large, sprawling state, he first suggested that the area to be defended be reduced by evacuating the Sea Islands. A galley and a support vessel would be placed at the mouth of each inlet to prevent incursions by the enemy and a strong garrison would anchor a string of smaller forts that would be built along the frontier from the Altamaha to the Savannah River, less than a day's ride apart. Using the forts as their headquarters, mounted troops would make raids into enemy territory, keep in contact for defensive purposes, and maintain "Constant [co]mmunication & Intelligence" with the main army, stationed near Savannah and ready to move when needed.[39]

So fond was McIntosh of his plan that he suggested it could be applied to the whole American frontier. It *did* have many desirable features. The bulk of the army would be in well-protected defensive positions, yet would have the necessary mobility if a small force were to defend a large area. Unfortunately, even this scheme was beyond Georgia's ability. Fort Barrington, on the Altamaha, was ideal as the primary garrison, but most of the other forts would have to be built. That would take men and money, and Georgia had little of either. As a result, only posts that were deemed most necessary were ordered erected and the others were postponed, leaving large gaps in the defensive perimeter.

Determined to implement as much of his plan as possible, McIntosh ordered a garrison stationed at Beards Bluff, up the Altamaha from Barrington. From these outposts scouting parties ranged and watched, and their initial success in gathering information indicated how the plan might have worked had other forts been constructed. McIntosh also attempted to secure the inlets with galleys, but again the shortage of money and supplies prevented full implementation. Directed by a faction-beset government that lacked the capacity for swift, decisive action, Georgia's defenses languished in the heat of Indian summer.[40]

To add to McIntosh's worries, recruiting was going slowly, and with the decline in the ranks due to expiring enlistment terms there were fewer than 200 Continental troops to use in the defenses.[41] Fortunately, Congress again responded to the critical situation and in the fall of 1776 authorized the creation of a Georgia brigade and appropriated $50,000 to pay the troops, plus a $20 bounty and land grants for those who enlisted for the duration. It also notified the state that Lachlan McIntosh had been selected to serve as the brigadier general.[42] Laurens, in Congress, and instrumental in McIntosh's appointment, was overjoyed and wished that his friend "had an army worthy [of his] command;"[43] but even with these additional incentives both men knew that that wish would be hard to fulfill.

Late in October the British struck. A force of Loyalists and Indians crossed the Altamaha, bottled up Fort Barrington's eighteen-man garrison, and set to plundering St. Andrew's and St. John's parishes. Immediately upon learning of the attack, McIntosh sent word to Major Leonard Marbury, who commanded a troop of horse in the west, to rush to aid the besieged outposts. Meanwhile he assembled what troops could be spared from Savannah's defenses and at dawn on October 31 began a forced march southward.[44]

It was well after sunset when his relief column reached the distressed area and was confronted by the victims. Jamming the road in a confusion brought on by fear and fatigue, scores of families (mostly women and children) carried what little remained of their belongings.[45] Refugees from a war in which Georgians fought Georgians—different only in their loyalty from the women and children whom McIntosh had earlier driven from their East Florida homes—they struggled along the road, fleeing from enemies who not long before had been neighbors and friends. As the army moved around and through them, some of the uprooted turned and fol-

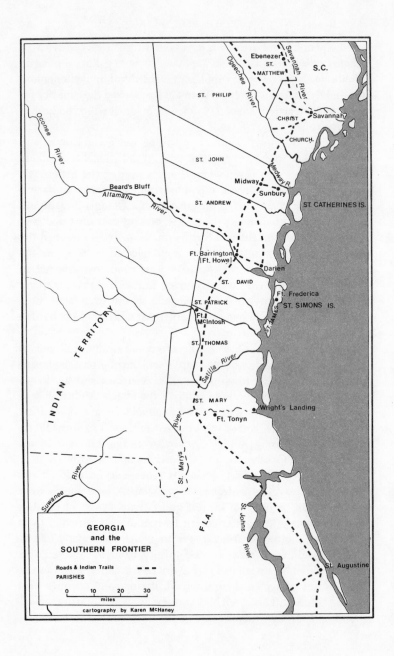

GEORGIA
and the
SOUTHERN FRONTIER

Roads & Indian Trails - - - -
PARISHES ———

0   10   20   30
miles

cartography by Karen McHaney

lowed the soldiers south, but others, with nothing to return to, plunged into the darkness.

Although the enemy retreated before his forces, McIntosh did not know how to deal with the invaders. Reports indicated that Loyalists were the main element in the attack, with Indians playing a second-ary role. Since, at that time, the Indians had only destroyed property and had killed no one, McIntosh questioned if punishing them was worth the risk of setting off a full-scale rising. But there was no decision to make: the troops he had brought south were insufficient to pursue the enemy into his own territory. After wast-ing almost two weeks waiting for Marbury's cavalry, the exasperated general returned to Savannah, where he finally made contact with the delinquent major, gave him the worst of his Scottish temper, and once more turned to matters of supply and defense.[46]

But Georgia's failure to pursue them had increased the Indians' confidence, and by December their attacks were killing people as well as destroying property. McIntosh issued orders that the "assa-sins" be hunted down and killed, and to secure the southern frontier against further encroachments he had Fort Barrington and the stock-ade at Beards Bluff reinforced. Work was also begun on two new outposts on the Satilla and St. Mary's rivers, where, deep within East Florida, Georgia horsemen could raid and collect information with greater efficiency. The fort on the Satilla, little more than a weakly defended observation post, was named Fort McIntosh.[47]

The general was encouraged to extend his southern defenses because, to a small degree, Georgia's recruiting efforts had finally borne fruit. The First Georgia Battalion reported 538 soliders, scattered in defensive positions around the state. There were also two artillery companies, of about 40 men, and Colonel William McIntosh's regiment of light horse numbered about 300. The latter was the key to General McIntosh's frontier defenses, even though many were freebooters who were interested only in loot. No enlist-ees had arrived for the Second and Third battalions, and the state was dangerously low in military necessities. Nevertheless, there were more Continental troops under arms in Georgia than ever before.[48]

Even with the new fort and more men in the ranks, Georgia's

defenses remained fragile. Mounted scouting parties were constantly ordered out, but the Floridians had become more wary and intelligence proved of little use. An attempt to negotiate a settlement with the Indians failed, and McIntosh had difficulty explaining this failure to his superiors. Indian raids continued, and the garrison at Beards Bluff deserted in the face of the enemy.[49] Though McIntosh, upon hearing of the American victory at Trenton, longed for the "opportunity [to] follow their Examples," such an opportunity was not in the offing.[50] As the gray of winter descended, Georgians watched, and waited, and tried to make the best of an increasingly bad situation.

The new year began with the usual scouting parties and vague reports of Indian activity. Georgia's troop strength remained about the same and McIntosh concluded that recruiting could go no further. Money problems plagued the province and a few officers, including Major Marbury, resigned because they were not paid. In addition, some Continental units had to be broken into small detachments so they could be supplied, and often they were forced to live off the land, which McIntosh found "Grievous & Intolerab[le]" but necessary. Time and again, too few men and insufficient material forced plans to be altered, delayed, or abandoned, and Georgia's defenses remained weak and disorganized.[51]

No enemy who was worthy of the name could fail to see how vulnerable Georgia was. It was simply a matter of finding the weakest spot and attacking. On the morning of February 17, 1777, a force of over 300 British regulars, Loyalists, and Indians struck the small garrison at Fort McIntosh. The general organized a rescue expedition, but the enemy, with reinforcements from the south, proved too strong. The fort held out for two days and then surrendered. Fear that the attack was the beginning of a new British offensive proved unfounded and McIntosh, though wounded in the fighting, was able to hold his line of defense on the Altamaha. Nevertheless, the enemy's success caused the cry for an expedition against St. Augustine to be raised again. The argument was the same as before: Georgia could not be safe as long as that city was in enemy hands. This time, however, more people were listening.[52]

CHAPTER FIVE

Mounting Mermaids on Alligators

Other parties arise who I fear have other Vie[ws] than equal & Just
Government & the hap[piness] of Mankind.

Lachlan McIntosh to George Walton, July 11, 1776

Demands for a new expedition against St. Augustine were motivated to a large degree by political considerations. Shortly after
Wright's expulsion, the Provincial Congress adopted the Rules and
Regulations of 1776, a simple, temporary constitution that was
designed to legitimize the status quo. It did not, however, legitimize
the consensus, for soon the compromise that launched McIntosh's
military career was dealt a severe and ultimately fatal blow. Moving
to take advantage of the absence of Gwinnett and Hall, as well as to
exploit the relative inexperience and lack of organization of many of
their followers, conservatives patched up old alliances and were soon
on their way to regaining their former power. Radicals, apparently
unable to counter the opposition's gains, were left with little to do
but protest.[1]

During the summer of 1776 the inability of this conservative-led
government to improve the dismal military situation provided ample
fuel for its critics, and since it was impossible to criticize the war effort without criticizing the army, McIntosh soon found himself in
center of the controversy. Smarting from radicals' volleys, which he
may have taken more personally than they were initially intended,
the commander turned to his conservative friends for support and
consolation, which they readily gave. The radicals, seeing this as
evidence of McIntosh's partisanship, increased their attacks, and
although the commander protested that he wished to keep the army
nonpolitical, few of his critics believed him.[2]

However, it was not until fall of 1776 that the radicals were able to
turn their uncoordinated opposition into a meaningful political

movement. The key to this transformation was Button Gwinnett, who, returning from signing the Declaration of Independence, fully expected to be appointed general in the newly created Georgia brigade. But this appointment was to be made by the Continental Congress, where Gwinnett's influence was not as great as it was in Georgia. Conservative supporters in Philadelphia united and the commission went to McIntosh. Bitterly disappointed, Gwinnett adroitly shifted his emphasis to exploit what he perceived to be the vulnerable conservative political position.[3] Making the most of the disastrous attempt on St. Augustine, this radical stalwart breathed life into the coalition of "western members," Savannah dissidents, and St. John's "excludeds," which had been all but leaderless since his departure for Philadelphia, and welded it into a new faction which was dubbed, accurately enough, the "popular party."[4]

Everyone knew what was at stake. New elections had been called and the new legislature would be charged with writing a permanent constitution for the state. Seeing this as an opportunity to create a Georgia in their own image, both factions abandoned all pretense of cooperation. The resultant campaign was marked by innuendos, insults, libels, and, in at least one case, violence. Major Joseph Habersham, an outspoken conservative and close friend of General McIntosh, had challenged an attempt by Edward Langworthy, a radical, to cast a proxy vote. Habersham later demanded to see the ballot, at which time Nathaniel Hughes intervened in support of Langworthy. Insults flew, then blows, and in the ensuing struggle Hughes was stabbed with Habersham's sword and died. The major claimed it was an accident and was later cleared of all charges, but Hughes was a martyr to the cause of the radicals—their first but hardly their last.[5]

The election was a turning point for the conservatives, for they found that methods and measures which previously had persuaded rural elements to accept their leadership did not work anymore. Unable to counter the radicals' promises of wider voter participation and popular government yet unwilling to attempt to control the movement by force, the conservatives turned to other quarters, particularly the military, to try to restore their declining influence. As a result, their efforts appeared devious, often hypocritical, and in the final analysis conspiratorial, though in reality they were none of these. But as the radicals' strength grew, conservatives' options narrowed, until they were reduced to calling for a limited government controlled by the "better sort"—at the very time that Georgians were demanding governmental expansion and action, as well as insisting that people in general have a greater voice in what was done. In the end, the conservatives found themselves on the wrong side of most of the issues that were important to the new, emerging majority, which made it easy for the radicals to denounce them as self-serving at best and, at worst, as Loyalists in disguise.[6]

Soon it was clear that nothing could be done to check the radicals, at least not for the moment. Their time had come, and when the Provincial Congress met, the "popular" party underscored its victory by electing Langworthy secretary, Gwinnett speaker, and placing other radicals in key positions. Moreover, the issue upon which all ambitions hinged was the new constitution, and the radicals left no doubts as to their intent. Gwinnett himself headed the committee, composed largely of his supporters, which did most of the writing and revising, and what they produced was as revolutionary as the separation from Britain.[7]

A directly elected, one-house legislature, the House of Assembly, was to dominate the new government, with little to check its power except a vetoless Governor and his Council, both chosen by the Assembly. Representatives were to be selected from newly created counties, apportioned so that the radical coalition's majority would become even more difficult to unseat. Voter qualifications were lowered, and though the process was hardly democracy, it was a dramatic step in that direction.[8]

McIntosh had seen the confusion wrought by a weak government that tried to act swiftly in a crisis and for that reason, if no other, felt that the Rules and Regulations needed revision; but the new constitution raised grave doubts in his mind. Many of its features were good, he confided to his friend George Walton, but overall the new system was too elaborate. "We are but a few people," he wrote, "and a plain Simple Form of Government with few Offices or Temptations will . . . suit us best." This constitution and its many new positions seemed to him the product of the "Lust after the old flesh

Pott," which, conservatives felt, motivated radicals' efforts.[9] Expressed with little of the caution one might expect from a man in his position, McIntosh's partisan opinions on the new government, if widely known, were sure to make him even more the object of radicals' scorn. Although he kept his views private for the moment, he was not a man to be silent long.

Even before the constitution was written, the radicals, with the civil government coming increasingly under their control, moved to extend their influence over the military. It would seem an easy matter, inasmuch as the militia was clearly under state direction and the Continental forces were sworn to serve under the civil authority except in certain instances. Though soon to become controversial, the Continentals' oath seemed of little consequence for the moment. Fearing, perhaps justly, that conservatives in the army would ignore orders from a radical-controlled state, as radicals had done at times when the conservatives held power, Gwinnett and his followers set out to purge the military of opposition—and that meant the McIntoshes.

In December 1776 the radicals made their move, but to the surprise of many it was not against the general. They charged that during the fighting which followed the St. Augustine expedition, cavalry, led by William McIntosh, had deserted the area south of the Altamaha.[10] It seemed that some of the citizens of St. John's had attempted to plunder Loyalist settlements in East Florida, and when the British retaliated they charged that William had failed to protect them. Though William was later acquitted, the strain of the controversy wrecked his health, which was already weakened by months of campaigning in the swamps and forests. He resigned his commission and was replaced by Captain John Baker, the candidate selected by St. John's Parish. Many of William's officers, angered by the appointment, resigned in protest, creating new vacancies which were quickly filled by radicals.[11]

General McIntosh was outraged at his brother's humiliation. He and William had exerted a powerful and often harmonizing influence on the Continental and militia forces, and in so doing, McIntosh believed, had alienated those who wished to control the military for their own ends. William, who was unquestionably responsible to the state government, was the most vulnerable to partisan intrigues and so he came under attack first. But the general felt that his own destruction was the ultimate aim. His fear was plausible, for with William McIntosh discredited, Lachlan McIntosh, William's brother and superior officer, would also be subject to criticism and pressured to resign. Thus the general saw himself as the focus of a radical plot, and though he did not name who he thought was responsible, one need not look far to find him. The source of his brother's and therefore his own trouble was St. John's Parish, center of power for Button Gwinnett.[12]

Weeks dragged on as the wary general tried to defend the state and himself. Meanwhile the Provincial Congress, having adopted the Constitution of 1777, adjourned in mid-February, leaving the government in the hands of President Archibald Bulloch and the Council of Safety, which included Gwinnett and George McIntosh. But it was a short-lived arrangement; before the month was out, Bulloch suddenly died. The obscure circumstances surrounding his death spurred rumors of poisoning, but foul play was never proved. To replace Bulloch, the Council elected Button Gwinnett its President with only one dissenting vote, that of George McIntosh.[13]

British activity in the south was Georgia's most pressing concern and its new President, whose powers as commander-in-chief gave him the military authority that had so long been denied, attacked the problem with all his energy. His solution was surprisingly unoriginal: St. Augustine must fall. Many Georgians, fearful after the recent loss of Fort McIntosh, were of a similar mind. The Council agreed, and on March 4 voted Gwinnett the authority to take the militia and proceed with an attack.[14] However, the Council's resolution did not include Continental forces; the part they were to play was left for Gwinnett to arrange as best he could.

President Gwinnett hoped to obtain support for the operation by appealing directly to General Robert Howe, the new commander of the Southern Department. In early March 1777, Howe arrived in Savannah to discuss Georgia's military situation and it was then that Gwinnett suggested the expedition. Howe was not impressed and pointed out that the plan contained many of the same flaws which had doomed the attempt in 1776. When his arguments failed to blunt

Gwinnett's enthusiasm, General Howe tried to delay a decision and finally went so far as to avoid the President entirely. Though hampered by his inability to get a quorum of the Council, due to the demands of the planting season, Gwinnett still pressed his case. As Howe became more negative, the President's determination grew. Through it all, McIntosh, recovering from his wound, remained on the sidelines and was not consulted by Gwinnett. The President wanted the Continental troops, but without General McIntosh.[15]

Then on March 14, 1777, everything changed. President Gwinnett had McIntosh's younger brother, George, arrested, put in irons, and placed in the common jail; the charge was treason. Gwinnett did not act on his own, however, but upon a recommendation from the Continental Congress. The basis for the accusation was an intercepted letter, written by East Florida Governor Tonyn, which revealed that George McIntosh, while serving on the Council of Safety, had secretly aided the British.[16]

The facts of the incident to which Tonyn referred were as follows. In May 1776 the younger McIntosh had formed a partnership with his brothers-in-law, Robert Baillie and Sir Patrick Houstoun, to ship a load of rice to Dutch Guiana. Just before the vessel sailed they were joined in the venture by William Panton, who was put in charge of the shipment. Panton, a known Tory, violated the strictures of the Continental Association by taking the boat to St. Augustine, where he changed its papers. He then sailed to the British West Indies and sold the cargo.[17] The incident not only involved the general's brother with three men whose loyalty to the American cause was at that time highly questionable, it implicated him in open trade with the enemy. If that were not enough, the East Florida Governor had praised George McIntosh as a man whose principles were "loyal attachment to King and Constitution" and who would aid the British with "all the service in his power." The evidence was too strong to ignore.[18]

Gwinnett acted well within his legal authority when he had George McIntosh arrested, but there is little to suggest that he found the duty unpleasant. In fact, McIntosh supporters complained that the methods were unnecessarily harsh and that the President was masking political and personal motives behind public responsibility.[19] Gwinnett denied this, but that did not alleviate the opposition's concerns. Conservatives saw it as another step in the suppression of their faction and the general saw it as one more move in the suppression of the McIntoshes. In many ways his fears were well founded. On the evening of the same day that George McIntosh was confined, Gwinnett met with Howe to discuss the matter. When asked if there were any charges against the general, the President replied that there were none, but pointing out the close relationship between the brothers, he speculated that the incident might raise doubts about the loyalty of the military. He suggested that, for the good of the state, General McIntosh should be assigned elsewhere.[20]

Gwinnett's proposal was not the first time that reassignment had been raised. During the past summer, General Lee had noted the close family connections between a number of Loyalists and Whigs, and his solution was to remove the whole Georgia battalion and replace it with troops from another state.[21] The conservative-controlled government had rejected the plan. Lee, an unpopular outsider, had suggested the removal of a force which at that moment seemed to be doing its duty as well as could be expected. Gwinnett claimed his suggestion was motivated by similar fears, but conservatives heard its political overtones. Whether planned or not, it appeared to opponents that the President was using George McIntosh's arrest to rid himself of the man who seemed to stand between him and total control of the armed forces in Georgia. If that was the plan, as the general and his friends believed, it failed; Howe rejected the proposal outright.[22] Gwinnett would have to find another way.

McIntosh's first concern was his brother's release. Expecting no sympathy from Gwinnett, he appealed instead to the Council of Safety and found that most of those who were present were not fully behind the President. In fact, Gwinnett had acted without consulting the Council for fear that it might prevent the arrest—an indication that the radicals had not completely consolidated their power. The Council convened and, over the President's protest, ordered the irons removed and the prisoner placed in more comfortable quarters. The following day, with Gwinnett out of town, the Council met again and released George McIntosh on £20,000 bail.[23] The President was outraged, but the action was legal.

Various radicals quickly pointed out that the full Council of Safety had not acted and that among those members who were present were the McIntoshes' brother-in-law, John Houstoun, and several of the family's close friends. Gwinnett's supporters noted with disgust that four of the Council members had helped to raise the bail.[24] This added a new dimension to the radicals' charges, for if conservatives were willing to support a "known Tory" openly, they must be Tories as well. With that, radicals' efforts to destroy conservatives took on the mantle of a patriotic cause: the defense of the state from its enemies. At this point many radicals began to equate opposition with treason.

The President, who had suffered a personal as well as a political defeat, led the way in denouncing the conservatives. Convinced that the McIntosh incident was a symptom of the disease which had weakened Georgia from the start, he spread it abroad that, had it not been for Georgia Tories and the supplies they provided, St. Augustine would have fallen long before. Traitors within the state, he claimed, had escaped capture through the aid of their "various Connections . . . who tho' inoffensive of themselves, yet [were] Tories by Consanguinity."[25] As Gwinnett saw it, Lachlan McIntosh was included in his definition. To eradicate this enemy, the source of his encouragement had to be destroyed, and that "source," the President pointed out, was St. Augustine.

Thus Gwinnett's proposed invasion became more than an effort to protect the Georgia frontiers; its purpose was also to promote internal security. But the radicals did not have a monopoly on this approach to partisan politics. Though conservatives had trouble classifying their radical opposition as pro-British, they denounced the radicals as self-seeking tyrants and as dangerous to liberty as any Tory. Their charges garnered little support, however, and the radicals, confident of success, prepared for an invasion which would secure themselves and the state from all enemies. Victory seemed within their grasp.

On March 17, President Gwinnett presented his full plan to General Howe, who rejected it as unnecessary and unworkable. Howe then called his officers to a council of war—which pointedly excluded Gwinnett—explained his decision, and announced that he was returning to Charleston. Gwinnett was outraged. As commander-in-chief of Georgia's forces, he felt it an insult that he was not included in the discussions. More important, Howe's rejection of Gwinnett's military scheme was a critical blow to Gwinnett's political scheme. It was as if Howe were working to obstruct his efforts, as if he were one of the opposition. If that were true, it would follow that Howe's refusal to cooperate was not a military but a political decision. Convinced this was the case, Gwinnett vowed to continue, since the "true friends of the State " felt the expedition was necessary.[26] The implications were clear. Howe was under the influence of men who did not have the state's best interests at heart, men who opposed the radicals. In short, Howe's visit was useless. "He came," Gwinnett later wrote to John Hancock, "he saw, and left us in our low Estate."[27]

CHAPTER SIX

"A Scoundrell & lying Rascal"

This great Hero that has set our Country in a flame cannot last long &
no gentleman could have suffered long under accusations trumped up
for time serving purposes.

George Walton to Lachlan McIntosh, April 18, 1777

O Liberty! why do you suffer so many of your faithfull sons, your
Warmest Votaries to fall at your Shrine! Alas my Friend! my Friend!

Lyman Hall to Roger Sherman, May 16, 1777

President Gwinnett had two forces from which to draw troops for
his invasion: the state militia and McIntosh's Continentals. The
former, poorly trained and undersupplied, were by far the inferior,
but with William McIntosh out of the picture they were firmly in the
radicals' camp. What these troops lacked militarily they made up for
politically, and to Gwinnett that was no small consideration. That
they could be depended on, therefore, seemed beyond question; that
they could succeed was not.

The Georgia Continentals had not been forbidden by General
Howe to participate, and under the terms of their "oath" they were
subject to state authority, but Gwinnett wanted no part of them.
One might argue that the case of George McIntosh caused the
President to question the propriety of having the brother of an
accused traitor lead the army against St. Augustine, but the move to
bypass McIntosh's Continentals in favor of Howe's had been made
well before George McIntosh's arrest.[1] The President did not want
to divide the command between himself and another Georgian,
especially one who was associated with the conservatives.

The options were clear. If the primary purpose of the expedition
was to take St. Augustine, the commander-in-chief should have used
all available units; but if the President hoped to use the invasion to

enhance his and the radicals' political position, he would have to go it alone. Gwinnett wasted no time. He decided to proceed without McIntosh and the Georgia Continentals. If the invasion succeeded, the radical Whigs would be hailed as saviors of the state. If it failed, the blame could be placed on Howe's refusal to aid them. The President was convinced that there was yet another reason for his problems with Howe. The general, he believed, did not wish to submit to Georgia's civil authority.[2] Since Howe was responsible to the Continental Congress and not to Gwinnett, the charge was not to the point, but reason was one of the early casualties of the struggle. Civil versus military was an issue to be called out when needed, and otherwise ignored.

Despite Howe's exodus and conservative opposition, Gwinnett was determined to proceed against St. Augustine by using only state militia. McIntosh realized that if the expedition succeeded without his assistance, his Continental forces would appear to be a useless burden to the impoverished state. Therefore he informed his officers that if the President requested aid, "give it to the ut[mos]t of your power & Corporate with him [i]n every measure which will promote [t]he good of the common cause."[3] But once preparations were under way, Gwinnett began to experience the difficulties that had plagued previous endeavors. Food, clothing, and ammunition were scarce, transportation facilities were inadequate, and when he called out the militia, only St. John's Parish responded. It was obvious that such a force had no hope for success. Faced with that certainty, on March 27 Gwinnett requested assistance from McIntosh.[4]

The general, though indignant that the President had waited so long to consult him, was satisfied with the turn of events and agreed to help. Continental troops were ordered to be ready to "march at the Shortest notice" and to aid in any venture which appeared to have a "probability of Success" or promoted the "Interest of this or the United States."[5] But McIntosh knew Gwinnett's mind, or at least believed he did. The Continental forces, he wrote General Howe, were called upon when no militia appeared "as a hole to creep out of & throw the blame upon the [mili]tary if nothing was done."[6] Convinced he was to serve as a scapegoat, the general nevertheless decided to join the expedition. Better to take part, though the chance of victory was small, than sit on the sidelines and be criticized no matter what the outcome.

One thing was immediately obvious: neither McIntosh nor Gwinnett intended to play a secondary role in the campaign. After a series of delays, for which each blamed the other, the troops began to march south. The main force reached Gwinnett's Sunbury head-quarters on Sunday, April 13, and when McIntosh arrived the following day, still in pain from the wound he received earlier, he was in anything but a cooperative mood.[7] Though resolved to aid the endeavor in his own way, he was disturbed over recent accusa-tions that he too had traded with the enemy. He wrote Henry Laurens that he expected "his detractors" to "trump up" charges against him as a result of the proposed invasion, and when they did, he hoped that the Continental Congress would hear his case.[8] Ex-pecting the worst from the men with whom he had agreed to cooperate, McIntosh set out to make the best of a bad situation.

From the moment the general arrived, the operation seemed to fall apart. Gwinnett called a council of war, which McIntosh refused to attend. Instead, McIntosh called his officers together and they re-solved that the calling of councils of war and courts-martial inter-fered with "the particular province of the Officers of the Military" and were "quite Improper for the President of the State." Though the officers agreed to consult with Gwinnett on all pertinent matters, their action was a direct slap at the President, who, despite McIn-tosh's belief that both sides agreed to this procedure, was not about to give in.[9]

On April 16 the troops prepared to embark, the officers took an oath of allegiance to the United States, and it appeared that at last the expedition would proceed. It did not. That same day Lyman Hall, Gwinnett's radical mentor, arrived at Sunbury and again raised the question of the right to call councils of war.[10] Trying to ignore the controversy that boiled around him, General McIntosh prepared to move the army southward, but when he called for the militia that Gwinnett had promised, he was informed that none was available. With that the advantage shifted to McIntosh and he immediately requested provisions so that his Continentals might conduct the expedition alone.[11]

Gwinnett understood what had happened. For the invasion to proceed as a purely Continental operation would have undone his whole plan. Success would be a major coup for the conservatives and failure could be blamed on the President and the militia. Therefore he ordered all preparations halted. In Savannah, the Council of Safety met to consider what to do, and McIntosh, fearful that the expedition would be used to discredit him, rushed to the capital to present his case. But the Council refused to hear him and suggested that, for the good of the state, the two leaders withdraw from the campaign. Both agreed, though the general, still suspicious of the radicals' intent, was less than enthusiastic.[12]

The Council of Safety then ordered Colonel Samuel Elbert to assume command and conduct the invasion. Elbert, bewildered that his orders came from the civil government rather than from his military superiors, asked McIntosh what he should do.[13] Although the general advised him to continue with the expedition, Elbert's "promotion" left McIntosh even more uneasy and, at times, irrational.[14] He had become as defensive as Gwinnett, seeing plots to remove him in almost every action the civil authorities took. The Council had refused to hear his explanation, and after he had voluntarily stepped aside, it put another officer in his place with orders to proceed with the operation. It was a move that some might interpret as meaning he was not capable of directing the expedition. That was an interpretation which General Lachlan McIntosh could not accept.

But the Council may well have done McIntosh a favor. Like the one that preceded it, the St. Augustine invasion was a disaster. Inability to coordinate the land and sea advance, lack of provisions, and oppressive heat combined to bring the operation to a halt. Finally, Elbert was forced to retreat with little accomplished.[15] McIntosh, meanwhile, remained in Savannah to ponder his fate. Always sensitive to personal affronts, the attacks upon his brothers and upon himself had driven him into a corner and convinced him that, for political reasons, Gwinnett and the radicals were working to humiliate him into resigning.

He was not alone in his suspicions. From Philadelphia George Walton wrote to the general about having been privately questioned "as to the firmness of [McIntosh's] principles in this great cause," but he explained that the attempts of the "rotten hearted designing enemy" to cast doubts on his loyalty had failed. The sponsor of this attack was Gwinnett. To Walton, President Gwinnett was a "self elected Demaugue," despised everywhere, governed by his vices, and loyal to no one except his radical crony, Lyman Hall. He concluded that Gwinnett pretended to be pro-American only to fulfill his own ambitions, one of which was to put himself in McIntosh's place.[16] Walton's attack had all the venom of those that radicals had leveled against conservatives, but to McIntosh, every word was true.

A confrontation was at hand. In May the first Assembly under the Constitution of 1777 was called to order, the factions began their maneuvers, and in the early stages the radicals suffered what seemed to be a setback. Gwinnett was defeated in his bid for the governorship by John Adam Treutlen, a man less radical than Gwinnett but certainly not a conservative.[17] Gwinnett may have been too controversial, even for some radicals, and so Truetlen emerged as a compromise candidate; but if that was the case the former President's more rabid supporters were not part of the compromise.

Once the executive was chosen, the Assembly set about examining the St. Augustine debacle and, immediately, tensions began to rise. Determined to exonerate their somewhat tarnished leader, radicals rose to Gwinnett's defense, agreeing with Lyman Hall that "the salvation of [the] State almost Depend[ed] on the Removl of Brigadr G McKintosh, to some other part of the Continent."[18] Conservatives were equally determined that McIntosh should remain in Georgia, and worked to have Gwinnett censured for mismanaging the campaign. The arguments were presented, debates conducted, and the vote was taken. The radical ranks closed and held firm; the conduct of the President and his Council was ruled to have been legal and correct. It was too much for General McIntosh. On the floor of the Assembly, he called Gwinnett "*a Scoundrell & lying Rascal*."[19] What had started as a political matter between two factions had become a personal vendetta between the two men.

On the evening of May 15, a written challenge was delivered to General McIntosh in which Gwinnett demanded satisfaction for the public insult and proposed that they meet at dawn the next day in Sir James Wright's pasture, outside of town. Perhaps to hide his apprehension, the general "humorously" replied that the hour was rather early but he agreed to be there, with pistols as his choice of weapon. McIntosh realized his dilemma. If he refused the challenge, his enemies would brand him a coward, unworthy of his commission; if he accepted and lost, the radicals would be rid of him. Yet if he killed Gwinnett, he could be prosecuted under the Articles of War.[20] Once again he found himself forced to act and seeing no way out, he agreed to meet his challenger. It was the only means by which he could maintain his honor and, at the same time, strike a blow against the personification of all his troubles, Button Gwinnett.

McIntosh and his second, Colonel Joseph Habersham, were first to arrive at the appointed spot. Gwinnett, with George Wells to assist him, soon joined them. If it was one of the beautiful May mornings so common along the Savannah, no one noticed; the only matter discussed was the business which brought them there. After the pistols were checked, some spectators appeared, causing the adversaries to move down the meadow to a spot out of view, where Gwinnett asked that McIntosh set the distance. "Eight to ten feet," replied the general, a clear indication of his serious intent, but Habersham protested that it was too close and so another pace was added. It was then proposed that they begin back to back, but McIntosh refused, suggesting that they face each other to "let us see what we are about."[21] At last, Lachlan McIntosh was convinced that his and his family's honor could be cleansed only by Gwinnett's blood.

When the preparations were completed, each man took his position and agreed to "fire as they cou'd," and the two shots sounded as one. Gwinnett fell, his thigh broken. McIntosh remained standing, but Gwinnett's ball was lodged in the flesh of his leg. Thinking Gwinnett no worse wounded than himself, the general asked if he would care to exchange another shot. At this point the seconds intervened and declared that both men had done their duty as gentlemen. They shook hands and departed.[22]

Gwinnett was carried home and put to bed in serious condition.

The weather was extremely hot and "a Mortification came on." Three days later, on the morning of May 19, he died of complications from the wound. Despite his attitude on the morning of the duel, McIntosh was distressed at the news and agonized over the events that led the "unfortunate man to his own destruction." For a brief time it seemed that shock had caused the sober men of both parties to pause, reflect, and realize that they, as the ones who had supported the quarrels, shared McIntosh's guilt. McIntosh, the wounded combatant, had even written his friend Laurens that it seemed "our unhappy divisions were thereby at an end." [23]

To McIntosh's relief, most people seemed to believe that Gwinnett's death was "owing to the unskilfulness of the doctor," and therefore no one seemed overly angry with him. For the moment, no efforts were made to prosecute the general; members of both parties visited him, and, according to McIntosh, Mrs. Gwinnett "publicly declared [him] innocent and altogether blameless, and often inquired after [his] health." [24] Then, as if by a signal, the truce ended. Toward the end of May, party jealousies reemerged and McIntosh realized, to his dismay, that nothing had changed.

To the radicals, the loss of Gwinnett was personal as well as political, and so it took little urging from Lyman Hall and his new lieutenant, Joseph Wood, to turn the faction's fury against McIntosh. The two men and their supporters attempted to bring criminal charges against the general, stirred up feelings against Colonel Habersham for acting as his second, and continued to press the case against McIntosh's brother, George. [25] The motives behind these actions have been lost within the maze of partisan attacks which accompanied them, but one factor emerged as a prominent concern for both sides: the old issue of civil versus military authority was trotted out again for the convenience of the radicals.

To his friends, Gwinnett had "lost his life in endeavouring to maintain the civil Power in opposition to the cunning & subterfuges of a designing man," Lachlan McIntosh. To the general, the issue was much the same, but the emphasis was different. "Unless," he wrote Laurens, "the Congress fixes some line between the government of their army and the interference of the civil government of this restless and unsettled State, it will not only become useless, but a nuisance to the inhabitants."[26] The matter appeared simple: the radicals wanted civil (meaning their own) control of the army; McIntosh did not. Civil control had often hindered his operations, but civil control by the radicals threatened him personally. Never a strong party man, he protected the army's independence so as to protect himself; the two had become inseparable.

With Gwinnett gone, the radicals quickly reorganized and, over conservatives' opposition, selected Joseph Wood to go to the Continental Congress. Then they unleashed their fury on McIntosh. The general had been released on his own recognizance and allowed to resume his command on the promise that he would appear before the Assembly in the fall, an intolerable situation for the Hall-Wood faction. Relying on their "grass roots" support, the two men circulated petitions calling for McIntosh's removal. In Chatham, Effingham, Liberty, Richmond, and Wilkes counties the radicals collected 574 signatures which they presented to the legislature.[27]

The conservatives could do little except claim that the petition lists were forged or a misrepresentation of popular sentiment. The old radical arguments of "treason by consanguinity" and opposition to civil authority reappeared, but the conservatives could deal with those charges. However, this tactic, pressure by weight of numbers, was something McIntosh's friends had little success combating. They complained that "Gentlemen of ability, whose characters [were] well established," were the only ones the radicals attacked, which put Georgia "into the Hands of those whose ability or situation in Life [did] not entitle them" to govern. They protested the "Stark Naked Democracy" which threatened to ruin the state, but the "people," to whom conservatives tried to appeal, saw these arguments as evidence that the radicals were right: conservatives were opposed to the popular will.[28]

Working through an organization called the Liberty Society, Hall and Wood left no stone unturned in their attempt to discredit McIntosh. Charges were brought against Captain John Berrien, the general's aide-de-camp, for "Speaking Disrespectfull" of Georgia's Assembly. Although they were subsequently dropped, the accusations gave support to the radicals' contention that the general's antigovernment views were shared by many officers.[29]

Finally the Liberty Society made its most dramatic move of the campaign. To McIntosh's dismay, Mrs. Gwinnett, still "in her [widow's] weeds," presented a petition to the Assembly, which was eventually forwarded to Philadelphia. The document, which the general's supporters claimed was "made out for her to move pity and compassion," denounced McIntosh in the strongest, most emotional language yet used, and it had the desired impact. Although the exact numbers will never be known, it is probable that a majority of Georgians now agreed with the contention that "while the Command of the Continental Troops remains in the hands of the McIntoshes, our People will never think themselves safe."[30] The radicals were winning.

If the general's problems were not enough, there was also the unresolved plight of George McIntosh. With the aid of their close friend, John Wereat, the brothers prepared and circulated pamphlets designed to prove the younger brother's innocence. But highly partisan in their arguments and supported by affidavits from the very men with whom George was accused of dealing, the pamphlets did not alter the government's position. The younger McIntosh finally obtained permission to take his case to the Continental Congress, but when he learned that he was to proceed to Philadelphia under armed guard, he broke parole and, until he escaped the state, was "hunted through the woods and swamps like a partridge in *Liberty* County," while his brother did everything in his power, legal or not, to prevent his capture.[31] The general's actions only prompted more charges that he was interfering with the civil authorities, charges that were difficult to deny.

The radicals' victory was at hand, but it was won at a terrible cost. Army discipline was shattered, morale was gone, and for a large segment of the population all faith in Georgia's Continental forces and their commander had disappeared. Since the radicals had also elected Edward Langworthy to the Continental Congress, they were assured of having three of the five Georgia members and control of the delegation.[32] The general must have known that if things were not altered by the time the next Assembly met, his career was at an end.

Fortunately, McIntosh still had friends who would come to his aid. Early in August, Walton and Laurens began to exert pressure to have McIntosh transferred to the main army. Congress was willing, and since one of Washington's brigades was without a general officer it was agreed that McIntosh would assume the position, enabling him to leave Georgia and his enemies behind.[33] It was not that simple, however, for before he learned of his transfer the Georgia Assembly had met and passed a resolution removing the general from his Continental command. Insulted, McIntosh stood his ground and refused to "dishonor [his] master the Continental Congress" by giving up the office it had bestowed on him.[34] Elbert, who was picked to replace him, refused to accept the promotion so long as McIntosh remained commander under the orders of Congress, thus negating the radicals' hopes to use his ambition to check the general and emphasizing once again the uneasy position in which ill-defined lines of authority placed the army and its leaders.[35]

Frustrated, the Assembly drafted a petition denouncing McIntosh's refusal to submit to its will and called on Congress to remove him (the main objective, after all). But before their efforts could bear fruit, the general received his new orders and began his journey northward.[36] Although it had not happened as his enemies planned, the state was finally free of McIntosh's influence; but the relief felt by the radicals could not have been greater than his own.

As for George McIntosh, whose arrest had precipitated the affair, his case also was resolved far from its origin. In early October, about the same time the general learned of his transfer, his brother presented his argument to the Continental Congress. Because most of Georgia's radical delegates were absent, it took less than a week for Walton and Laurens to obtain a resolution stating that "there is not sufficient cause before Congress for the detention of the said George McIntosh," and with that brief phrase the case ended.[37]

Or did it? Though George McIntosh was not found guilty, neither was he exonerated, and the clouds of suspicion were heavy. Even such a McIntosh supporter as Henry Laurens was skeptical, and confided to John Wereat that George's defense contained evidence to indicate that he, the youngest McIntosh, "may be charged to have been [a] willfully high criminal." Laurens also assigned the general a share of the blame for the events which followed the arrest, for "if he had taken a wise part in the beginning, if he had not attempted to knock down suspicions too well founded much trouble might have been saved."[38]

Laurens was speaking well after the events, and outside the emotional climate which accompanied them, and he knew it. Gwinnett was dead, the reputations of the McIntoshes were badly damaged, and Georgia was in turmoil. For Congress to have found George McIntosh guilty would only have strengthened the radicals, and since Laurens had no love for them or their politics, he had worked for acquittal. Still, as so often in the past, the South Carolinian saw things more clearly than those around him. "To judge charitably," he wrote the general, "your brother gave way to temptation and to say lastly acted very indiscretely, he seems to have been in the class of those who wished the American cause very well but not *so well* as to make any sacrifice of his investment."[39]

George McIntosh went home to his native state. His health broken and his reputation ruined, he never attempted to return to political life. Few records exist to indicate how he spent his last years, but in December of 1779 he died.[40] In another way, his brother's fate was equally harsh. He lived to learn that the same jealousies and factions that he had hoped to leave behind in Georgia appeared in slightly different forms wherever he went. His journey to Washington's headquarters was, in reality, a retreat. It would not be his last.

CHAPTER SEVEN

New Commands, Old Problems

As party animosity, personal prejudice & misunderstanding have unhappily created some divisions in Georgia and General McIntosh among others may in consequence have undeserved censures cast upon him, I think it but justice to him to say that he ever appeared to me to have the warmest attachment to the cause of America, to have endeavored by every effort to promote its service, and that I have not the least doubt that his zeal and spirit will be of benefit to the common cause.

General Robert Howe to John Hancock, November 3, 1777

[I] beg leave only to inform your Excellency that General McIntosh is unfortunate enough to be universally Hated by every man in this department both Civil & Military.

Colonel Daniel Brodhead to General George Washington,
January 16, 1779

Relieved to be free from Georgia factionalism, Lachlan McIntosh began his trek north. Passing through the seasons as he rode, he left summer in Georgia, autumn in Virginia, and in early December 1777 arrived at his destination, where he was greeted by the Pennsylvania winter, General Washington, and Valley Forge. After the battle of Germantown the American army had moved to the high banks above the Schuylkill River to wait for spring. Less than 25 miles to the southeast the British settled down as well—in Philadelphia. Secure and warm within the fallen capital, the army of George III rested, hardly realizing the drama that was being played out just beyond its reach.[1]

What happened in Valley Forge that winter has become so deeply embedded in the saga of this nation's birth that there is a tendency, in this cynical age, to treat the accounts of suffering, privation, and courage as romantic tales, embellished with each new telling. But Valley Forge was real—as the men whom McIntosh found cramped in unfinished huts or huddled for warmth in tattered tents knew all too well. Fully a third of the approximately 10,000 soliders in Washington's army were incapacitated for want of clothing, shoes, and blankets.[2] The men were tired, discouraged, and restless. If the army was to exist when spring came, it would take a monumental effort, and its leaders knew it.

On December 20 Washington placed McIntosh in charge of the North Carolina brigade, the sickliest and worst-clothed unit in an army that was characterized by illness and exposure. Troop returns showed that of the 2,700 men who manned the brigade at full strength, only 928 were in camp. Of those, 327 were sick and 164 were "unfit for duty for want of cl[othin]g."[3] So short of manpower was McIntosh's new command that he was forced to enlist the "walking sick" to erect shelters, but it seemed to do little good. As the snows deepened, casualty lists lengthened, though not a shot was fired by the enemy.

During January and February 1778, the North Carolina brigade averaged 88 sick in camp, 219 sick in hospitals, and 199 unfit for lack of clothes; not once during that season did the unit record over 564 able-bodied men available for duty.[4] Any decline in the number of sick was usually accompanied by the grim notion that death, not recovery, had ended their suffering. In view of the "skeleton" medical corp (at one point only a doctor and his assistant), it is remarkable that the record was not worse, but it was bad enough.[5] As his men crouched around their fires and hoped for warmer days, McIntosh exhausted every means of bettering their situation.

In the end, his efforts produced scant results. North Carolina Governor Richard Caswell tried to help, but the scarcity of money, the cost of supplies, and the distance between Valley Forge and the brigade's home state all but negated his attempts.[6] Meanwhile, efforts to obtain provisions in the immediate area met with opposition from the residents, who preferred British coin to Continental script, and morale dipped as men went hungry in a state where food seemed plentiful. Congress, characteristically, set up a committee to investigate. Reorganization of the Commissary Department was finally ordered and conditions improved somewhat, but by then it was spring and the worst was over. Surprisingly, the army's desertion rate had been lowest among the North Carolina troops. Distance from home and lack of proper clothing for the trip were surely primary factors, but one must give credit to the officers who supported their men through the ordeal.[7]

Because of its weakened condition, the North Carolina brigade was seldom called on to perform military functions. Every effort was made to keep the men together, until, at the suggestion of McIntosh and his officers, the brigade's nine regiments were reorganized into three battalions and the surplus officers were sent out to recruit new troops.[8] As spring came, the unit, still undermanned, was given the responsibility of collecting intelligence on enemy movements, in anticipation of an early offensive. The enemy, it turned out, was not moving, and so the assignment mainly involved protecting a herd of cattle that was brought in as provisions for the army. The animals were important, especially to men on short rations, but it was not the type of duty from which military careers are made. Still, McIntosh gave it his full attention and delivered the beef as ordered.[9]

In April, Washington removed the Georgian from his brigade command and ordered him to inspect all Continental hospitals in New Jersey and Pennsylvania. McIntosh was to send back lists of patients and attendants, remove all unnecessary personnel, rectify inefficiency and neglect, and make suggestions as to where new hospitals might be located. Washington had long been dissatisfied with the operation of the medical corps and McIntosh was chosen as the "discreet Field Officer" who was capable of carrying out what was, in reality, a housecleaning. Although the new assignment lacked the glamor of a field command, the discretionary instructions gave him the most personal authority he had enjoyed since he left Georgia. Setting out as soon as he received his orders, the general spent almost two months traveling from hospital to hospital. Few significant changes resulted from his visits; no major reforms were ordered and the American medical corps continued in its generally inefficient course.[10] Yet his conduct impressed General Washington, for it was not long until McIntosh was given the greatest opportunity of his career.

In early May 1778 the American war for independence began to take a turn for the better. The army had survived Valley Forge and was being welded into a sound, confident fighting force. This confidence continued to grow as the soldiers learned that the United States was no longer alone in the struggle; France had formally joined them.[11] Yet even before the Franco-American alliance was announced, Americans were making plans to enlarge the scope of their operations.

In late April commissioners from Virginia and Pennsylvania met at Fort Pitt, America's strongest western outpost. They discussed how best to defend the frontier from British-sponsored Indian attacks and concluded that the surest way was to send an expedition against Fort Detroit, the headquarters of British western operations. This suggestion was transmitted to Congress, where on May 2, 1778, it was considered and approved. To carry out the proposal, Congress authorized the raising of two regiments from Virginia and Pennsylvania recruits.[12]

Washington had been interested in the Ohio Valley (whose security was the object of the Detroit expedition) since his involvement in the Ohio Company prior to the French and Indian War. Plans to ensure that it remained free from foreign control were to occupy his thoughts throughout the Revolution.[13] But the capture of Detroit promised to create as many problems as it solved. Both Virginia and Pennsylvania claimed the area and their conflicts (which predated the Revolution) had so hampered the efforts of General Edward Hand, commander of the Western Department, that he had asked to be relieved. Congress accepted his resignation; then, on the same day it approved the Detroit expedition, it authorized Washington to appoint a replacement. The man he selected was Lachlan McIntosh.[14]

In recommending McIntosh, Washington stressed the Georgian's "firm disposition and equal justice; his assiduity and good understanding," which made him "an officer of great worth and merit," with whom his commander parted "with great reluctance." Washington also "imagined" that previous experiences had given McIntosh "knowledge of negociation in Indian affairs" which would be useful on the frontier. But these qualifications, though excellent in themselves, could have been duplicated in other commanders.

Washington was looking for something more, and Lachlan McIntosh was judged able to provide it.[15]

The expedition was filled with pitfalls, the major one being the participants themselves. Fort Pitt was to serve as headquarters, but three-quarters of the troops were to be drawn from Virginia. Thus, it was hoped, neither state could use the anticipated victory to reinforce its claims. But since almost all who were involved, with the exception of McIntosh, had some interest (usually personal) in who owned the land, there was little reason to believe that the balance struck by Congress would overcome the differences. The Georgian was about to step into a maze of state claims, land-company schemes, colonization enterprises, and speculators which confuses historians to this day. To do nothing more than prevent conflicts within the American forces promised to be a major undertaking.[16]

Clearly, such a joint effort could succeed only if its commander kept peace between all parties and held himself above charges of favoritism. Washington believed, or at least hoped, that McIntosh could perform the task, and later informed Pennsylvania officials that it was primarily for his "disinterested concern" that the Georgian was selected.[17] And so, for the second time in his career, Lachlan McIntosh was chosen to keep quarreling parties' energies directed against the British. His record in the previous attempt offered little encouragement for success.

McIntosh realized that it was the most prestigious assignment he had yet undertaken, but it is doubtful that he, or anyone else, anticipated how important it would be. The operations of the next year would go far toward deciding which nation would permanently occupy the territory beyond the Appalachian Mountains, and the part the Georgian played was essential to fulfillment of the American dream of being more than a nation of small states crowded between those mountains and the Atlantic Ocean. Territorial expansion was second, and remained second only to independence in the minds of American leaders, especially Washington. In a very real sense, their hopes rested on Lachlan McIntosh.

Accompanied by Lackie, now a captain in the army and assigned to his father as an aide, the general journeyed to York, Pennsylvania, where the "fugitive Congress" was meeting. Reaching York in late May 1778, he found that the Board of War had made almost no arrangements for supplying the expedition or for recruiting the two regiments that Congress had authorized. Reports that Indians had launched scattered attacks along the frontier made matters even more urgent; so McIntosh, realizing there was no time to raise new troops, requested that Washington provide him with men already under arms.[18]

Understandably upset with the expedition's lack of progress, Washington promised to provide what aid he could, which he pointed out might be little, if any. With the enemy still in Philadelphia and American ranks showing only a small numerical increase, the fact that he released any men at all indicates the importance he placed on the Ohio Valley. The Eighth Pennsylvania Regiment, under Colonel Daniel Brodhead, was ordered to join the operation, along with the Thirteenth Virginia Regiment under Colonel John Gibson, part of which was already at Fort Pitt.[19] Thus both states were represented and McIntosh had his army.

Brodhead was selected, it seems, because he was competent, available, and above all a Pennsylvanian. Gibson, who represented Virginia, had been transferred from another assignment because of his knowledge of the language and customs of the Indians in the area.[20] McIntosh needed such talents; so it is hardly surprising that he came to rely heavily on Gibson's advice and judgment, and consulted him on a wide variety of matters. The attention he paid the Virginian was hardly overlooked by the Pennsylvania delegation, and was to cause the general considerable grief in months to come.

The two regiments gave General McIntosh a solid core of experienced troops, but not enough to launch the invasion. Others realized this and came to the expedition's aid. Among them was Colonel George Morgan, the Indian Agent for the Middle Department, who, like so many people operating in the west, was a land speculator interested in the Ohio Valley. Morgan believed that 1,500 Continentals, plus militia, could—in the proper season—capture what he claimed was a nearly defenseless British headquarters. He also asserted that once this objective was accomplished, the hostile Indians, whom he estimated at no more than 300 warriors, would join the American cause through "fear & interest," and the frontier would be secure. This evaluation, from the man who was supposed to have the best grasp of the situation, no doubt helped influence the Board of War.[21]

On June 11, 1778, Congress received the Board's recommendations and resolved that "an expedition be immediately undertaken . . . to reduce, if practicable, the garrison of Detroit." An army of 3,000 Continentals was to be provided and McIntosh was authorized to raise as many as 2,500 Virginia militia if needed. In addition, Congress appropriated $932,732⅓ for provisions.[22] From all appearances, it was to be the best-manned and -supplied operation ever to serve in the Western Department, and of course the largest command ever assumed by General Lachlan McIntosh.

McIntosh quickly set about organizing the expedition, for if his army did not reach Fort Pitt by September 1, little could be accomplished before winter set in. Immediately, however, obstacles began to mount. Virginia authorities, disappointed with the role assigned them, protested that they could provide neither the men nor the provisions Congress required. Their attitude, combined with supply problems that plagued the expedition from the start, slowed efforts almost to a halt. "Really ashamed" at the delays, the general cajoled, argued, complained, and threatened those he felt were responsible, but the results were minimal.[23]

As the expedition floundered, the entire complexion of the frontier changed. In mid-July a new wave of Indian attacks struck the Wyoming Valley and soon the western side of the mountains, from New York to Virginia, was in an uproar. Colonel Morgan, who argued that the neighboring tribes were friendly and deserved protection, insisted that the attacks came from hostile forces farther west. Frontiersmen, who refused to make such a discrimination, saw the attacks as evidence that Morgan's peaceful policy had failed. Convinced that the real enemy was the Indians Morgan shielded, they demanded that the expedition against Detroit be abandoned until hostile towns along the frontier could be destroyed. Then the invasion might be launched without fear of attack from the rear.[24]

Morgan's critics had yet another argument. The raids forced McIntosh to send Brodhead's regiment to the aid of some of the distressed areas, thus delaying the rendezvous at Fort Pitt and making the prospects for a successful expedition against Detroit that season even more remote. Meanwhile, however, an expedition against the Indian towns could do much to secure the frontier before the snow came. Colonel Morgan, seeing his entire Indian pacification policy threatened, argued that such a move would only hurt America's friends and benefit her enemies. But the critics were too strong. On July 25, Congress abandoned the Detroit expedition and ordered McIntosh to attack the Indian towns.[25]

McIntosh was on the march when Congress made its decision, and he crossed the mountains and descended to the fork of the Ohio still thinking his objective was Detroit. Arriving at Fort Pitt on August 6, he was sure he had plenty of time to launch the expedition and was disappointed when the news of the change arrived. Reluctantly changing his plans to conform to the new orders, he evaluated the local defenses, which consisted mainly of small stockades scattered among the settlements and, seemingly, located more for the protection of particular individuals than for the population in general. These, he felt, should be broken up.[26]

The suggestion was not greeted enthusiastically by county officials, but McIntosh was determined. To replace local garrisons, the Georgian proposed a chain of forts along the frontier and west of the settlements, designed to serve everyone. The plan, complete with ranging cavalry, was very much like the one he had proposed for Georgia. Since his army was busy, he suggested that the counties begin erecting these posts on their own, promising to help as he could. But county officials, already overburdened with advice and suggestions from the new commander, were not receptive to his idea. So while McIntosh prepared to move against the Indian towns, the local inhabitants procrastinated.[27]

General McIntosh left little doubt that he did not intend to tie his army down with county defenses. But as preparations for the westward incursion moved along, new problems appeared. George Morgan, the disgruntled Indian Agent, had been made purchasing commissary for the Western Department—an office upon which the success of the expedition depended. Since the local population claimed, with much justification, that it was unable to supply the provisions in the quantities needed, the goods had to be brought over the mountains. The difficulty of the journey, combined with poor planning and execution, resulted in the loss or spoilage of large quantities of food. Complaints became so persistent that McIntosh ordered a full investigation, but little was done to alleviate the mismanagement. The most lasting effect of his inquiry was the tension it created between commander and supply corps.[28]

As supplies trickled in and men, horses, and wagons crowded the fort, spilling into adjacent fields, McIntosh turned to other matters. The neighboring Delaware tribe—who through the efforts of Morgan, some Moravian missionaries, and their chief White Eyes remained friendly to the United States—had been invited to the fort. Past agreements, worked out by Morgan, had kept the warriors neutral, although they supplied information on enemy activities. But recently the British had "given the hatchet" to most other tribes, and the isolated Delaware needed firm allies. McIntosh, who also needed allies, was ready to bargain.[29]

The previous June, Congress had appointed commissioners to treat with the Indians; Virginia was allotted two representatives and Pennsylvania was given one (which it failed to select). The two Virginia commissioners, Andrew and Thomas Lewis, were at Fort Pitt when McIntosh arrived. It was on their advice that the Delaware were invited to the fort to negotiate the treaty. The Indians, led by White Eyes, agreed to come, and McIntosh began the talks on September 12. One week later, the Treaty of Fort Pitt was signed and Colonel Morgan's long-standing policy of Delaware neutrality was reversed.[30]

What was established instead was a military alliance, defensive and offensive, between the parties. In return for their aid in combating the British, the Delaware were to enjoy American protection, trade, and all the benefits of civilization. Their land was guaranteed to them forever and American representatives indicated that it might, in time, become a state in the union. (Much of this, of course, was subject to the approval of Congress, which was never obtained.[31] In fact, it is possible that neither McIntosh nor the American delegation believed that it would be. This, the first Indian treaty negotiated in the name of the United States, set the tragic standard for so many that would follow.)

Apart from the Delaware, the one who lost the most in the Treaty of Fort Pitt was George Morgan. As the architect of the program of Indian neutrality, he felt that it was an error to abandon it. Yet, having seen the strength of his opposition in the debate over the Detroit expedition, he realized that the Fort Pitt negotiations would end as they did. Not wishing to be a party to this new policy and involved with pressing duties elsewhere, Morgan stayed away from the meetings and let Colonel Gibson act as interpreter in his place. The results may have been worse than he expected.[32]

The events at Fort Pitt badly damaged Morgan's reputation, for the treaty not only rejected Indian neutrality, it also rejected Morgan as the Delaware's spokesman. He must have realized that to restore himself and his policy, the treaty would eventually have to be discredited. As one might expect, McIntosh was pleased with the negotiations and the prominent part he played. He rewarded White Eyes with the title "Lieut. Colonel of all the Indian Nations between the rivers Ohio, Mississippi & the Lakes," and then, assured of Delaware support, set about making final preparations for his incursion into hostile country.[33]

McIntosh's new orders were to invade the Indian territory and destroy their towns, but exactly how he was to proceed was left to his discretion. After some thought, he concluded that simply to invade and destroy would provide only a temporary solution. Once such a mission was completed and the army returned to Fort Pitt, the Indians would move back to their towns, rebuild them, and renew their attacks more fiercely than before. Rather than strike and withdraw, he proposed, once again, a chain of forts, but distinct from those he had proposed to defend the counties. These forts would be built in a line directly into the heart of the Indian country, close enough to support each other, and designed to serve as bases from which excursions against the Indians could be conducted.[34]

This new proposal took the season into consideration; it could be started that fall, halted for the winter, and continued in the spring without serious damage to the overall objective. Since the distance between the forts could be easily regulated in terms of time and space, problems created by the irregularity of the terrain could be overcome. (Incidentally, the forts fulfilled one of America's promises of the Treaty of Fort Pitt: establishment of a post to protect the Delaware.) There was one additional factor which must not be overlooked. The proposed chain of forts was along one of the roads which led to Detroit, an objective that had never been fully dismissed from either McIntosh's or Washington's mind.[35]

Fall colors had already begun to dot the mountains and the nights were growing cooler when, on September 10, Colonel Brodhead's Pennsylvania Continentals returned from their assignment.[36] McIntosh now felt the army was strong enough to proceed. Supply problems still existed, but the Commissary Department had been able to stockpile enough goods to provide for the initial phase. The cost had been high, especially in the immediate area, since some of the inhabitants engaged in what was becoming a universal practice, war profiteering. As a result, there was serious talk of "impressing" the necessary goods, but the general, remembering Georgia and not wanting to create animosity among the local population, held back.[37]

Convinced that he had to move quickly and assured that the supplies necessary to keep the expedition going would follow shortly, McIntosh ordered Brodhead to take his troops and proceed to the site selected for the first fort. The main army soon followed, and after marching about 30 miles west of Fort Pitt they arrived at the chosen location. On a high bluff on the northern side of the Ohio River, about a mile below the junction of that river and Beaver River, the stockade was erected.[38] Irregularly shaped, with its longest side facing the river, and dominated by large blockhouses, the post, which enclosed more than an acre, was an imposing sight. Named Fort McIntosh (modesty never having been one of the general's virtues), it was the first United States military post established on the northern, or Indian, side of the Ohio River. There McIntosh brought together the largest force assembled on the western side of the mountains during the Revolution—over 1,300 troops (mostly

Virginians). It seemed that if the promised supplies arrived and militia units could be kept intact, his prospects for success were excellent.[39]

But while Fort McIntosh was being built, supply problems became critical. Complaints of high prices, scarcity, and profiteering finally forced the reluctant general to allow impressment on a limited scale, which, predictably, was not very successful. The most immediate problem was forage for the animals. The cost of grain had more than doubled, and even at that inflated price there was little available. What grain there was had been bought by distillers, who in turn raised the price of whiskey. This increased the army's operating expenses even more, for with winter coming, McIntosh knew the troops would need an ample supply of what he termed that "very necessary article."[40]

Pleading with local officials to set prices and to prosecute speculators did little good, but the situation was not entirely due to their inaction. During the Indian raids, crops had often been destroyed or planting delayed; so there were shortages everywhere. Still, the army needed supplies and McIntosh was not inclined to excuse the failure to provide them. Pointing out to county officials that he had been accused of favoritism for allowing their militia to serve at home while Virginia troops manned the expedition, he insisted that, to balance the hardship, Pennsylvanians were expected to sacrifice their goods. But the logic of his demand had little effect, and the officials held back and waited.[41]

McIntosh's dilemma was evident: without forage, the expedition would have to be called off, but full impressment would alienate the citizens. Necessity, as it so often did for the general, soon forced a decision. Specifically excluding family provisions, he ordered the supply agents to impress goods when necessary and left it in their hands. He could delay no longer, for a large portion of the militia was on short-term enlistment that was scheduled to expire January 1. If those troops were to be used, he had to move quickly.[42]

In early November McIntosh prepared to march the army farther west and establish the second fort in the chain, in the heart of the Delaware nation. He believed that in the process the army would make such a show of force that any Delaware who doubted the wisdom of their alliance would doubt no more.[43] The motives behind the second phase of the expedition were sound but the conditions under which the army would have to labor were far from ideal. When the march began, McIntosh did not have sufficient quantities of salt, flour, whiskey, and forage to take the army the full distance. But not wanting to delay, he ordered purchasing agents to buy the necessary provisions and stockpile them at Fort McIntosh, to be sent to the army as needed.[44]

McIntosh's decision to proceed was based on two assumptions: the Commissary Department could obtain the supplies and it could get them to the army. Even though the agents guaranteed that provisions would be delivered,[45] if one considered the general scarcity of goods, the transportation problems, and the overall record of that department, the belief that the supplies would reach the army was an act of faith. In the final analysis, General Lachlan McIntosh's decision to advance meant that he was taking a poorly supplied force through potentially hostile territory with winter fast approaching. The construction of Fort McIntosh had been a success from every standpoint, and he should have stayed there until spring. In choosing to try to construct a second fort, the Georgian was courting disaster.

CHAPTER EIGHT
The McIntosh Expedition

He [McIntosh] struck me as one of those who excel in the Regularity of still Life from the Possession of an indolent uniformity of soul. The little Eagerness he shewed to go thence when every Thing almost depended on Vivacity gave no good Omen of his success.

Gouverneur Morris to General Washington, March 14, 1779

I beg leave to add, that General McIntosh's conduct, while he acted immediately under my observation was such as to acquire my esteem and confidence; I have had no reason since to alter my good opinion.

General Washington to the President of the Continental Congress,
May 11, 1779

Autumn colors were fading and the bare branches of winter could be seen in the mountains when in early November 1778 the army of approximately 1,200, more than half from the northwest counties of Virginia, began its march west.[1] Colonel Richard Campbell, with 150 men, remained at Fort McIntosh to forward supplies as they arrived; but the supplies did not come. Though the column pushed on, the lack of forage soon made it impossible for the horses to travel more than four miles without rest. Slowly they pressed deeper into Indian territory and as the danger of raids increased, McIntosh prohibited unauthorized hunting and stressed the necessity of staying close to camp. But the independent-minded frontiersmen, who made up a large segment of the army, paid little heed.[2]

Soon the general's fears became reality. Two men, hunting against his orders, were killed and scalped a short distance from camp. With that, McIntosh began to enforce discipline with an iron will. Courts-martial were held for men who fired guns, hunted, or strayed from camp without permission; and trading with Indians was strictly forbidden. Punishments ranged from fines to flogging with a hickory switch, and in one case the commander overturned a

court's decision on the grounds that it was too lenient and reprimanded the officers in charge.[3] The policy was necessary, but to
men who wished to hunt in order to supplement their dwindling
supplies, it was another hardship on an expedition which had more
than its share. Naturally, their anger centered on their leader.

The Commissary Department continued to promise supplies, and
even sent lists of goods on hand, but promises and lists did not feed
the men and animals. In Fort McIntosh, Colonel Campbell did all he
could to move the agents to more productive efforts, but without
success.[4] As the expedition advanced, the relations between the
army and the commissary deteriorated. Colonel Campbell complained; Colonel Morgan and his assistant, Colonel Archibald Steel,
made excuses; and General McIntosh's men suffered.

To make a bad situation worse, winter came to the Western
Department. Snow and freezing rain forced the expedition to an
even slower pace, and the longer the men marched, the more
supplies they used. On November 18 the army arrived at its destination, the headquarters for the Delaware nation on the Tuscarawas River. The once-powerful force had been reduced to a tired,
ragged body of men, subsisting on a daily ration of "4 oz. of injured
flour and 8 oz. very poor beef." It was hardly a display to convince
the Indians of the strength of American arms.[5]

Ignoring the impression his army made, McIntosh, with all the
assurance of a conquering hero, called the Indians together and
announced that he had come to build the fort they requested. But it
was not for their defense alone that the army had come. The general
explained that the fort was to be only one of the chain which would
be placed along his "path to Detroit." The reference to an attack on
British headquarters may have been nothing more than an attempt
to assure the Delaware of American determination to destroy the
tribe's enemies, but the fact remains that, despite the orders from
Congress, Detroit was on the Georgian's mind.[6]

The general closed his speech with an ultimatum. The Delaware
were told to send word to neighboring tribes that they had fourteen
days to come to camp and treat with him. If they refused, they
would be declared enemies and hunted down. The irony of what he
said was too much for the Indians. They heard the threats and

boasts, looked at the ragged army, and when McIntosh finished "they Set up a General Laugh." [7] It was a fitting response to a march which should never have begun.

To McIntosh and his troops, it was not a laughing matter. The supply situation was critical, and neither the Indians nor authorized hunting parties could provide the needed provisions. December was upon them and the men were anxious to return to Fort McIntosh before their enlistment ran out. The general, realizing he could not hold them beyond their prescribed time, reluctantly agreed to postpone further operations and to start back once the fort was finished. He named the new outpost after his old friend Henry Laurens, now President of the Continental Congress. Colonel John Gibson, by now one of McIntosh's most trusted officers, was left with 150 men to garrison the post, and the army began its withdrawal. [8]

The return to Fort McIntosh was anything but orderly. Militiamen broke ranks and straggled back in small bands, subsisting at times on nothing more than roasted cowhide. Snow was falling on Christmas Eve, when the main force reached Fort McIntosh. The hard campaign over, the general relaxed discipline and ordered that each soldier draw two days' provisions and a half pint of whiskey. The men were "generally poor and emaciated," and the liquor "flew to their heads," causing most of them to become "quite inebriated" and rowdy. When order was restored, McIntosh refused to punish them. Instead, observing that "a hair of the same dog is good for the bite," he ordered the same ration for the next day. The incident was not repeated. Within a week, most of the militia had been discharged and the general returned to Fort Pitt, leaving Colonel Brodhead to command Fort McIntosh. [9]

Even though one might question McIntosh's judgment in some of his undertakings during the fall of 1778, one must also say that he accomplished something. The Delaware had joined the United States in a formal alliance, an expedition was launched, territory was occupied, and outposts were established. It had not been done without criticism, but his efforts had the support of General Washington, and to McIntosh, that was what mattered. Washington, with his eye still on Detroit, was even willing to allow the expedition to continue through the winter, and when that proved impossible, he

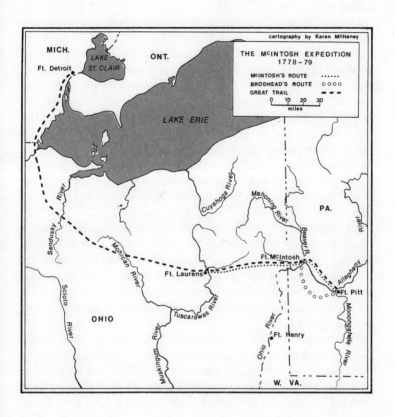

cartography by Karen McHaney

THE M^cINTOSH EXPEDITION
1778-79

M^cINTOSH'S ROUTE ·······
BRODHEAD'S ROUTE ooooo
GREAT TRAIL — — —

0   10   20   30
miles

MICH.

Ft. Detroit

LAKE
ST. CLAIR

ONT.

LAKE ERIE

Sandusky River

Mohican River

Scioto River

OHIO

Cuyahoga River

Mahoning River

Beaver R.

PA.

River

Allegheny

Ft. McIntosh

Ft. Laurens

Tuscarawas River

Muskingum River

Ohio River

Ft. Henry

Ft. Pitt

Monongahela River

W. VA.

sent the Georgian detailed instructions for the preparation and execution of a spring offensive. It was not unqualified approval of all of McIntosh's actions, but it was enough support to give him the confidence to carry on.[10]

Despite McIntosh's accomplishments, the new year found the Western Department far from secure. Most of the Indians were still under the control of British agents and in no way inclined to accept what had been done. Fort Laurens, difficult to supply and reinforce, was the obvious place for the enemy to strike, and McIntosh could not have been too surprised when he learned that the notorious Loyalist, Simon Girty, was leading a band of Indians against the post, and had sworn to "get Colonel Gibson's scalp." Late in January, Girty's men had ambushed a provisioning party out of Fort Laurens, killing two soldiers and capturing letters that revealed how poorly supplied the Americans were. Bolstered by that information, Girty prepared for what appeared would be a quick and easy conquest.[11]

The news of Girty's activities, linked to rumors that the Delaware might join the British, spurred McIntosh to act. After conferring with his officers, he ordered a relief expedition, under Major Richard Taylor, to proceed by the Muskingum River to the threatened outpost. He then issued orders for raising militia in case additional aid was necessary, all the while working diligently to prevent the loss of his Indian allies.[12]

As days passed with no word from Taylor's expedition, conditions at Fort Laurens grew increasingly grave. Finally, on March 3, McIntosh learned that Girty's forces had attacked and were laying siege to the fort. McIntosh was sure that the enemy would not have attacked had they not eliminated Taylor's relief column first. It was therefore up to him to act or Fort Laurens would surely fall. The general was working feverishly to raise men and supplies for a second relief expedition when Taylor and his men unexpectedly returned. Unable to navigate the river because of high water, they had turned back and arrived in camp just in time to join the new operation.[13]

It still took over a week to get Taylor's men resupplied, but by March 19 McIntosh and some 500 troops were on a forced march to

Fort Laurens. In the meantime, conditions at the besieged outpost
had become desperate. Food was gone and the men were eating their
moccasins; it seemed only a matter of time before the garrison would
fall. Then, to the surprise of everyone, Girty and his Indians withdrew, and when the relief column arrived it found no resistance at
all. Gibson's men, overjoyed to see the Americans, fired their guns in
welcome. The noise panicked the pack animals, causing much of the
badly needed flour to be scattered and lost, but the fort was safe, for
the moment.[14]

Why had Girty retreated without making even token resistance?
Apparently, McIntosh felt it was from fear of the relief party and he
pursued the matter no further. Not until later was it revealed that the
Loyalist had learned that an American army under George Rogers
Clark had taken the British stronghold at Vincennes. That news was
accompanied by reports of harsh treatment accorded to Indians who
carried scalps of white men. It was enough to cause Girty's Indians
to decide that the time might not be right for a confrontation; so they
retreated. Clark had a general idea of McIntosh's activities and the
Georgia general may have had some knowledge of his, but there is
nothing to indicate that the two cooperated in any way. Luck was a
large factor in most successfully coordinated ventures in the American Revolution, but in this case it was more than a factor, it was
everything.[15]

The victories at Fort Laurens and Vincennes seemed to open the
door for the long-awaited attack on Detroit, but if it were to come, it
would be without Lachlan McIntosh. Even as he marched to Fort
Laurens, efforts to have him relieved of his command were reaching
a climax. The general had left Georgia to escape the petty jealousies
and political squabbles that had threatened both the army's ability to
function and his career. He found much the same in the Western
Department. His new troubles arose from three separate but related
sources: Colonel Morgan, Colonel Brodhead, and the Pennsylvania
civil government. For different reasons, the three united behind a
common objective: the removal of General McIntosh.

Morgan's animosity toward McIntosh was born when the Treaty
of Fort Pitt discredited his policy of Indian neutrality, and it ma-
tured during the conflicts between the commissary and the com-

mander over the difficulty of supplying the army. In January 1779, the matter came to a head. General McIntosh ordered Archibald Steel, the commissary's chief purchasing agent, to be court-martialed for neglect of duty, and Morgan rushed to his defense. At the trial, Morgan charged that the negligence lay not with Steel but with McIntosh, whose "ignorant, absurd, and contradictory conduct" had caused the supplies to be wasted. The court, in an effort to calm passions on both sides, held that neither Steel nor McIntosh was at fault, but that the rugged terrain and lack of money had caused the problems.[16] Neither man was satisfied and the hatred between them grew.

Daniel Brodhead's dislike for the general sprang from other sources. Apart from cutting the road to Fort McIntosh, his regiment had generally served as a garrison force, while Gibson was allowed to exercise an independent command at Fort Laurens. The situation was too obvious for the Pennsylvanian to ignore and his disgust with the role assigned him grew into general opposition to the conduct of the entire operation. Naturally, the bulk of his criticism was directed at McIntosh. In mid-January, during Steel's trial, Brodhead wrote General Washington that McIntosh was "unfortunate enough to be almost universally Hated by every man in this department, both Civil & Military."[17] He gave no grounds for his charges, but events soon made it clear that he was not alone in his sentiments.

McIntosh's use of Gibson was merited to some degree. Gibson was a competent officer, knowledgeable in Indian languages, and as a Virginian he seemed equipped to command Virginia troops, the bulk of the army. But this preference for Virginians, though in many ways a product of necessity, did not sit well with Pennsylvania's civil authorities. Moreover, since the campaign began, McIntosh had done little to gain their support. He constantly criticized the local officials for their failure to provide men and supplies, and even took it upon himself to warn Pennsylvania's Vice President, George Bryan, that if the west were conquered by Virginia troops, Pennsylvania's claims in that area would be greatly weakened.[18] Pennsylvania's government, already hard pressed, did not need to be lectured on problems beyond the mountains, and McIntosh's efforts to build up his forces produced only animosity.

In late January the general's critics began to unite against him. The Delaware Indians, most likely under the direction of Colonel Morgan and the Moravian missionaries, announced that McIntosh and Gibson had tricked them into giving up their neutrality through the Treaty of Fort Pitt. Morgan immediately declared his support for the Indians and promised to take them to Congress to plead their case.[19] About the same time, he wrote Colonel Brodhead that he hoped the Pennsylvanian would soon take command of the Western Department and save it from the "Blunders & Absurdities" committed by McIntosh.[20] Brodhead and his friends in the Pennsylvania government quickly accepted Morgan as an ally, not because of his support for the Indians but because of his opposition to McIntosh. It was a marriage of convenience that would dissolve once its aim was accomplished.

Discrediting McIntosh proved no easy matter. Washington dismissed Brodhead's accusations as insufficient to merit action on his part and he continued to support the Georgian. He promised to watch McIntosh's movements closely, but Brodhead, unsatisfied, continued his attack. In a new series of charges he asserted that McIntosh's ambition had caused him to disobey orders and push for Detroit, rather than work to secure the frontier. The result, Brodhead claimed, was "the very romantic" Fort McIntosh, "built by the hands of hundreds who would have rather fought than wrought." It was this misuse of manpower, the colonel later charged, that caused the expedition to fail.[21]

How successful the attacks on McIntosh might have been will never be known. Early in 1779 the general learned that Savannah had fallen to the British and that his family was in enemy hands. Without hesitation, and perhaps with relief, he requested to be allowed to resign from his command and to be reassigned to Georgia.[22] Congress granted the request and in his place Washington appointed Daniel Brodhead. The commander-in-chief made the choice with genuine reluctance, but pressure from state officials made the selection of the Pennsylvanian almost inevitable. Informing Gouverneur Morris of his decision, Washington made it plain that he still supported McIntosh and that Brodhead would not have been his choice if the department were conducting any important military operations at the time. "Once [and] for all," Washington bluntly wrote of Brodhead's appointment, "it may not be amiss for me to conclude with this observation. That, with such means as are provided, I must labour." [23]

In early April, Brodhead assumed his new command and McIntosh left for Philadelphia. Visibly altered by the strain of the past months, he delayed only long enough to request a formal investigation of the charges against him. His hopes for official vindication were quashed, however, when it proved impossible to call witnesses away from their duties to testify. Gathering what evidence he could and sending it to Washington, who continued to voice his support for the Georgian, McIntosh prepared for his journey apprehensively. A short while later he received his orders and left Pennsylvania, never to return. [24]

General McIntosh's career as commander of the Western Department had been plagued with problems, many of his own making, but when one considers the conditions under which he worked, his accomplishments were remarkable. Just before his arrival at Fort Pitt there had been serious talk of abandoning the settlements west of the mountains. Upon his departure, forts had been built in the Indian country and the raids had almost ceased. No matter how just the criticism against him, McIntosh was the only commander at Fort Pitt during the Revolution to occupy and hold enemy territory and erect posts beyond the Ohio. Though Fort Laurens was eventually abandoned, Fort McIntosh remained an important outpost throughout the war. [25]

Although not as spectacular as Clark's capture of Vincennes, McIntosh's expeditions and forts did much to guarantee that the Ohio River Valley would not be left uncontested in British hands. All of this was accomplished despite personal and political opposition, inadequate supplies, temperamental soldiers, and harsh winter conditions. Had he been given the support which he, as the commanding officer, expected and deserved, he might have made it to Detroit. Nevertheless, the gains he made are a tribute to Lachlan McIntosh and the men who marched with him.

As he made his way back to Georgia, McIntosh learned that Colonel Brodhead, who soon supported the Detroit expedition he once opposed, was beginning to experience many of the problems which had plagued the general. Colonel William Crawford, one of the Virginia officers at Fort Pitt, wrote his former commander that nothing had really changed and that "envy and malice" raged in the Western Department. He wished McIntosh good fortune and expressed the hope that the general would find better conditions in Georgia than he had at Fort Pitt.[26] Lachlan McIntosh hoped so too.

CHAPTER NINE

The Siege of Savannah: On the Outside Looking In

I can not avoid representing to you the Deplorable situation I find this
unfortunate state in.

McIntosh to General Lincoln, August 4, 1779

General McIntosh sent to Prevost requesting liberty for his Wife and
family to come out of Town, he returned for Answer that he would
not permit it, that there were none but Women and Children in the
Town and those our friends and that if we chose to burn the Town
and destroy them we might begin as soon as we please.

Joseph Habersham to "Bella," October 5, 1779

In the summer of 1779 there were few places where American
prospects were more dismal than in Georgia. Arriving in late July,
McIntosh found a state whose most populous and productive areas
were in enemy hands. What was left of the Whig government had
fled inland and set up makeshift operations in Augusta. The army
was in a similar state. Of the 158 men on the muster rolls of the First,
Third, and Fourth Continental battalions, only 42 were present.
The other battalions were probably in similar condition. In addition, the Whigs had fewer than 600 militia available, and they were
scattered in small forts along the frontier.[1] Demoralized, with some
of its best officers in enemy hands, the Georgia military establishment was pitiful to behold.

McIntosh's uneasiness over returning to the state which had
"exiled" him was hardly alleviated by the condition in which he
found the army he was expected to command. He set to work
immediately, but the task seemed more than one man could handle.
Troops from Virginia had arrived in the state "without a Single

Tent," which, the general noted, made him "uneasy for their Healths this rainy Season in a Climate they are not accustomed to." Poorly housed, clothed, and fed, the army seemed to melt under the August sun, while McIntosh, wishing he at least "had some Liquor for them to keep their Spirits up," pleaded with General Benjamin Lincoln, commander of the Southern Department with headquarters at Charleston, for help in remedying the "Deplorable situation." [2]

Lincoln, however, could offer little more than sympathy. Because Georgia's treasury was empty and its supplies depleted, McIntosh was forced to turn to an exhausted population for aid. Enough supplies were borrowed so that scouting parties could be sent out, but the people, hard pressed themselves, offered little more. Impressment seemed the only sure means of provisioning the army, but, remembering Pennsylvania, he was loath to take that step. Instead, he continued to plead with the local inhabitants for what they could spare, and to stress to General Lincoln that, with the enemy in Savannah, preserving the Whig cause in Georgia was more essential than ever. Lincoln, well aware of the enemy's posture, hardly needed reminding. [3]

In spite of the dismal military situation and Georgia's need for someone to repair its defenses, the apparent ease with which General McIntosh was able to take control of the army and the lack of political opposition to his appointment seem paradoxical, in light of the violent opposition which had accompanied his departure. The basic reason for this change in circumstances, however, was simple enough. With the British in Savannah and the rest of the state under siege, help from anyone, even McIntosh, was welcomed. But if necessity alone was not enough (and for some it was not), the general's return was made easier by the fact that, for the moment, his enemies were out of power.

What had taken place was this. In the confusion which followed the fall of Savannah, a body, calling itself the Convention, met in Augusta to keep alive at least the concept of Whig government. Since it never represented all the counties of the state, it did not claim the authority of the Assembly, yet it carried on general governmental functions through an executive committee. While this body held power, radicals were replaced (apparently with little fanfare) by a coalition of moderates and conservatives who were much more receptive to the general's return.[4] About the time that McIntosh arrived this executive committee was superseded by a new organization, called the Supreme Executive Council. This governing body, dominated by low-country conservatives who had fled Savannah, seemingly marked the defeat of what was left of Gwinnett's faction. Its membership included many of McIntosh's former supporters and its President, John Wereat, was his closest and most trusted Georgia friend. This was a government to the general's liking and one with which he could work.[5]

Encouraged by this friendly civil authority and hailed by it as a potential savior, Lachlan McIntosh enjoyed an exhilarating period of civil-military cooperation. The Supreme Executive Council set up a committee to confer with the general on command problems and the lines of communication were kept open, busy, and largely free of conflict. When McIntosh's pleas to Lincoln for aid produced little in the way of positive results, the government exerted what influence it possessed and, as a consequence, South Carolina advanced Georgia a loan of $100,000. Though not enough to take care of all its needs, the money eased some of the state's burdens. Meanwhile, much to the relief of the Georgians, the Indians did not aid the British to the extent expected, and McIntosh had the time to organize the meager forces on hand. Although he and the Supreme Executive Council did not agree on everything, their cooperation prevented additional problems from arising in a state which had more than its share.[6]

Early in September, the general's attention shifted from the back country to Savannah. Ever since the fall of the capital there had been debate as to the best means of retaking the city. When Washington proved unable to provide Continental troops for the task, it was suggested that Congress apply to Count d'Estaing, who commanded a French fleet that was operating in American waters. The French Minister protested and Congress gave up the idea, but South Carolina's Governor, John Rutledge, not feeling restrained by the Minister's objections, forwarded the request to d'Estaing.[7]

On September 1, to the surprise of the Americans and the British, the French fleet, made up of twenty-two ships of the line and with

4,000 troops, appeared off the Georgia coast. Lincoln learned of the arrival three days later and immediately sent a messenger to McIntosh at Augusta with orders to collect all the men he could within the next twenty-four hours and march "with greatest dispatch" to Ebenezer, about 30 miles upriver from Savannah. There he was to join Lincoln's army, coming from Charleston. The general issued the call for troops and the militia responded with an enthusiasm that amazed witnesses. The chance for an American victory in Georgia was better than it had been in several years, and few wanted to miss it.[8]

Everything seemed to point to an American advantage, but speed was essential. Lincoln urged McIntosh to move as quickly as possible and, if the infantry proved too slow, to send the cavalry on ahead. In Savannah, General Augustine Prevost, the British commander, and the returned Royal Governor, Sir James Wright, made every effort to prepare the city's defenses for the attack they knew was coming. At the same time, Prevost sent a frantic request to Lieutenant Colonel John Maitland, stationed at Beaufort, South Carolina, to bring his 800 regulars to aid the city; but time was against them.[9]

If the Americans or their French allies were able to attack before reinforcements arrived or before the city's defenses were completed, Savannah seemed sure to fall. Stressing again the need for haste, Lincoln ordered McIntosh to secure flatboats and barges to carry his troops across the river. Such vessels were not available, and when the two armies met on September 11, the only boat on hand was a canoe. As a result, two valuable days were lost while rafts were built and the men were ferried to the south side of the Savannah.[10] Meanwhile, an impatient d'Estaing landed a force of 3,500 well-equipped French troops. Lincoln's army, when it finally came together and moved toward the city, consisted of 1,500 men, many of whom were soldiers in name only. McIntosh's contribution to this force consisted of three militia companies, the Georgia Continentals, and a few Virginia troops—in all, fewer than 300 men.[11]

By September 16, 1779, the American and French armies had set up camp outside the city and d'Estaing sent a message to the British demanding their surrender. Prevost requested terms, then asked for time to prepare a reply, and d'Estaing agreed. In allowing this delay, the French commander committed a major blunder, for in the intervening time Maitland and his troops were able to slip into the city. Prevost, now with nearly 2,500 troops in protected positions, felt he could hold out and rejected d'Estaing's demands for surrender. The allies reacted by sealing off all approaches to the town and entrenched themselves opposite the British lines. The siege of Savannah had begun.[12]

McIntosh was concerned with more than siege operations. The major reason for his return to Georgia was that his family was in British hands, and he had come to Savannah hoping for a speedy reunion. Prevost's refusal to surrender changed all that. Realizing that a siege would mean bombardments, and that cannonballs did not distinguish between civilians and soldiers, he searched for a way to free his loved ones. On September 29, largely because of McIntosh's urgings, the Americans requested that all women and children, including Prevost's family, be allowed to leave the town.[13]

The British, thinking the allies might not shell the city at the risk of hitting the noncombatants, refused the request; but they underestimated their adversaries' determination to regain the capital. On the evening of October 3, much to the general's apprehension, the allies began the bombardment, creating "great Mischief both in town and in the enemy lines." The shelling continued for three days, during which time Prevost's family hid under feather beds in their cellar, while Mrs. McIntosh and her family "suffered beyond description" from the constant threat of death from the sky.[14]

Finally, realizing that no advantage was to be gained by keeping the women and children in the city, Prevost sent word to the allies that he was willing to have them evacuated. It was then the allies' turn to refuse, hoping that the danger to his own family might weaken Prevost's resolve to hold out. But once again, one side underestimated the determination of the other. While each blamed his enemy for the danger to the civilians, the shelling continued, and the noncombatants endured it as best they could.[15]

As the siege dragged on, d'Estaing became impatient. Finally, informing his allies that to stay at Savannah any longer was not in the best interest of his country, he insisted that the city be attacked.

Some of his officers strongly objected, saying that an assault would be rash, but d'Estaing argued that his duty to support the Americans and to uphold the honor of France made it impossible for him to leave without striking a blow against the enemy. Lincoln had little choice but to agree with his superior; so plans were drawn up for an assault on the British right flank, apparently their weakest point. The French were scheduled to lead the charge and the Americans, commanded by McIntosh and Colonel John Laurens, were to provide support. The attack was to come no later than four on the morning of October 9, and the key to success was to catch the enemy by surprise.[16]

By this time the British had thrown up impressive earthworks which the bombardment had not measurably damaged. The right of their line, guarded by an emplacement called the Spring Hill redoubt, was hard against Yamacraw Swamp, and it was through those marshy woods that the Franco-American force planned to move. Once in position, concealed by the undergrowth, they would wait till false attacks on the British left and center signaled them to advance. If all went as planned, the surprise would be complete and the enemy lines would crumble.[17]

But all did not go as planned. During the night the British learned, through spies, deserters, or civilians, that the assault was imminent and they made preparations to repel it. As the allies massed in the predawn darkness, they were greeted by the eerie skirl of bagpipes which seemed to rise from the very spot at which the attack was aimed. Aware now that the enemy knew their plans, their apprehension grew as delays postponed the attack till well past its 4:00 a.m. deadline. Finally, at 5:30, just as the sun began to rise behind the British position, the sound of firing was heard. With that signal, the French sprang into action. Out of the mist they swarmed, across the open ground, and into the fury of British resistance.[18]

For a moment the outcome hung in the balance as a detachment of French grenadiers broke the line, but their effort, like the entire assault, was poorly coordinated. Striking to the left of their target, the grenadiers were not in a position to be reinforced; they faltered, the British closed their ranks, and the retreat began. D'Estaing rallied his troops. They charged again and the enemy replied with musket and cannon. The result was devastating. The white uniforms of the French were red with blood, and the fate of their American allies was similar. Trapped in the entrenchments near Spring Hill redoubt, they were cut in ribbons.[19]

McIntosh, leading his Georgia troops and the First and Fifth Carolina regiments, arrived at the "Scene of Confusion" just in time to witness the final retreat. Approaching the French commander, the Georgian informed him, through an interpreter, that his own troops were fresh and ready to serve. But d'Estaing, who must have realized the end was near, ordered the Americans simply to move farther to the left, out of the way of his disorganized forces. This meant that McIntosh had to take his troops through Yamacraw Swamp, and "while struggling through [that] Morass" they heard the firing slacken and the drummers beat retreat. By the time the Americans reached their station, the battle was finished.[20]

Behind the British lines, joy reigned. Meanwhile, in the French camp, d'Estaing, his casualty list growing with each new report, announced that he planned to raise the siege immediately. Having no alternative, the Americans agreed. In less than an hour on that October morning, the French had lost 521 men, killed and wounded. American casualties were set at 231. Although the British reported only 18 killed and 39 wounded, it had been one of the bloodiest days of the war.[21]

With the French decision to withdraw, everyone knew the siege was over. Lack of coordination and cooperation had done as much to defeat the allies as the battle itself. Had they attacked when they first arrived, the city might have fallen; every day's delay after that only made the outcome more certain. Distraught by his inability to free his family, McIntosh made preparations to withdraw his dispirited troops. But many of those who survived the fighting melted into the countryside. Provisions were nearly exhausted, sick and wounded were everywhere, and the force of able-bodied men was so reduced that it was difficult to find soldiers to serve as guards or to repair roads. What had begun with such hope had come to an inglorious end.[22]

On October 18 the Americans began to break camp and retreat from the city. The following day the French started to embark and by November 2, 1779, their last ship was gone. Lincoln returned to Charleston with the bulk of the American army.[23] McIntosh reluctantly withdrew also, leaving his family behind—safe, he had learned, but still in British hands. Slowly, the remainder of his forces wound their way back to Augusta, where Georgians pondered what steps should be taken to keep the Revolution alive.

CHAPTER TEN

The Siege of Charleston:
On the Inside Looking Out

General Lincoln informed the General Officers privately that he
intended the Horn Work as place of retreat for the whole Army in
Case they were drove from the Lines.—I observed to him the impos-
sibility of those who were Station'd at the So. Bay and Ashly River
retreating there in Such Case, to which he replyed that we might
Secure ourselves as best we could.

McIntosh's Journal of the Siege of Charleston, April 29, 1780

The journey from the humid lowlands around Savannah to the pine
hills of Richmond County was accomplished quickly and with little
opposition from an enemy that was content to watch the American
forces retreat. Contrasting sharply with the river towns along the
coast, Augusta, on the cutting edge of the frontier, was more like the
villages of McIntosh's youth: raw, untamed—an earthy mixture of
the primitive and the civilized. It was into this remote pocket of
temporary security that the Whig cause had been forced, threatened
on all sides by a victorious enemy that now seemed capable of
quickly finishing the conquest begun nearly a year ago.

When one considers the state of Georgia's revolution, it would
seem that the time had come for Whigs to put aside personal and
party differences, work together, and try to restore confidence in at
least the potential of their movement. But when McIntosh arrived in
town he found just the opposite. Whig factionalism, which had been
retarded but not destroyed during the general's exile, reared its ugly
head once more.[1] At a time when unity seemed essential, Whigs
emerged who felt that to win independence would be meaningless if
the victory was not on their terms. Even in the darkest hours of the

war, the goals for which Georgia Whigs were fighting were still being measured by local, not continental, standards.

In the confusion which followed the failure at Savannah, the Supreme Executive Council, most of whose members had accompanied McIntosh to the coast, was challenged by a rival body which called itself the Assembly. Using tactics perfected by the old "popular party," this new movement declared itself the state's legitimate government. Although the influence of the eclipsed Hall-Gwinnett faction was evident, this Assembly represented more than a resurrection of the St. John's radicals. The "western members" who had filled the ranks of the radicals in 1777 emerged, in that fall of 1779, as leaders, not followers, and what greeted McIntosh when he arrived from Savannah was a coalition bent on stripping power from the low-country elite once and for all.[2]

But McIntosh failed to realize how "revolutionary" this new movement was. Since the new Assembly had elected his old friend George Walton as Governor, it would seem he had little to fear from that quarter. Therefore, he resolved to remain neutral, keep his own counsel, and devote his time to rebuilding the army. Rumors were flying and "nocturnal Combinations" were forming, but McIntosh stayed aloof, believing he could avoid the appearance of supporting either faction and thus prevent a repetition of the conflict that earlier had driven him from the state.[3]

In late December the general left Augusta and, joined en route by his brother William, headed south in another attempt to free his family. His leaving was hastened by reports that, despite his efforts, some of his officers had begun taking sides in the political disputes and that the army's neutral posture was rapidly disintegrating. As the brothers rode and talked, the weather worsened, chilling men and horses to the bone and slowing their pace, to the increasing irritation of the general. He had not seen his wife and children in nearly two years, and the hours seemed to hang suspended as they wound their way along the narrow, twisting road.[4]

Late in December, on "the Coldest night [of the] year," the McIntosh party took shelter in a hut just off the road. The servants, aching from the cold, rushed inside to build a fire, leaving the horses fully loaded outside. As the travelers warmed themselves in the half-dark cabin, they were startled by the noise of their mounts' being moved, but before they could react a band of armed men forced the door and burst into the room. Springing to his feet, the general seized a weapon that was pointed at him (which, fortunately, misfired) and immediately the room came alive with struggling men, half illuminated by the fire.[5]

In the fight, one intruder got off a shot, but the general deflected the assailant's aim and the shot passed harmlessly overhead. Apparently the McIntoshes offered more resistance than their attackers expected, for in the confusion the general's party slipped through the back door and into the woods. Their baggage, however, was plundered, and all their personal effects and papers lost. Shaken by the experience and his nerves frayed from the strain of the past months, General McIntosh saw more in the attack than a simple case of robbery. The real objective, he was convinced, was to take him prisoner, but he refused to reveal who he suspected was behind it. He vowed to be more careful in the future and turned again to matters at hand.[6]

The first month of 1780 was a busy one for McIntosh. His ill-fated brother George had died in December and his estate had to be settled. The unhappy task was offset by news that the British had finally realized there was no advantage to be gained by holding his family. Released with little more than the clothes they were wearing, they were greeted by a relieved husband and father, who quickly took them across the Savannah to South Carolina. After reporting to General Lincoln in Charleston, McIntosh was able to enjoy only a few days of uninterrupted family life.[7] In early February 1780, a British fleet appeared off Charleston and America's war for independence entered a new, critical phase.[8]

On February 14, McIntosh received Lincoln's orders to repair to Charleston. For safety he took Mrs. McIntosh and the children to Camden, in the back country, where Joseph Kershaw, an old friend, agreed to provide for the family and to work the general's few remaining slaves with his own, on shares. McIntosh stayed in Camden until March 8 and then began his journey to Charleston.[9] By then the British had blockaded the harbor, and many of the land approaches to the city were cut off. Fighting had begun in some quarters, and as the general approached, the sound of cannons "made [him] impatient" to join the fray. With little trouble his party passed through a gap in the enemy lines and, arriving at Lincoln's headquarters, learned how perilous the city's position was.[10]

Lincoln put McIntosh in command of some South Carolina country militia and the Georgia general set about securing the section of the perimeter assigned to him. The enemy had erected a battery on James Island and a number of their ships had crossed the bar into the harbor, giving them a means of bombarding the American positions from land and sea. Since the city was not fully encircled, General McIntosh was able to make brief visits to his family, but enemy movements were becoming more menacing and skirmishes between the two armies increased in frequency.[11]

As McIntosh became accustomed to his new post, some disturbing news reached him. Samuel Huntington, President of the Continental Congress, wrote that Congress, on the recommendation of George Walton and the Georgia Assembly, had suspended him from command. Outraged, McIntosh took the letter and the accusations and laid them before Lincoln and South Carolina Governor John Rutledge. After examining them, they concluded that since the general was in command of South Carolina militia and therefore responsible to Governor Rutledge, it would "be improper for [him] to leave the garrison until the siege was over." For the moment, the matter was resolved, but McIntosh knew that he had not heard the last of it.[12]

For the remainder of March and into early April the British continued their relentless pressure. They shelled the American positions almost daily and in one exchange hit McIntosh's headquarters, without injuring the general. Some of the shells also fell on the city, and soon civilian casualties were recorded with those of the army. It was obvious to almost everyone that the advantage belonged to the enemy, so that morale was dangerously low when, on April 10, Sir Henry Clinton sent a message to General Lincoln demanding that he surrender.[13]

The American commander, according to McIntosh, answered "immediately & without consulting anyone . . . that his duty and inclination led him to hold out to the last extremity." [14] But if Lincoln planned to defend the city at all cost, he was ignoring the reality of his position. With 2,650 Continentals and an equal number of militia to hold three miles of lines against a British force nearly twice its size and with many times its firepower, the odds were against him. There was still an escape route open, across the Cooper River, and if Lincoln moved quickly, the army at least could be saved. But the American general, displaying the same lack of initiative that had doomed the siege of Savannah, delayed his decision. All the while the British were closing the circle. [15]

With the situation growing more critical every day, Lincoln and his generals requested that Governor Rutledge and part of his Council leave Charleston to preserve the government in case the city fell. Their concern was justified, for on the morning of April 13 the British, with their batteries completed and many of their ships in place, unleashed a full bombardment on the city. The Americans returned the fire as best they could, but the damage within their lines was great and more civilians were killed. [16]

This sudden escalation of the fighting moved Lincoln to call a council of war, where he gave his officers what McIntosh described as their "*first* idea of the State of the Garrison, the Men, the provisions, Stores, Artillery, etc." and pointedly told them that there was little hope for aid. The Engineer Corps, under Colonel de Mons Laumoy, revealed that the American fortifications "were *only Field* works, or lines, & could hold out but a few days more." After comparing the strength of the two adversaries, Lincoln concluded that he was compelled to consider evacuating the city. [17]

McIntosh, who could hardly have been as surprised at the news as some of the junior officers, quickly offered his opinion. If things were as bad as Lincoln said, then the Georgian believed the Americans "should not [lose] an hour longer in attempting to get the Continental troops at Least out," since there was still an open route across the Cooper. He insisted that the safety of South Carolina, and probably the south, depended on such action. Although the other officers agreed, Lincoln hesitated. Vacillating, he asked them to retire and "consider maturely [the] expediency & practicability of such a Measure," promising to consult them again. But not everyone

was willing to risk staying in the city, and that same day Governor
Rutledge, with some of his Council, slipped across the river to
safety.[18]

If Lincoln had moved quickly to ensure that the evacuation route
remained open, there might have been time for the army to get away.
But he did not, and the delay was costly. The next day a British unit
under Lieutenant Colonel Banastre Tarleton surprised the American cavalry posted at Monks Corner and closed the last avenue of
escape.[19] The Americans began to search for an alternate route of
evacuation, but it was no use; Charleston was surrounded. If the
army was to survive, it would have to fight its way out.

The enemy was closing in rapidly and by April 19 was within 250
yards of the American flank and moving upon the left. Faced by
those critical conditions, Lincoln called another council of war,
which met at General William Moultrie's quarters since the commander's quarters were too exposed to the shelling. Lincoln explained the deteriorating state of supplies and again raised the idea of
evacuation. All agreed that it would be extremely difficult, but
McIntosh, his Scottish blood boiling, favored trying. He proposed
that the militia guard the garrison and cover the escape of the
Continentals, but Colonel Laumoy objected, feeling that the time
had come to ask for "Honl. terms of Capitulation" which would
allow the army to withdraw. But they had to act quickly, for if they
waited until their position weakened further, Clinton might not be
willing to make such a generous concession.[20]

The other officers agreed with Laumoy and were about to draw up
the terms when South Carolina's Lieutenant Governor, Christopher
Gadsden, stormed into the meeting. Gadsden, whose timely arrival
McIntosh felt might not have been accidental, "appeared surprised
& displeased" at the plan to give up the city. He agreed to consult his
Council on the matter, but it was evident that he opposed evacuation
and capitulation, since either would put Charleston in enemy hands.
After Gadsden's outburst the council of war adjourned; but when it
met again that evening, surrender terms were put to a final vote.
McIntosh, who still preferred to fight rather than surrender, asked to
be allowed to vote last. But when he saw that all the others favored
Laumoy's plan, he made the vote unanimous.[21]

No sooner was the decision made when Gadsden and four of his Council members interrupted the meeting. Outraged at the proceedings, Gadsden "Used the Council [of war] very Rudely" and protested "that the Militia [was] willing to Live on Rice alone rather than give up the Town on any Terms." He argued that old women were so used to the enemy bombardments that they walked the streets without fear, but if capitulation had been agreed upon, he happened to have his terms in his pocket.[22]

Gadsden and his Council made their position clear: the choice was either surrender on favorable terms or hold out to the end. One of the Councilors even went so far as to warn that the townspeople had set sentries near the boats that were assembled to evacuate Continental troops, and that if Lincoln tried to use them, he swore "he would be among the first who would open the Gates for the Enemy and assist them in attacking [the Continental forces] before [they] got on board." With that outburst, Gadsden and the Council stormed from the meeting, leaving the officers alone with their decision.[23]

Shortly after the departure of the civil authorities, Colonel C. C. Pinckney, one of South Carolina's most outstanding soldiers, arrived from Fort Moultrie to lend his support to those who opposed evacuating the city. McIntosh rose in agreement. Though "hurt by the repeated Insults given the Commanding Officer in so public a manner" (which he felt also insulted the other officers), he declared he still "was for holding the Garrison to the last extremity."[24] Colonel Laumoy, however, objected once again. It was true, Laumoy admitted, that fighting "to the last extremity" was the honorable way, but he felt that the Americans had already reached that point, and if those who were present "were not of that opinion, [he] desired to know what [they] called the last extremity." Laumoy received his answer when, in the final vote, McIntosh's views prevailed among the officers.[25]

But Lincoln decided otherwise. The following day he called a council of war and announced that the city could not hold out, and that the enemy was too strong for evacuation to succeed. Even if they broke out, Lincoln explained, the army would be so weak that it would easily be overtaken and defeated. He therefore proposed that before American affairs "became more critical," terms of capitulation be suggested to Clinton "which would admit of the army with-drawing and afford security to the persons and property of the inhabitants." Once again McIntosh requested to vote last, and again, faced with the prospect of being the only one in opposition, reluctantly voted for the plan.[26]

But it was too late. Clinton knew that the city could not last much longer and refused to accept the terms offered by the Americans. Instead, he issued counterproposals, amounting almost to unconditional surrender, which were unanimously rejected. With that, the brief truce that accompanied the exchange of notes came to an end and the shelling became more intense than ever. Charleston was at the point of collapse. Rations were cut and the houses of civilians were searched to uncover those who were hoarding provisions. Enemy trenches were so close to the American lines that the armies were able to shout insults at each other. Finally, on April 26, General Louis Duportail slipped through the enemy's lines with bleak news from Philadelphia: there was no prospect for relief or reinforcements. The American officers knew it was only a matter of time before the city fell.[27]

Charleston went about its business like a man in the last stages of an incurable illness, preparing for the end he knows is coming. Tar barrels were burned to discourage night attacks and the men were instructed to retreat inside a centrally located emplacement, called the Horn Work, if their lines were overrun. McIntosh, whose troops were too far away to use this fortress of last resort, asked what was to become of his men. The burden of defeat weighed heavily on Lincoln as he replied that they should "Secure [them]selves as best [they] could." There was little else that could be done.[28]

Meanwhile the enemy continued his relentless pounding. Slaves were pressed into service in an effort to repair the crumbling defenses, but the damage was too extensive. Then, on May 5, Fort Moultrie, which guarded the harbor, surrendered and the ocean approach to the city was open to the entire British fleet. It was a crushing blow to morale, especially among the civilian population, for many had believed the fort impregnable. The will to resist was dying in Charleston.[29]

Clinton, knowing the end was near, again sent his surrender terms to Lincoln. The American commander refused and the shelling continued, while many in the army and in town believed the terms had been rejected because of the influence of wealthy Charlestonians who were trying to protect their property and of officers who wanted to protect their careers. Supplies had reached the critical point, and soon the day came when the army had no rations at all and there were "Hungry guts in the Garrison." Desperate soldiers became "more active than the Commissary" in rounding up provisions, and few were immune to their searches for food. Units of the militia, totally demoralized, abandoned their positions and refused to return.[30]

It was war at its worst. The glory was gone and the heroics displayed so early in the campaign had been reduced to a base struggle for survival. During the final days the generals exchanged notes, terms were negotiated again and again, and the city lived from truce to truce. Finally Lincoln bowed to the inevitable. At three in the afternoon of May 12, what was left of the army marched out of the Horn Work and laid down its arms.[31]

During the last, frantic days of the fighting, the British overran McIntosh's position and he became a prisoner of war. That event marked the end of his active service as an American officer. In an ironic way, his capture was a fitting end to a career that had been directed by the best of motives and destroyed by the worst of circumstances. This confinement was just another hardship to be endured until an exchange was made under the terms of capitulation. It would soon pass.

But his capture was not the only reason for the termination of his service in the field. The congressional resolution that suspended him from command meant that, prisoner or not, he could no longer lead soldiers of the United States. The vague yet powerful set of values he called his honor had been insulted once again, but this time the quick emotional reaction was denied him. Forced to sit and wait for the opportunity to exonerate himself, he had the time to brood and prepare his defense. He knew that freedom, when it came, would mean little unless the stain on his character were removed. When the long-awaited release came in the summer of 1781, he was ready.

CHAPTER ELEVEN
"Implacable Mallice of Implacable enemies"

New plans for persecution are formed and will be pursued with unrelenting malevolence against some men who will be convicted of having pretty good possessions acquired by many years industry and on which some of our boisterous Patriots look with evil and longing eyes—I have been told that one of them made use of the following expression: Campbell and Mc— possess too much property in their place – I have bled in the service of this country and by G– must have part of it. Can you expect justice from one who is capable of making use of such an expression.

Wereat to McIntosh, January 19, 1780

The circumstances that led to McIntosh's suspension from his Continental command were in many ways similar to those which drove him from the state in 1777. In both, his assocation with one political faction led to his denunciation by the other, which produced the demands for his removal. But while that may explain what happened to the general, it does not make the complex issues and events surrounding the matter understandable. What was actually happening was a major shift in political power that witnessed, among other things, the assumption of leadership roles by back-country radicals. And as had happened before, McIntosh, not entirely the innocent victim, was caught in the middle.[1]

The radical–conservative conflict which predated McIntosh's initial appointment had been, at the outset, a low-country, "aristocractic" affair. Despite their avowed animosity, the social-economic-geographic compositions of the antagonists were essentially the same. In other words, though there were many factors to consider, the primary reason for their struggle was that St. John's Parish was out of power and wanted to be in, while the Christ Church coalition was in control and proposed to keep it that way. But as we have seen, the St. John's led radicals won, and their victory carried Georgia's internal revolution into a new phase which promised even more dramatic changes in the future.

The radicals' victory in 1776–1777 was achieved through the creation of the "popular party," which brought rural, back-country elements into the ruling councils of government—but, it must be noted, as junior partners. Control of the state remained firmly rooted in the coastal ricelands. One set of low-country "elites" had replaced another, and although the "western members" were given a taste of power, their appetite was hardly satisfied. That their actual status had not been measurably increased was not difficult to ascertain, even for politically unsophisticated "frontiersmen." But for nearly two years they were unable to alter the situation significantly.

Then, in December 1778, Savannah fell to the British and what remained of the Whig movement was driven into the back country, taking refuge in Augusta, seat of power for the "western members." In the confusion, representatives from the frontier counties of Wilkes, Richmond, and Burke met in Augusta to "keep up a show of Government." Calling themselves the Convention, they set up an executive council to carry out basic administrative functions. With William Glascock as its President, this committee maintained at least the illusion of Whig authority during the critical first six months of 1779, when it seemed the British would overrun the entire state.[2] During that time the men of the back country held the line, controlled the government, and preserved the Revolution. It seemed that the day of the frontiersmen had arrived.

But had it? On July 10, 1779, Glascock wrote the Continental Congress of the steps he and his Council were taking to ensure that at least part of Georgia would have a Whig government. Although upset that the state had no representative in Congress, there was nothing in the letter to indicate that he and his associates were not in control. Then, two weeks later, Glascock's administration was out of office. Exactly how this was accomplished is unknown, but its implications were clear. Even though Savannah and the Chatham

County stronghold were in enemy hands, the deposed conservative faction was about to make a comeback.[3]

As best as can be told from skeletal records, a group of some twenty-five men met in Augusta in July. Although each county was represented, when it was found that they were too few to act as an Assembly, they set up a nine-man committee to keep the government in operation. It was the same tactic used by the previous "Convention" but the outcome was dramatically different. The new committee, designated the Supreme Executive Council, was dominated by the same tidewater conservatives the popular party had displaced more than two years earlier.[4] And as they moved to the forefront, Glascock and the western members retreated—but not for long.

John Wereat was chosen to head the Council, which included such conservative stalwarts as Joseph Clay, Seth John Cuthbert, William Gibbons, and Joseph Habersham. Still, the remaining members were from inland counties, which gave the new government at least the impression of being a nonpartisan coalition. Absent, however, were any who could be classified as hard-line radicals. McIntosh, recently returned from Fort Pitt, attended the Council's meetings and heartily approved of the proceedings. These were "Men whose Character [he] trusted and with whom [he] was so fortunate as to have the best understanding"; now he had every reason to believe that civilian–military clashes could be avoided. Everything seemed to indicate that the general's decision to return to Georgia was the right one.[5]

But this change in government was not accomplished without opposition, especially from Colonel George Wells, commander of the lower Richmond militia and a radical leader since the early days of the Revolution. McIntosh paid such rumblings little heed. Things seemed to be going well—so well, in fact, the general apparently forgot that in a state that was struggling for its life, any display of sympathy for those who were suspected of supporting the enemy was, in the eyes of many, treasonous. No doubt remembering his brother's suffering and never one to forget old friends, McIntosh threw caution to the wind and openly defended some whom the radicals had branded Tories. The Council gave him a sympathetic hearing, but rather than issue the general pardon he requested, it promised safety for the families and property of the accused, and that each case would be considered on its merits. Aware that the climate of opinion would not tolerate what was being asked, Wereat and his associates did as much as could reasonably be expected; but on this issue, reason hardly dictated McIntosh's conduct. Not only did the general defend Georgians who were suspected of treason, but, while doing so, he chose to reside at the home of one of the accused, his old friend Andrew McLean. To many this seemed a bold insult to the cause for which they fought, and old charges that a McIntosh was as dangerous as any Tory were soon heard again.[6]

At the same time, opposition to Wereat's Council was growing. In mid-August it had ordered General McIntosh to remove Colonel Wells from his command, a task he could hardly have found unpleasant since Wells had been Gwinnett's second and a leader of the anti-McIntosh petition drive which followed the duel. Already critical of the Council, a body that was not authorized under the Constitution of 1777, which he had helped to write, Wells emerged from this confrontation convinced that Wereat and his supporters, including McIntosh, were out to reestablish conservative control and undo the work of the "popular" party. Soon there rallied around him a growing, vocal opposition, fully prepared to assume control if the Supreme Executive Council faltered. Meanwhile, aware that the besieged back country was likely to follow the faction which could provide it protection, Wereat and the Council worked to avoid sensitive issues, keep order, and govern as well as the unsettled circumstances would allow.[7] Lachlan McIntosh would have done well to follow their example.

Despite this opposition, the Supreme Executive Council apparently believed it had the situation under control. Therefore, when news reached Augusta that the French fleet was off Savannah, the Council showed little hesitation in joining the "enthusiastic" march to the coast, no doubt sensing that victory there would all but guarantee their controlling the Assembly once elections were held. But victory was denied them, and in the confusion that followed, George Wells and his allies made their move. With more support

than often has been credited them, this new coalition set up in
Augusta a government that they attempted to render legitimate with
the name Assembly. The fact that westerners Wells and Glascock,
with old-line radicals like Richard Howley, were leaders of the
movement surprised no one, but when George Walton was elected
Governor by the new body, the effect upon many conservatives
must have been devastating.[8]

Walton's role in this affair still poses more questions than answers.
Though never one of the Christ Church "aristocrats," he had early
attached himself to the conservative cause and had risen swiftly in its
ranks. Serving with distinction in the Continental Congress, he
proved an able defender of the McIntoshes and a vehement critic of
Gwinnett and the radicals. Therefore, when the "popular" party
came to power, one would expect Walton's head to be among the first
to roll. It was not. Perhaps his signature on the Declaration of
Independence insulated him from its wrath, or perhaps his skill at
adapting to changing political situations allowed him to survive.
Somehow, he was able to finish his term in Congress and return to
Georgia in anything but disgrace. Once home, he was given command of a militia unit and during the British attack on Savannah in
1778 he served bravely, was wounded, and was taken prisoner when
the city fell.[9]

Walton remained in British hands until October 1779, when
General Lincoln notified him of his exchange. A few days later,
Lincoln wrote him again, suggesting that it was in the best interest of
the state for the Assembly to meet as soon as possible and that
delegates be sent to Congress. But if Walton took this to mean, as
later claimed, that he was to go to Augusta and raise a government to
replace the *extralegal* Supreme Executive Council, he kept his intent
from the one man with whom the new government would have to
work: the commander of the American forces in Georgia, and his
good friend, Lachlan McIntosh. Immediately upon his release,
Walton visited the general, but in their discussions he apparently
gave no hint of Lincoln's suggestion.[10] It is possible, of course, that
General Lincoln's second letter had not reached him as yet (this is
doubtful, though the timing of events is difficult to determine), or
perhaps Walton did not wish to jeopardize his plan by telling it to

Wereat's close friend. What is more likely, however, is that at this point Walton simply was not sure what steps he was going to take. Augusta was his destination, but he knew little of conditions there. The one man he could trust to give a candid analysis of the situation was Lachlan McIntosh.

After a short, cordial visit, Walton left for Augusta, where he discovered something nature, and George Walton, abhorred—a vacuum. With Wereat's Council absent, Howley and Wells were attempting to consolidate their position, but some Whigs, realizing that these two had no more right to govern than the Supreme Executive Council, were uneasy. At this critical juncture Walton arrived, and provided the legitimacy the coalition needed—Lincoln's letter, which seemed to authorize an Assembly in place of the unconstitutional Council. That this tactic seemed to fly in the face of earlier radical arguments against military involvement in civilian affairs mattered little to Howley and Wells. Here was their opportunity, and they seized it. For his part, Governor Walton may well have been trying only to give Georgia the stable, constitutional government many felt Wereat's Council could never provide; of course, he may also have been trying to restore his career, which had been in limbo for nearly a year. Motive, in this case, is difficult to assign. One fact, however, remains: in the fall of 1779 George Walton changed sides, and that change put him on a collision course with Lachlan McIntosh.[11]

The failure to take Savannah at a time when everything pointed to victory convinced many back-country Whigs that the Supreme Executive Council lacked the will to prosecute the war to its fullest. Furthermore, charges that Tory influence was responsible for the defeat made sense to a people who had seen their commanding general defend Loyalists and who remembered that Wereat's Council had refused a blanket condemnation of those who were accused of treason. The circumstantial evidence was such that Walton's faction had to do little more than point out the coincidences to make its case. Toryism was easily linked to McIntosh, whose close association with Wereat and the Council seemed to prove that all shared a common lack of resolve. With memories of earlier British incursions and Loyalist reprisals still fresh in their minds, it was easy for what remained of the Whig movement to agree that Walton and his Assembly offered the best hope of protection.[12]

Thus McIntosh arrived in Augusta early that December to find "Divisions instead of being mended, in a worse State than ever."[13] Colonel Richard Parker, who assumed command in the general's absence, now refused to surrender his post, siding instead with the Assembly, which later endorsed his action. McIntosh, though outraged at Parker, did not press the issue as he might have. Instead, he seemed to take stock of the situation, hoping to discover what role, if any, he was to play.[14] The matter was complicated by the fact that his return coincided with the election of the first constitutionally sanctioned Assembly Georgia was to have in over a year, and in an effort to legitimize their earlier assumptions of power with a popular mandate, both parties were engaged in the most bitterly partisan contest since the 1776 election, which vaulted Gwinnett to power. And in this election, as in the earlier one, Lachlan McIntosh was not a candidate but an issue.

Under such circumstances, it was impossible for the general to "stay clear of either party & mind [his] military duty alone," as he had intended.[15] His association with Wereat's Council, which by now he obviously favored over Walton's Assembly, placed him squarely in the middle of the controversy. But earlier Loyalist affiliations made him a liability to his friends' cause and the new "popular" party swept the election. Still, despite all that had occurred, McIntosh felt he could work with Walton, as he indicated on December 11, when he wrote to Lincoln for advice as to which government he should apply if the need arose before the new, clearly legitimate Assembly met in January. That dilemma was avoided, however, for no sooner was the letter written than the general learned that his family might be released from British captivity. The news overshadowed everything else and he hurriedly left Augusta, apparently believing that Walton and his followers were content simply to let him go. He soon realized how wrong he was.[16]

The rest of December was spent attending to family business, and in early January McIntosh reported to General Lincoln in Charleston, where he was shown a "most extraordinary Resolve of *Governor* Walton's and Six of his Council."[17] Declaring "the People at Large in

[Georgia had] such a Repugnance to Brigadier General McIntosh, that in the event of any Offensive operation on the part of the Enemy . . . they would not turn out under his Command," his detractors recommended that McIntosh be employed in some other department and that Lincoln appoint a replacement. "Good God," the general wrote Wereat after reading the document, "will the Mallice of these people never be at an end [?]" Convinced that these sentiments did not reflect popular opinion, McIntosh reasoned that his critics were acting out of the same lust for power that motivated the Gwinnett faction. He further concluded that his only failure was to do what he now felt Walton had done: shift with the political tides. For him, it was better to stand charged for that reason than to betray his friends and his honor. Feeling that, despite the new Assembly's pro-Walton majority, he could get a fair hearing, the general asked Wereat to seek justice for him in the Assembly and turned his attention to the security of his family.[18]

Apparently Lincoln did not possess the most damaging material that McIntosh's critics had sent to Congress: a letter date November 30, 1779, and supposedly written "Pursuant to the command of the General Assembly." Although most of this document dealt with Georgia's defensive problems and her need for aid, the next to the last paragraph was directed specifically at McIntosh. Stressing the same "common dissatisfaction" emphasized in the Council's resolution, the letter deemed it "highly necessary that Congress would whilst [General McIntosh was] in the service of the United States direct some distant field for the exercise of his abilities." This request, signed by William Glascock, Speaker of the House, carried the weight of a body Congress believed to be Georgia's duly elected Assembly. It was not easily ignored.[19]

Also in the package was a letter from George Walton, who apologized for the trouble all this had caused Congress. Assuming the stance of one slightly above the fray, the Governor assured the delegates in Philadelphia that it was all true—"that a general and settled Aversion" prevailed against McIntosh. He was quick to point out that he did not "Mean to Suspect the integrity" of the general, and that he still counted himself "very much his friend," but as it was "the Practice of Nations not to continue any Officer in Command longer than he preserves the confidence of the People," it might be best to remove McIntosh to another post and replace him with Samuel Elbert.[20]

Walton may well have seen himself acting simply as he had in 1777, when he was instrumental in securing McIntosh's transfer from Georgia to escape the wrath of Gwinnett's supporters. At the same time, there is no reason to doubt that the Governor was sincere in considering himself "very much" the general's friend. If McIntosh could remain on good personal terms with Loyalists, though their politics differed, why could Walton not continue his friendship with the general, even though they were on opposite sides? Knowing that Wells, Howley, and their supporters feared and hated McIntosh, Governor Walton may have seen this secret request for the transfer as the best means of easing his old friend out of the picture with minimal embarassment for all involved. Times were unsettled, and the sooner that such divisive symbols as General Lachlan McIntosh were dispensed with, the easier it would be for the state to defend itself.[21]

But if this was Walton's intention, he made a fundamental mistake: he neglected to tell the general. What had been done in 1777 was accomplished with McIntosh's full knowledge and approval, but in the fall of 1779, although the general was willing to work with the Governor, Walton did not take him into his confidence. Between November 30, the date on the Assembly's letter, and December 15, when the material was sent to Congress, there were numerous opportunities for him to inform McIntosh of the attitude of the Assembly and of the plan to have him transferred to a post where his talents could be fully utilized. But the Governor, perhaps fearing repercussions from his new allies, did not act, and when McIntosh saw the resolution he was stunned.[22]

Meanwhile, a more realistic John Wereat offered the general little hope for vindication in the new Assembly. Howley had been elected Governor, the former Governor was picked as a delegate to the Continental Congress, and lesser offices were created and passed out to their supporters in numbers and at a cost far exceeding the conservatives' wildest fears.[23] It was clear that neither Wereat nor his associates ever enjoyed the support and trust of Georgians outside the occupied areas. Having failed to gauge the impact of revolutionary rhetoric on popular expectations, they found themselves defenseless against charges that their Council was an attempt to overthrow the Constitution of 1777 and thwart the will of the people. Finally, when the failure to take Savannah combined with suspicions that some of their number were in reality Loyalists, their position became untenable. Deposed and discredited, Wereat left no doubt as to whom he felt was responsible for their condition. "Can you believe," he wrote the general, "that this wretch . . . would sacrifice and destroy his best friends to accomplish any favorite point he had in view and in short that Nero of infamous memory was not a greater tyrant than G[eorge] W[alton] [?]" [24]

Though his friend's sentiments did not fall on deaf ears, General McIntosh, safely out of Georgia, seemed for the moment more concerned with the growing threat to Charleston. Then, on March 17, he received the letter from Samuel Huntington, President of the Continental Congress, informing him that, without so much as a hearing, Congress had resolved it "inexpedient to employ [him] at present in the Southern Army, and that [his] services in that Department [were] dispensed with until further orders of Congress." The decision was based on the papers Walton had sent to Philadelphia. A subsequent resolution, calling for him to "repair to head quarters," in lieu of suspension, was proposed by McIntosh's friends, but Congress seemed to have had enough of the controversial general. The move was defeated. The news reached Charleston just as conditions were worsening, and so his superiors ordered him to remain at his post; but McIntosh knew that soon he would have to answer to the charges, or his career and reputation would be lost. [25]

Ironically, Congress may have gone further than Walton wished. The former Governor surely knew McIntosh's sensitivity on matters where his honor was concerned, and was aware of how his single-minded dedication to that principle had brought Gwinnett to his end. What Congress had done guaranteed that General McIntosh would not be quietly transferred to another post. No way remained for the general to salve his wounded pride without discrediting his accusers. McIntosh set about doing just that. Gathering what material was available to support his case, he sent it to Georgia and demanded an explanation. The results far exceeded his expectations, for apparently the Assembly's request for his removal had been kept a secret—even from its members. The source of this revelation was none other than Speaker William Glascock, who, upon hearing that his signature was affixed to the document, declared it "a flagrant forgery" and denied either direct or indirect knowledge of it.[26]

The Assembly, Glascock contended, had never passed such a resolution, and, contrary to Walton's assertions, the "reputable" people of the state gladly served under the general.[27] In fact, he was to testify some time later that "every Matter that was . . . carried in the House of Assembly . . . was first Settled and determined upon, in a private Club held at Geo. Wells's Lodging, and composed of the Governor Elect, the new Counsellors, some Select Members of the House & others whom they gained by Offers and picked out to Suit their purposes, and prevented the entrance of all others, their proceedings were kept in the profoundest Secrecy, even from the other Members of the House, except some trifling Matters carryed in to Amuse them." It was in such a meeting that the Assembly's letter was written.[28] In short, Glascock vowed that McIntosh had served Georgia well and "ought to receive the Grateful testimonials of Publick approbation, instead of the malicious insinuations of Private Slander." Outraged at having been used by a few men "governed by Design or Self-Interest," the former Speaker, a strong Whig since the days of the First Provincial Congress, threw partisanship to the winds and, on the same day that Charleston fell, sent his vehement denial to Philadelphia.[29]

During his confinement McIntosh was allowed to prepare his case, which consisted mainly of collecting affidavits in his favor. Glowing though they were, the testimonials were hardly objective assessments, and he knew it. His main hope rested on Glascock's denial, and so he waited as the wheels of justice slowly turned. Meanwhile the general's mind was drawn away from his troubles by those of his family. British activity had forced them from Camden and in the next few months they were constantly on the move. Lackie stayed with them the entire time, endearing himself even more to his father, who clearly singled him out as his favorite, but even his efforts failed to relieve all their hardships.[30]

Finally, in September, Glascock's denial was presented to the Congress, but both Walton and Howley had been selected as delegates from Georgia and were well prepared to defend themselves. Citing conditions which forced legislators to "set in council by day and scout against the enemy at night," Walton defended his actions as a product of circumstances. The denunciation of McIntosh, he asserted, was the sense of the Assembly, and Glascock had authorized his signature to be added to it. Howley supported Walton's explanation, as did George Seegar, clerk of the Assembly at the time. The delegates at Philadelphia knew well what it meant to try to carry on the functions of government with the enemy close at hand; so McIntosh's supporters, with little more than Glascock's letter, were overwhelmed. On September 25 the committee that had been set up to investigate the charges reported in favor of Walton.[31]

Distressed at the news, McIntosh vowed to continue the struggle, and so, aided by Wereat, who had been taken prisoner when the British entered Augusta shortly after Charleston fell, set to build a case that could not be ignored.[32] Parolled in the summer of 1781, the general gathered his information and headed for Philadelphia, spoiling for a fight. His request for a new inquiry was quickly granted, but Congress, with little apparent desire for a protracted debate, was willing to go even further. It seemed that McIntosh's friends had used the intervening time to the general's advantage, for on the same day his request was made, the hearing was held and the resolution suspending him was repealed. Walton and Howley tried to add an amendment barring McIntosh from commanding troops in Georgia, which was what the former probably wanted from the start and what the latter, at this point, would be happy enough to get. That attempt was defeated, nine states to one; only its sponsors voted for it.[33]

But Congress's "Act of Justice" hardly satisfied McIntosh. The months of confinement had built up a reservoir of hatred that now spilled out in a bitter request for a new investigation to root out those who were responsible for his disgrace.[34] It was his substitute for the pistol and ball. But Congress, having spent enough time on Georgia's political problems, was not inclined to review the issue. By fall, Walton and Howley had returned to Georgia, and with them went much of the general's desire for a congressional investigation. With his major antagonists absent, revenge would not be quite so sweet.

Though formally exchanged by February 1782, McIntosh did not return to Georgia immediately. Because his personal funds were exhausted, he decided it was best that his family return to Camden, where they would be cared for. During his stay in Philadelphia he lived in an army barracks, rejoiced with his fellow soldiers at news of the victory at Yorktown, and kept an eye on political developments at home. Finally, in July of 1782, the British evacuated Savannah and the general began his long journey. Hardly expecting a hero's welcome, he knew he was returning to a state where his fortune and his reputation lay in ruins. Despite the outward display of "gaiety" that amazed those around him, the future weighed heavily on his mind.[35]

CHAPTER TWELVE

"This Cursed War has ruin'd us all"

When I see a man, surrounded with what the world calls more than
Difficulties: Exiled from Country, Splendid fortune, from family,
with wants of almost every kind into the bargain, when such a man
bears all this not only with constancy, but laughs at it with gaity, you
must not blame me if I envy him, when I feel myself & see most of the
World beside me incapable of it.

Aedanus Burke to Lachlan McIntosh, October 28, 1781

I have Just taken in all the Crop Henry made for me this Year,
Consisting of not quite five bushels of Nubin Corn & not a single
bushel of pease—a horrid prospect of Subsistance.

Lachlan McIntosh to John McIntosh, September 23, 1786

Like a vengeful demon, Lachlan McIntosh descended on Georgia in
that hot August of 1782. Caring little that the careers of Walton and
Howley, in the words of John Wereat, were "as much depreciated as
paper money," or that the new leaders of the state were more
concerned with postwar recovery than with renewing old rivalries,
he served notice to all that he expected Georgia to exonerate him, as
Congress had done. Implicit in his attitude was the belief that, to
clear his name, the guilty had to be brought to justice.[1] Even the
formerly all-consuming passion for economic security was pushed
aside as he plunged headlong into the battle for his honor.

But not everyone was as enthusiastic or as committed to the cause
of "justice" as the general. Wereat, whose dislike for Walton was
understandable, agreed to aid in a suit against the former Governor,
but John Houstoun and James Jackson, both rising stars in state
politics, refused to lend their names to the revival of partisan causes.
Jackson was even so blunt as to admit to Wereat, his friend and
longtime adviser, that fear for his political future overrode all other
considerations—a confession which outraged Wereat. Legal aid

finally had to be sought in South Carolina, but though the Assembly approved Charles C. Pinckney, Thomas Pinckney, and Edward Rutledge to plead before the Georgia bar, their distance from Savannah and the expense their services would incur virtually guaranteed that McIntosh would not be quick in bringing suit.[2]

Seeing his predicament, the general appealed to a less than receptive Assembly, which, with no real choice in the matter, agreed to hear his case. On January 18, 1783, a committee composed of William Gibbons, William Few, and the chastened James Jackson began to review the evidence. Pleased with the committee, since they considered none of its members Walton men, McIntosh and Wereat presented an even stronger case than they had in Philadelphia. Overwhelming critics with petitions, letters, and affidavits, McIntosh soon left little doubt that he had enjoyed far more support than his detractors claimed and that the Glascock signature was unauthorized, a forgery. So stunning was the presentation, it seemed—in the words of one witness—that instead of having been "dispised," McIntosh was "universally esteemed and Respected, except by George Walton."[3]

Walton and, to a lesser degree Howley, emerged from the testimony as the principal villains in the affair. Samuel Stirk, who had been secretary of Walton's Council, testified that McIntosh's failure to desert the Wereat faction and acknowledge Walton as the executive of the state prompted the Governor to declare that "he had made General McIntosh and he would be *Damned* if he would not break him." Summoned to answer the charges, Walton disregarded the order, sending instead a letter which cited the anti-McIntosh sentiments of Colonel Parker, since killed in action, and called on the committee to consult the explanation he had given Congress. Howley appeared before the committee but, according to McIntosh, "evaded giving any evidence" and was allowed to depart. With that, the investigation came to a close.[4]

On February 1 the committee returned its verdict, and after a brief debate the Assembly resolved that Walton's letter and his Council's resolution were "unjust, Illiberal and a misrepresentation of facts." It further held that the Glascock letter was a "forgery in Violation of Law and Truth," and that the Attorney General should look into the matter to see if grounds for charges existed. To the general's dismay, however, Walton and Howley were never brought to trial, but perhaps that was for the best. Except for McIntosh and a few of his friends, old wounds healed quickly. The radical–conservative conflict that did so much to bring Georgia into the Revolution waned after 1779 and by war's end was eclipsed by other forces.[5] Georgians' efforts to rebuild the state's shattered economy were creating new alliances, based on sectional concerns and on personalities rather than on the rivalries with which McIntosh was associated. Under these conditions, old issues were simply in the way, and General Lachlan McIntosh was an old issue.[6]

It was therefore understandable that the Assembly had no desire to discredit Walton (now one of the leaders of an increasingly powerful Augusta-based coalition) and risk creating a new conflict that would deter Georgia from more important matters. Thus the day before McIntosh's vindication it made Walton Chief Justice of the very court in which such a trial would be held.[7] Outraged by what they perceived as a miscarriage of justice, the general and his friends vowed to continue the fight, and soon the air was full of accusations that quickly spilled over into the *Georgia Gazette* in one of the most vigorous and (for the readers, no doubt) entertaining exchanges to grace that paper in many years.[8] Matters reached such a fevered pitch that William McIntosh, the general's third son, who had inherited more than his share of his father's temper and absolutely none of his restraint, drew up a petition which pledged its signers "to assist in pulling [Walton] of [f the] Bench," which, he asserted, "ought to be filled with an Unblemished Character."[9] But the petition apparently gained little support. William McIntosh would have to find another way to make the Chief Justice pay "for his own infamous and personal behavior to [his] Father."[10]

This avenger of the family honor did not have long to wait. While walking one day with some of his friends, William encountered Walton and Dr. Nathan Brownson. Immediately flying into a rage, the young man took a horsewhip he was carrying and began striking the Chief Justice. To escape the blows, which William proudly confessed were "well Laid on," Walton took flight, leaving his dignity—but not his assailant—behind. Like the hound after the hare,

William followed, swingly wildly, until the magistrate, his pride as wounded as his back, broke down a gate and escaped. No doubt distressed that the violent strain that brought down Gwinnett had passed from father to son, the general prepared to defend his offspring against the charges he was sure Walton would bring. But the Chief Justice, for reasons of his own, never retaliated.[11]

William McIntosh's may have been the only physical assault on Walton, but political attacks were numerous. In March 1783, a Chatham County grand jury, which included Wereat, the general, and a number of McIntosh supporters, issued a ringing denunciation of the Chief Justice. Declaring (among other things) that it was inconsistent with their duty to themselves and to their country "to act under a Court whose presiding Magistrate [was] liable to a criminal prosecution," they called on the Assembly to remedy the situation. Stung by this attack from the low country, Walton refused to accept the findings and, as the controversy boiled around him, dissolved the grand jury.[12]

Unwilling to give up, the jurors took their case to the Attorney General, who recommended that Governor Lyman Hall suspend the Chief Justice so that the jury could complete its functions. Hall agreed and Walton was relieved of his duties, but in the next session he returned to office. McIntosh was to make one final gesture of defiance. Just before the grand jury met he had received a note from "Hercules Wormwood," a contributor to the anti-Walton letter campaign, pointing out that in 1742 a group of citizens had refused to serve as jurors for a judge who was under indictment. The general acknowledged the precedent, and when he was called the next year to serve on the grand jury, he failed to appear. The act may have given him some personal satisfaction, but it cost him a £10 fine.[13]

The Assembly's action produced more satisfying results in other quarters. After Congress learned of his vindication in Georgia, it was not long before McIntosh received news of his long-overdue promotion to major general.[14] Once again he was the state's ranking officer and another blot on his honor was removed. Still, his victory was not complete, nor would it ever be. The men who had slandered his name, had forced him to spend time and money defending his honor, and had nearly ruined his career were still free. In fact, the whole affair had surprisingly little effect on his adversaries. Walton continued as Chief Justice, and later became Governor, United States Senator, and a Superior Court judge. Howley, though never as prominent as his colleague, also was apparently hurt little by the investigations, for in the fall of 1783 he was named acting Attorney General.[15] If McIntosh was to play a role in the development of Georgia as a part of an independent nation, he would do so surrounded by constant reminders of the most trying events of his life.

By now the general was losing his will to continue the fight. Not fully comprehending the effect revolutionary politics had on the distribution of power in Georgia, at first it was difficult for him to understand the postwar issues and influences which helped resolve his case. Finally he realized that he had done all he could, and decided to give up the struggle. Drained by the experience, he wanted simply to gather his scattered family and return to the life he had known before. But that, too, was denied him, for early in 1783 his beloved Lackie had taken ill and died in Camden.[16] Always his father's favorite, the young man's sense of responsibility and attention to duty made it appear that once again a second son would emerge as family leader. With Lackie gone, much of the warm, human side of the general seemed to fade. His concern, of course, was for the living, but it is doubtful if he ever fully forgot the dead.

Living, however, was no easy matter. Finding that his rebellion had destroyed much of the world that he had committed treason to preserve, the general was forced to resort to new devices to survive, and Lachlan McIntosh had never been much of an innovator. In his postwar condition one can see many of the elements that led to the political and economic decline of coastal Georgia and enabled the back country to rise in its place. Slaves were gone, barns and houses burned, fields flooded, dams destroyed, and the palmetto and sawgrass had returned with a vengeance. The land was fertile enough, but putting it into production was another matter. Repairs could be made, crops planted, and new markets found; all that was needed was capital, which McIntosh felt he would soon have. Convinced that most of his losses could have been prevented had he been less attentive to Georgia and more concerned with his personal welfare, the general was confident that the state would not only restore what he had lost but also reward his diligence in its defense. What he received, he reasoned, would enable him to rebuild.[17] But others also were gathering to divide the spoils, such as they were, and each felt his contribution more worthy of recognition than that of the next.

So it was that, in addition to a generally disrupted economy, Georgia faced a deluge of claims against her. Scant records had been kept during the war, making the actual extent of its debt unknown; thus, in an effort to meet the demands on its nearly exhausted treasury, it was ordered that those who had claims against the state should have them audited. If the claims were approved, the auditor would issue "audited certificates" for the value, which could be used to pay up to one-half on the purchase of confiscated Loyalist estates. Audited certificates that were not used to buy property could be exchanged for "funded certificates," which were much more popular since they paid 7 percent interest per annum in specie and were redeemable after seven years. The method solved some problems but created others, for the interest payments increased Georgia's already excessive debt. In a state whose finances were so uncertain, individuals who sought relief were at a disadvantage from the start.[18]

Aware of the state's limited resources, McIntosh knew it was essential to present his case as soon as possible. Therefore, in July 1783 he sent the Assembly a memorial which argued that the state owed him £12,170 for funds spent and damages incurred in the war. Although he had lost most of the vouchers and other evidence to substantiate his claims, he had the support of Wereat, who had become state auditor, and some of the leading members of the House, and so he hoped for the best.[19] The Assembly, however, was of another mind. "In confidence of his veracity," it agreed to compensate the general for debts contracted when he had been forced to cover the cost of food, forage, and pay for his troops with money from his own pocket. This sum would be credited toward purchases from the state that he and his son William might make. But the state refused to compensate him for the losses suffered on his plantation during the war. Noticeably absent from the state's grant was specie, the very thing that the general's depressed financial state needed most.[20]

The failure of the Assembly to pay his full claim was a bitter disappointment, and McIntosh continued to press the matter. Not content simply to wait while the legislature listened to his pleas, he persuaded creditors that it was only a matter of time before he would be paid in full. In this way he got them to postpone payment on his outstanding debt, and in some cases even obtained additional credit. Had this been applied to the restoration of his existing plantations, the general might have made a major step toward financial solvency. Displaying the same inclination toward economic indiscretions that Laurens had condemned so long before, McIntosh took the money, bought more land, and moved even closer to becoming one of Georgia's "landed poor."[21]

Part of this new property was on Skidaway Island, and there, close to his Savannah friends and connections, he established a plantation which was to become the center of his postwar life. He retained the property near Darien, but it was turned over to his sons to manage, which they did with mixed success. The decision to desert the Altamaha must have been difficult, and, since it made him just one more impoverished planter in an area that had more than its share, it may not have been the wisest move; yet in it one finds a glimmer of recognition by McIntosh that times had truly changed. Still, by tying himself to the coast, McIntosh made it clear that he did not accept the shift of power that had taken place. Old ways died hard, and despite this new venture, begun with a declared willingness to take risks he had long avoided, General Lachlan McIntosh's future was firmly rooted in the past.

Continuing to equate land with financial security, and finding this commodity the state's most available means of compensation, McIntosh accumulated large blocks. But what may have been wise policy in colonial Georgia was now questionable. New state land taxes were more demanding than quitrents and the would-be planter soon found himself extended beyond his means. Creditors were pressing from all sides, and the prospect of fields idled in the spring by a lack of capital seemed an increasingly real possibility.[22] Yet, after a fashion, the state did come to the general's aid. Less than two weeks after the Assembly had given only partial satisfaction on his claims, he was selected to serve on the Board of Commissioners, which was set up to examine claims against confiscated Loyalist estates. Though hardly the most lucrative appointment, it offered the promise of a much needed income, and so he took it.[23]

The position may have been offered, and accepted, for another reason as well. The issue of confiscated estates was volatile, as many Georgians felt the state's economic salvation was possible through the sale of these lands and others saw it as the opportunity to punish traitors. This latter attitude distressed some, particularly in the low country, who had old friends among the charged, and it thereby threatened to turn the matter into an emotionally charged political issue. McIntosh, whose views and connections were well known, may have been selected to calm such fears—not to mention his own.[24] Whatever the motives, it was one of the few political positions General McIntosh would occupy in Confederation Georgia.

In spite of this appointment, the Assembly's attitude toward McIntosh seemed contradictory at best. It cleared his name and praised him for services to the state, but when special land grants were given as rewards to certain officers (beyond their military bounty grants), McIntosh did not receive so much as an acre.[25] It was as if the Assembly was not quite sure what to do with him. To treat the general as a hero might vault him into politics and stir up the old factionalism that many sought to minimize. It seemed safer to keep him away from the center of power—to honor him, but not too much. Thus he could lend the state his talents and his prestige, but on a controlled basis. The old war horse was being put out to pasture, but McIntosh, fifty-six years old and beset with financial problems, appeared more relieved than upset.

Meanwhile, the general's association with the Board of Claims did little to alleviate his economic distress, and 1783 drew to a close with hope for financial solvency as dim as ever. The commissions that were granted for his services did not meet his needs, and as spring planting approached, creditors grew impatient. The only recourse was to sell some of his land, and so, reluctantly, part of his Altamaha island property was put on the block.[26] It was not enough, and more land was offered, but because land was not a rare commodity, prices never reached expectations. Soon further evidence of his plight began to appear in the *Gazette*. His "famous Horse Rochester" was advertised at stud for four guineas per mare (one dollar for the groom), while oysters and "slip potatoes" were offered for sale at his Skidaway plantation. Meanwhile he continued to apply to the Assembly for the funds he felt were his by right. But the leaders of Georgia, pressed at every quarter, were not able to satisfy his demands.[27]

Despite these hardships, life was not without rewards, and high among them was the role McIntosh played as spokesman for veterans of the Georgia Line. After he helped found the Georgia Society of the Cincinnati, those officers whom the organization honored responded by electing him its first president, an indication that among them, at least, he was still widely admired.[28] Though the Society professed no political intent, he hoped it might exert some pressure to speed up benefits promised the army, but even if that were not accomplished, the simple fact that he had been singled out to lead so prestigious a group did much to restore his confidence. He prized the organization's selectivity and protested efforts to broaden its base as tending to make membership "too cheap."[29] Furthermore, activities within the Society kept him in close contact with all the men who had served under him, and since their problems were also his, he gladly became their champion.

The veterans of Georgia's Continental battalion were angry. Although the state had given them certain advantages in the purchase of confiscated estates, they argued (with some justification) that, as in the past, the militia was receiving preferential treatment. In an effort to equalize matters they petitioned the Assembly for additional land on the basis of a refugee warrant, given for service outside the state. The Assembly refused on the grounds that the line had been paid and given bounties for working in their "chosen profession," and since one area was the same as another to a military man, they could not be classified as "refugees." General McIntosh, who had been active in earlier efforts to obtain relief for his troops, protested the Assembly's ruling and threw himself into the fight with all the enthusiasm his enlightened self-interest could muster.[30]

The focus of the army's demands soon shifted. In February 1784, the Assembly created the counties of Franklin and Washington from the land between the Ogeechee and Oconee rivers that had been ceded to the state by the Creek Indians in the Treaty of Augusta in 1783. Since the treaty had not been accepted by all the Creek nation, the state was anxious to validate its claim by populating the area. One of the most readily available groups for that purpose was the Georgia veterans. With that in mind, the land between the north and south forks of the Oconee River was set aside for those who were due military bounties from either Congress or the state.[31]

Reserved for twelve months, the land was free except for clerical fees, and there were no cultivation requirements; it seemed a logical solution for all. But McIntosh and the veterans felt otherwise. Disappointed at being restricted to one particular reserve and at having to wait till the land court opened in Augusta before they could survey their claims, they again protested—to an increasingly unsympathetic Assembly, which flatly rejected their demands. Having no other recourse, the veterans agreed to abide by the regulations as written and set about grumbling over the "quality" of land they were to receive.[32]

Although wishing that more preference were given to his men, McIntosh was generally pleased with the fact that he was authorized to receive, according to his estimate, 3,450 acres. If the quality of the land were good, enough might be realized from its sale to pay off his debts and revitalize his plantations. Hopes soared even higher when he learned that his officers had voted to allow him first choice of the reserve as a token of their esteem, which seemed to guarantee that at least some of his financial worries would soon be behind him. Thus bolstered, he spent the time prior to the land court's opening preparing for the event, and offering advice on how the process should be handled—most of which was courteously ignored.[33]

Perhaps they should have listened. Though preparations went forward in an orderly fashion, when the court finally opened and warrants for survey were distributed, all semblance of order disappeared. Like vultures, the applicants descended—pushing, grasping, in a mad rush to have their claims processed. Document clerks were assaulted as tables crushed under the numbers and duplicate grants were often issued as money secretly passed from speculator to surveyor. With chaos and corruption the hallmarks of the event, it is hardly surprising that when calm was restored, few were satisfied with the results.[34]

General McIntosh was among the disappointed. Angered by speculators and surveyors who maneuvered to buy soldiers' warrants at reduced prices, and faced with an attempt by one combination to lay claim to the best part of a grant issued to him, McIntosh turned to the courts for a *caveat* against further encroachments on his property. The strategy worked and the land was his, but again the result seemed hardly worth the effort. After examining what he had received, he headed home, declaring the entire military reserve "the ordinariest Tract of Land that could be found in [the entire] Cession."[35]

As one might expect, restricted personal finances meant a restricted public career. In February 1784, as the question of the military reserve was coming to a head, the Assembly, still following a bewildering policy toward the general, chose him as a delegate to Congress.[36] Nothing could have been more poorly timed. Although he accepted the post, McIntosh quickly realized that he would be unable to play a role in the land-grant controversy if he were in Philadelphia—which may have moved the Assembly to select him in the first place. Facing the dilemma squarely, General McIntosh decided to stay home and tend to his own affairs. He was not reelected.

Although his hopes for the military reserve were never realized, McIntosh's decision to remain in Georgia seems to have forced the legislature to come to terms—if for no other reason than to get him off its back. In April Wereat certified that the general was due £3,471 13s 1d, and the Assembly apparently agreed to honor some of these additional claims. Since this represented less than one-fifth of what he felt was owed, the general was far from happy, but he took it, and applied what he could to his ever mounting debt. It still was not enough, and soon a notice appeared offering his house in Savannah for sale or lease—an unhappy testament to the severity of his plight.[37]

Through early 1785 McIntosh's finances improved only slightly, and though his creditors were less persistent than in previous years, he was unable to do little more than break even. It seemed that once one crisis had passed another appeared. Minor problems relating to some "shady" business dealings of his son Jack had to be smoothed over, but the main threat to his holdings came when he learned that his failure to register his and Laurens' land south of the Altamaha meant that it might be declared vacant. After a frenzy of activity, the general obtained the renewal certificates and ownership was preserved, but not without expenses that he could ill afford. Still, the friendship between the two men proved as strong as ever, though their interests were never as intertwined as before the war. The Altamaha matter proved to be one of the last recorded business dealings in their long and amicable relationship.[38]

No doubt McIntosh missed the advice and admonitions of his friend. His inability to separate the important from the trivial, his almost blind belief in the legitimacy of his cause, and his growing lack of faith in many of the men who governed the state added to the general's woes. As political power shifted from the tidewater to the back country and as his taxes rose, he became more distressed. Political events swirled about him, new men and issues came and went, and old power alignments seemed to matter little, if at all. The day of General Lachlan McIntosh had come and gone—almost without his realizing it.

CHAPTER THIRTEEN
The Postwar Public Servant

I was glad that Congress had Interposed it's Authority & that in
Consequence we should Settle all our differences in an Amicable
Manner the expectation of which determined me to Meet you with a
full representation of these Nations for effecting so desirable a purpose. Meantime while I was waiting for the Second Advices, I
received Authentic information that yr. Georgians were resolved to
Embarass the Commissrs. in the execution of the trust Committed to
them by Congress.

Alexander McGillivray to Benjamin Hawkins, July 30, 1786

Tempting as it is to blame the general's lack of postwar political
activity solely on pressing financial obligations and the action of state
officials bent on minimizing previous factional divisions, one must
not forget that even before the Revolution McIntosh had shown only
occasional interest in direct political involvement. During those
years, he sought or accepted offices only when it was in his interest to
do so, and after the war that same standard continued to apply.
True, none of the posts that he was offered allowed him a real voice
in state policy, nor were they such that one might use them to launch
a political career; but though these restrictions were important to
state officials, they seemed to matter little to McIntosh. Simply put,
when it was to the state's advantage, General McIntosh's services
were requested, and when it was to the general's advantage, those
services were given.

One case in point involved the state's attempt to establish its claim
to land east of the Oconee River. Aware that during the Revolution
most Indians had allied themselves with the British, Georgians were
anxious to regularize relations with the tribes. But Alexander
McGillivray, the brilliant, cosmopolitan, half-breed chief of the
Upper Creeks, resisted efforts to negotiate and instead sought aid
from the Spaniards in Florida. Faced with this opposition, Georgia

was able to persuade only a small band of Creeks (led by two minor chiefs) to meet with state commissioners at Augusta in 1783. There, on November 1, the Indians signed a treaty that gave the state full control of the land east of the Oconee.[1]

General McIntosh had been selected to serve on that first treaty commission, but as the appointment came at the time when personal and financial burdens were heaviest, he followed his earlier inclination, opted to see after his own, and declined the appointment. No sooner was the treaty signed than it came under fire. McGillivray was quick to denounce the agreement, pointing out that only two Creek towns were represented at the talks. Georgians, however, accepted the cession as valid and proceeded to carve Franklin and Washington counties from it. Planning to populate this land with settlers who would help revive Georgia's war-torn economy, state leaders saw the Indians as a threat to their very survival. The Indians saw Georgians in the same light.[2]

This controversy did not pass unnoticed in Congress. In May 1784, a committee report on Indian affairs for the Southern Department suggested that Congress should assume complete control of Indian relations. The southern delegates, reluctant for the states to give up any authority, blocked the measure. There was, nevertheless, a well-substantiated feeling among many that if something were not done soon, encroachments into the disputed territory would result in a full-scale Indian war.[3] Tension between Indians and Georgians did not ease during the summer of 1784, and when Congress reconvened in November the southern Indian problem was brought up again. Moving slowly, Congress did not reach a decision until March 1785, when it adopted a compromise report which put less emphasis on the central government's role in Indian relations. Congress then appointed three commissioners (Benjamin Hawkins of North Carolina, Daniel Carroll of Maryland, and William Perry of Delaware) to negotiate with the Indians, authorizing them to apply to the southern states for their expenses, which would be credited to the states' 1786 requisitions.[4]

Some states, including Georgia, felt that the action represented a violation of their right to deal with their internal affairs and were disturbed that only one of the commissioners was from the lower south. To minimize the protest, two additional commissioners, Andrew Pickens of South Carolina and Joseph Martin of North Carolina, were added. This left Georgia as the only deep south state that did not have a representative on the commission, a fact that was not overlooked by her leaders.[5]

Fearing the federal negotiations might overturn the Treaty of Augusta, Georgia decided to have a boundary line surveyed and fixed before the federal commissioners arrived. McIntosh, Elijah Clark, and Benjamin Hawkins were selected to serve as state agents, but Hawkins, who was not a Georgian but was a member of the federal delegation, eventually declined. Thus it was left to Governor Samuel Elbert's old comrades in arms, McIntosh and Clark, to defend Georgia's rights, and since both men had claims in the military reserve, which was part of the contested land, the Governor seemed sure they would serve the state well.[6] Realizing where his interests lay, McIntosh accepted the appointment, but soon the issue was thrown into confusion and the general, once again, became the center of controversy. Shortly after he received the state appointment, Congress selected him to replace the ailing Daniel Carroll on its commission.[7] That gave Georgia the representative she so badly wanted on the federal body, but it put McIntosh in the uncomfortable position of having to decide which master to serve.

Still believing it would be "a capital point gained" if Georgia could survey the boundary before the federal delegation acted, Elbert pressed on; but time was running out. The federal commissioners arrived in Charleston in May and the next month shifted operations to Georgia. Aware of federal intentions, the Indians refused to cooperate with state efforts, forcing Elbert to abandon his plan and reluctantly announce that the federal conference would be the time for establishing the boundary. Meanwhile, the Governor did not exert himself on the federal commission's behalf. When Hawkins requested $2,000 to defray his delegation's expenses, Elbert pointed out that only the legislature could grant such a sum and that it would not meet till the next year. No efforts were made to obtain money from other state sources.[8]

Soon after the arrival of the federal agents, McIntosh made his decision; he resigned from the state commission.[9] Since Georgia's opposition to the congressional agents was fast reaching a fevered pitch, his decision—apparently not one to endear him to local officials—seemed yet another example of his inability to gauge political situations. But there may have been meaning in what seemed madness. He and Georgia were of like mind on this matter, and his services on the state delegation would have had little real effect. As a member of the federal commission, however, he could serve as a force for state interests as well as his own. His presence might make little difference as well, but it was worth a try. Meanwhile the state appointed Edward Telfair, William Few, and James Jackson to attend the negotiations, with instructions to "protest against any measures which [the federal agents might] adopt contrary to the Articles of Confederation and the Constitution and the Laws of the State." But Few and Jackson proved unable or unwilling to go; John King and Thomas Glascock were chosen in their place, and finally Georgia had a delegation.[10]

On October 24 the federal commissioners arrived at Galphinton on the Ogeechee River and found only a small party of Indians. McGillivray, attempting to play the Spaniards against the Americans, was not ready to enter serious negotiations; so he kept most of the Creeks away. The federal commissioners refused to treat with such an unrepresentative number, but before they withdrew they showed the Georgia delegation a draft of the treaty they hoped to offer, which the Georgians protested as violating the rights of the state. After the federal agents left, the state representatives negotiated a treaty with the few Indians who were present, confirming the Treaty of Augusta of 1783.[11]

The federal delegation proceeded to Hopewell, South Carolina, on the Keowee River, where they signed treaties with the Cherokees in December and with the Choctaws and Chickasaws in January 1786. Those treaties also drew protests from Georgia, but to no avail. On the whole, McIntosh played only a minor part in it all, for after the Cherokee treaty was concluded he withdrew from the commission and returned to Georiga. Efforts to get him to return proved futile.[12] With the Treaty of Augusta confimed, his interests were taken care of. There seemed little reason for him to continue and to risk the possibility that his activities might alienate some state officials. Perhaps the general's years as a "political issue" had taught him something after all.

If McIntosh's aim was to divorce himself from the growing controversy, he was apparently successful. The federal commission's failure at Galphinton and his secondary role in the entire affair seemed to blunt any animosity toward him. As one might expect, the Assembly denounced the Treaty of Hopewell and those who negotiated it, but it paid most of the general's expenses. However, Georgia's Indian problems were far from solved, for McGillivray rejected the Treaty of Galphinton, as he had the Treaty of Augusta, and vowed to oppose its enforcement.[13] Georgians, on the other hand, were generally pleased that their agents had produced even a questionable treaty confirming their claims to the disputed land. Thus satisfied, the state was willing to let McIntosh quietly retire, no doubt to his relief.

During the Confederation period, General McIntosh "served" his state in yet another function—in settling the Georgia–South Carolina boundary dispute. That controversy turned on a disagreement as to the origin of the Savannah River, the accepted boundary between the two states. South Carolina argued that the river began where its two tributaries, the Keowee and Tugaloo, joined, thereby giving the Palmetto State the land between that point and the North Carolina border and stretching to the Mississippi River. Georgia contended that the head of the north branch of the Keowee was the source of the Savannah and, therefore that the disputed territory belonged to Georgia. South Carolina also claimed the area beyond the headwaters of the St. Mary's and Altamaha rivers, running to the Mississippi. Georgia disputed that claim also, and with both sides citing colonial charters and the Proclamation of 1763 to uphold their cases, the issue was drawn.[14]

In February 1783, immediately after having cleared him of all Walton's charges, the Assembly appointed McIntosh, along with John Houstoun and Edward Telfair, as "Agents to settle and adjust the northern boundary" of Georgia. It was as "nonpolitical" a post as could be offered, and, as was probably expected, little came of the commission that year. But soon both states began granting land between the Keowee and Tugaloo and tensions mounted. Early in

1785 the states agreed to appoint agents once more and again the general was selected. Georgia, and especially McIntosh, whose southern holdings might be affected, hoped South Carolina would quickly give up her claims there, leaving only the northern border to be settled, but South Carolina refused, clinging to her claims to both. Faced with that impasse, the states decided to ask that the final settlement be made by a special federal court set up by Congress.[15]

Congress agreed and South Carolina quickly presented her evidence, but Georgia was not so prompt. Governor Elbert found that much of the material for reinforcing the state's claims was in England, and when it proved slow in coming, the state requested that the court be postponed. The request was reasonable and a delay, till June 1787, was granted. It still was not enough. By February 1787, no documents had been sent and none seemed forthcoming. Apparently feeling his case was not strong enough to trust to a third party, newly elected Governor George Mathews informed his commissioners that the state must negotiate directly with South Carolina or delay the federal court once again.[16]

Over the years the Georgia boundary commission had seen many changes; so by 1787 it became the duty of McIntosh, John Habersham, and John Houstoun to find a solution—quickly. Citing the nearness of the court's sitting as a "sufficient inducement for [the state commission] to use every means in [its] power, that will not be injurious to the state, to have the claims adjusted," Governor Mathews charged McIntosh and his associates to produce as favorable a settlement as possible.[17] Mathews knew that the state's claims were weak, so he further instructed the commissioners that, though supporting papers would be sent them, their "own personal knowledge will be of equal advantage." Furthermore, he stressed that if a settlement could not be reached, every effort was to be exerted to delay the meeting of the court.[18]

But South Carolina was willing to negotiate, and on April 24, 1787, the delegations met at Beaufort, South Carolina. Five days later the Convention of Beaufort was signed and the dispute was ended. The boundary between the states was declared to be the Savannah and the Tugaloo rivers, giving South Carolina the land between the Keowee and the Tugaloo while Georgia got all the disputed territory west of the headwaters of the Altamaha and St. Mary's—ending the controversy in the sector that most concerned McIntosh. In fact, so complete was the settlement that it stands as one of the best examples of how states could solve their differences under the Articles of Confederation.[19]

Not everyone was happy, however, for John Houstoun protested that Georgia had gained nothing in the negotiations and he refused to sign. McIntosh and Habersham had no such reservations and added their names, pointing out that their main purpose was to end the animosity between the states, prevent future disputes, and save the expense of a court. In short, they claimed to have compromised for the sake of a settlement. The following year the Georgia and South Carolina legislatures approved the convention and the matter was put to rest.[20]

General Lachlan McIntosh's public career was coming to an end. In 1787 he was at last chosen a member of the Assembly, but he served without distinction and was not reelected.[21] The general was in his sixtieth year, and though apparently healthy, much of the old vigor had been lost. Financial problems continued to plague him, and nothing seemed to help his economic prospects. Apart from trying to cope with the general difficulties created by an unstable state economy, he spent considerable time trying to minimize the effects of his sons' "Don Quixot schemes," which threatened what little financial security the family had left. To make matters worse, crops had been so bad in 1786 that all of his working slaves ran away, either from the fear of "the short prospect of provisions, or the Shame of making so little." Most returned, or were returned, but it was a hard blow for a man who had always prided himself on his ability as a planter.[22]

The Confederation period—that era in which many of the essential principles of American revolutionary radicalism were tested, was coming to an end. Georgia's disenchantment with the Articles had grown to critical proportions during the negotiations with the Indians and, despite its avowed attachment to the basic concepts of state sovereignty and local control, the state was preparing, psychologically, to leap into the unknown of the new federal union. What was coming was, in a very real sense, Georgia's first secession from the United States.[23]

The Confederation period had been equally difficult for McIntosh. Financial burdens constantly hindered him and, although his political ambitions were slight, the state's apparent inclination to ignore him or, at best, offer offices with little real influence over public policy may well have been a blow to the McIntosh pride. Associated with old factionalism, which the new factions wished to forget, he was, to many, a relic of another era, a curiosity—a man who was respected for what he had done but, increasingly, was expected to do little else. The new order had few things to offer him and, in disdaining the demands of popular politics, he had less to offer it. Thus the future promised little more than a continued struggle, but he faced it with the confidence that characterized his entire life. He was growing old but he had no desire to do so gracefully. General McIntosh had always been a fighter and would continue to be.

CHAPTER FOURTEEN

The Last Years

> My Heart then fills with gratitud, And I seem to be really in Your
> happy Family, injoying with you, that improving Philosophic con-
> versation You used to indulge me with . . . O my friend what a degree
> of intellectual injoyment our nature is sassceptible of, when we turn
> our views frequently to behold and contemplate the Moral System
> impressed on the Human Mind, by the Divine Intelligence!
>
> *William Bartram to Lachlan McIntosh, May 31, 1796*

Late in 1787 General Lachlan McIntosh found his state once again
on the verge of rebellion, but this time her conflict was with an
American government—the Confederation. Ever since the Revolution, Georgia had been at odds with federal authorities over the
conduct of Indian affairs. The crux of the disagreement was that the
state wanted to negotiate without interference from congressional
agents, but once a treaty was signed, Georgia officials wanted federal
assistance in enforcing its provisions. Not surprisingly, Congress
rejected this role and refused to recognize the treaties drawn up at
Augusta and at Galphinton; so Georgia decided to have no more of
Congress. Just as tensions between state and the Confederation
reached a peak, a convention, meeting in Philadelphia, proposed a
solution—the Constitution.

Spurred by a newspaper campaign in which anonymous corre-
spondents damned and praised the proposed document, Georgians
prepared to run headlong into the arms of the new government.[1] But
Lachlan McIntosh, who had given his aid and approval to the revolt
against Great Britain, found that he could give neither to the
threatened break with the Articles. Although he had suffered finan-
cially under the Confederation, politically it fulfilled his desire for a
loose, limited government, and he questioned the wisdom of de-
serting such a union. Finding that Wereat had been chosen president
of the Georgia ratifying convention, the general, disappointed that

he was not selected to attend, felt moved to advise his friend on the matter at hand. What resulted was a remarkable statement of a minority position that would not come of age for over half a century—and then with the most tragic results.[2]

Conceding that "the Men who framed [the] Constitution [were] the Wisest & best that this, or perhaps any other Nation ever produced," and that indeed there were "pressing exigencies [in] National Affairs [that] requir[ed] Some Speedy & effectual remedy," McIntosh nevertheless cautioned against adopting the new system "in the Lump, . . . without enquiry or Limitation of time or Matter." On the whole, he found it "really astonishing to see people so reluctant lately to trust Congress with only 5 per Cent duties on Imports for a short time to pay the National Debt expressly, & so Jealous of the Sovereignty of their respective States so eager now to yield these & every thing else . . . & to become *the State*, instead of United States of America." Such an abrupt turnabout struck McIntosh's cautious, conservative soul as ill advised at best; at worst, it might be embracing a remedy "Worse than the Disease."[3]

Yet McIntosh knew that if the Constitution, or even part of it, was rejected, one could hardly expect "the last illustrious Members [to] Serve again & the determination of any others less dignified [would] not have the Same general influence." What he proposed, therefore, and what he hoped Wereat would present to the convention, was that the new system be adopted for a period of twenty years so that the states could "have a fair tryal of its Effects." "At the expiration of that time [the states would] be at Liberty & have it in their own power to adopt it again if they please for another period either without or with any Amendments they may find Necessary." Under this plan the work of the framers, whom McIntosh obviously admired, would not be rejected, yet Georgia would avoid putting herself under a government so fixed that "efforts made there after for redress of Grievances must be termed rebellion."[4]

It was in this last statement that the true source of General McIntosh's opposition was revealed. His distrust of government removed from the people was real enough, as was his reluctance to change simply for the sake of change, but he had studied the document carefully and knew that it was far easier to amend than the

Articles; as it was written, redress was clearly possible without revolution. But it was not what existed that McIntosh feared; it was what he saw in the future. In time, he predicted, "it will be impossible to obtain Amendments in the Mode proposed when the majority, which is observed will ever be against the Southern States, find it in their Interest to Continue [things as they are], & Men of influence are once fixed in their Saddles."[5] It was this shift of power that troubled him, for already there were indications, some in the Constitution itself, that once the realignment was complete, his way of life, and the prosperity of his state, might be threatened as never before.

"It is known," the general wrote his friend, "to have been long the intention of the, Eastern & Western States to abolish Slavery altogether when in their power, which however Just may not be convenient for us so soon as for them[,] especially in a New Country & hot Climate such as Georgia." "Let us," he continued, "therefore keep the proper time for it in our own power while we have it." Since the Constitution prohibited any interference in the slave trade for twenty years (and by implication protected that institution), McIntosh felt the same period should be set for states to examine the union and determine the conditions under which they would remain associated with it. Then, if the new majority tried to end slavery when the prohibition expired, the southern states would be in a position to respond.[6] Prophetically, Lachlan McIntosh saw what the issue was to be and understood, as few seemed to, that if some provision was not made for its resolution, what seemed a redress of grievances to one side would indeed be rebellion to the other.

But the prophet was ignored. Apparently Wereat did not introduce the plan, but even if he did, the convention was clearly of another mind. In January 1788 it ratified the Constitution without a dissenting vote, and Georgia, with her "peculiar institution," became part of the new United States. In an ironic postscript to the whole affair, McIntosh was selected to serve in the convention that was charged with drawing up the amendments Georgia's constitution needed to bring state government into line with the national government. Apparently he refused the post, for when the convention met another served in his place.[7]

For Lachlan McIntosh, the years after the Constitution's ratification seemed to pass rapidly, blurred by a consistency of activity with little that was noteworthy to punctuate the era. He was an old man, growing older. As had been the case during the Confederation, economic problems demanded most of his time and energy. The winter of 1788 was especially severe and, coming on the heels of a poor harvest, the McIntosh family had to endure hardships that were reminiscent of the war years. Food supplies were quickly depleted, forcing the general to hire out slaves to bring in a little money and to relieve the plantation of mouths to feed. What livestock he had accumulated over the years was either sold or slaughtered, and finally he was forced to apply to his son, John, for aid. Everyone in the family "Suffered Amazingly . . . for want of Clothing & provisions," most were sick, and the few slaves he kept became insubordinate. When spring finally came, McIntosh's meager resources were nearly exhausted but his creditors were as demanding as ever.[8]

The general tried every means at his disposal to revive his sagging finances. Attempts to sell or mortgage military reserve land failed and once again he turned to the state for assistance. That effort too was wasted, for the Assembly rejected his claims. Finally, fearing that his land might be seized and sold for his failure to pay his taxes, the general was forced "to apply the first time in [his] life, and much against [his] grain, for some public office." In February 1789 McIntosh wrote President-elect Washington of his plight and asked to be appointed collector of customs for Savannah.[9] Though the post went to John Habersham, McIntosh was not ignored. He was appointed naval officer for the port and served in that capacity for over ten years.[10] Learning to deal with any stigma he might have felt accompanied a patronage appointment, McIntosh soon applied for the position of deputy postmaster for Savannah, promising, in his optimistic way, that although the office had yielded little profit in the past, he would make it pay in the future.[11] But with so few spoils to pass around, it would have been foolish to give two offices to one man; thus it went to another.

Federal employment proved insufficient to solve all his financial problems; so McIntosh continued to watch state politics, hoping for some new mode of relief. But most state offices were elective, and since he refused to submit to "the management and Intrigues by which they [were] generally obtained," he effectively removed himself from contention.[12] Nevertheless, the general remained willing, if not anxious, to speak his mind when issues affected him, and by 1790, what seemed to trouble him most was the state's land tax. Expecting the sale of Georgia's western lands to bring enough revenue to allow taxes to be lowered, he was outraged when the Assembly proposed to deed a large section of that land to the national government for less than $200,000. Rising in opposition, he denounced the plan in a somewhat confusing but strongly worded statement that was published in the *Georgia Gazette*, but the state turned a deaf ear. In the end, however, the plan was apparently abandoned, and the general was satisfied.[13]

Despite his financial problems, McIntosh's social position seemed to have remained intact. A frequent guest at Savannah functions, he was elected president of the Society of St. Andrew and continued to serve as president of the Society of the Cincinnati. In the latter capacity, he played a prominent role in entertaining President Washington when he visited Savannah in May 1791—a function well suited to the general's love for pomp and pageantry. He was also one of the organizers of the Liberty County Jockey Club and served on its governing board. On the surface, it was the life of a retired gentleman, full, rich, and satisfying, but beneath the offices and the ceremony was the struggle to afford the life style, a struggle which seemed to grow more difficult each year.[14] Finally, McIntosh went so far as to appeal to Congress for relief, but John Wereat, who was in Philadelphia and presented the general's claims for wartime losses, was unable to obtain any form of satisfaction. The only hope, Wereat explained, was the Georgia Assembly, but that had already been tried, and McIntosh refused to humble himself again.[15]

Through these financial crises the McIntosh family remained close and aided each other when they could. His son William was often more trouble than help, and soon his quick temper and dueling escapades were well known. Perhaps reflecting on his own experiences, the general warned his sons of the dangers of a "quarrelsome character" and of the "anxieties" such activities gave their friends.

John apparently heeded the message; William did not, and bore the scars to prove it.[16] William's adventuresome nature led him to pursue a military career, and he performed bravely in Georgia's wars with her Indian neighbors. John, on the other hand, chose to devote his time to planting and was a partner in many of his father's enterprises. Although William courted death, it chose his brother first. John died in May 1792, and General McIntosh took control of most of his estate.[17]

Few records remain to reveal the extent of McIntosh's economic troubles, but there is a 1793 tax digest which shows something of the nature of his plight. That year he owned over 1,000 acres of tidal swamps that were suitable for rice culture, 4,000 acres of pine barrens of varying quality, 3,233 acres of salt marsh, and over 1,200 acres of Sea Island property that was suitable for growing indigo or corn. In addition, he held town lots, wharves, and other buildings valued at £450, and had eighty-four slaves with which to work his holdings. In all, his property was valued at over £7,560. Included in that inventory were all the ingredients for a successful planting operation: good land, labor, and facilities.[18]

But from the moment Lachlan McIntosh returned to Georgia in 1783, he had been hampered by a lack of hard money with which to finance his operations. Owing to a general lack of specie in postwar Georgia, almost all transactions were conducted by exchange or credit. What claims the state acknowledged were usually paid with land, credit, or bonds that fluctuated in value. Slaves were bought on credit, as was additional land, and crops were planted with borrowed money. The result was an economic cycle of year-to-year borrowing that is all too familiar to agriculture.

Lachlan McIntosh became one of the short-term borrowers for whom one bad crop could drain away what little money had been accumulated. The harvests of 1786, 1787, and 1788 proved disasters from which he never fully recovered. They exhausted his capital and forced him to curtail his operations, which made it even more difficult for him to raise the money to pay off debts and taxes. In 1793 his tax came to nearly £140, and the state was just as demanding as his other creditors. So, despite the extensive holdings shown in the tax digest, much of which had belonged to his dead son's estate, the general's expenses exceeded his income. Soon, notices that his property was being sold bore testimony to his inability to meet earlier obligations.[19]

Despite all that they had undergone, the general and his family still commanded considerable respect, as the creation of McIntosh County in 1793 indicates. The following year he was called on to chair a committee protesting British maritime policy and acts of war against American shipping, and in 1795 he led a full denunciation of Jay's treaty. It was the perfect forum for an aging military hero, and General Lachlan McIntosh proudly rose to defend the nation he had helped create.[20] In 1797 he was briefly involved in a canal-building scheme near Georgia's new capital, Louisville, but nothing came of the venture. Meanwhile he continued to receive an income from his position as Savannah's naval officer, but age forced him to neglect that post, for which, much to his consternation, he was reprimanded.[21]

Unable to devote full time to his various enterprises, the general began to divest himself of many of the responsibilities he had taken on over the years. He continued to serve as president of the Society of the Cincinnati and occasionally heard from old acquaintances, such as William Bartram, whom he had befriended when the naturalist visited Georgia prior to the Revolution. When possible, he stayed away from the hot island plantation during the summer months, but his life was far from the comfortable retirement for which he had hoped. Tax problems and debts continued to plague him, yet he was apparently willing to entrust them to his family and his attorneys.[22]

Early in 1799 McIntosh's faithful friend, Wereat, died; and before the year ended his fiery son, William, followed. Few of the old revolutionaries remained. Laurens had died in 1792; Howley was gone, as were William Glascock, Lyman Hall, and Samuel Elbert; and in February 1801 the general's brother, William, passed away.[23] It was almost over. Old factions made little difference as Georgia honored her dead as heroes and statemen, and waited for the others to join them. Walton died in February 1804.[24] As far as surviving records show, he and the general never settled their differences. McIntosh apparently ignored Walton's successful career, and he left no comment on his passing. Nevertheless, he must have felt some satisfaction in outliving his longtime adversary.

On February 20, 1806, shortly before his seventy-ninth birthday, General Lachlan McIntosh died in his home in Savannah.[25] The inventory of his estate revealed that he had been able to retain most of his personal property, which, when combined with the estates of his deceased sons, suggested a more extravagant way of life than actually existed.[26] He was buried in Savannah with all the honors due him. He would have liked that.

CHAPTER FIFTEEN

"But what good came of it at last?"

> Be Asshured I never Shall be Afraid or a Shamed to own I have been
> under obligations to a Worthy brave good man, General McIntosh.
>
> *Captain Thomas Farrell to Lachlan McIntosh, July 31, 1786*

In November 1947 the Georgia Department of Archives and History received the following notice from the American Library Service:

> We wish to offer, subject to prior sale, the following scarce item:
> Gwinnett, Button. Famous Georgia Signer. An autograph letter
> signed, written by the Man Who Assassinated Button Gwinnett in an
> Historic Pistol-Duel—General Lachlan McIntosh of Savannah,
> Georgia. . . . [1]

It had finally come to that—"the Man Who Assassinated Button
Gwinnett." The Altamaha frontier, Georgia's defense, Valley
Forge, the western campaign, Savannah, Spring Hill redoubt, and
Charleston were not worthy of mention. The political, military, and
economic struggles seemed forgotten. What occurred that May
morning in 1777 erased nearly eighty years of achievement, failure,
joy, and suffering. With one shot Gwinnett became a legend and
McIntosh was reduced to historic trivia, remembered only because
his bullet made his adversary's signature the rarest of the Declaration's signers. General Lachlan McIntosh spent much of his life
fighting to preserve his reputation and honor, yet if this advertise-
ment is an accurate indicator, he failed.

The real failure, however, lies not with the general but with later
generations, whose myopic backward glances produce praise for the
sensational and ignore the important. For over seven decades,
tumultuous years during which the fabric that was colonial America
was woven, unraveled, and rewoven into a new, more complex
tapestry, Lachlan McIntosh lived and worked. First and foremost a

Georgian, he and his family helped guide that colony through the agony of birth and development, creating for themselves, in the process, a social-economic-political dynasty that serves as a near classic example of how an aristocracy of ability formed and functioned. Though hampered, as the letters from Laurens clearly show, by limited commercial talents, McIntosh was able to exploit his opportunities to the extent that he was recognized by all who knew him as successful and important.

Molded by his Altamaha upbringing and its time of struggle, dislocation, privation, and hard-won successes, Lachlan McIntosh emerged as a cautious, conservative man, aware of the transitory nature of his wealth and status, and dedicated to the cause of keeping both. Elitist in politics (though he preferred to leave those duties and rewards to others whenever possible), provincial in outlook, dignified, and perhaps a bit overbearing, he appeared almost a caricature of the colonial country squire, and no doubt would be happy to know that this image survived. But he was no caricature. He was human, and though he strove for a standard of gentlemanly exclusiveness, his own humanity and the temper of the times often negated his efforts.

Yet of all the gentlemanly ideals that McIntosh took to heart, the one which did more to shape (some might say warp) his life was his acute sense of "honor"—an attitude he often translated into a near self-righteous faith in the validity of his own cause. Any challenger who questioned the motives or methods of himself, his family, or his friends was quickly answered, and often with serious consequences for all. Still, despite the self-assurance which seemed parent to this "honor," the general's actions were usually guided by the highest principles of his age, and he prided himself on that fact.

Reserved in public but warm and friendly to those he numbered in his inner circle, he held loyalties as frequently and firmly as he gave them. His wit and charm entertained the ladies and impressed other gentlemen, although the serious nature displayed to those who were other than close associates often led casual contacts to interpret his personality as cool, businesslike, and even dull. However, in the midst of political intrigues that split families, ruined reputations, and gave rise to some of the most overt examples of political hypocrisy to grace, or disgrace, the era, McIntosh's loyalty to friends (Loyalist and Whig) and to his principles serves as a refreshing, if politically naive, example of a man who refused to bend to expediency.

It is at this point that the supreme irony of Lachlan McIntosh's life is revealed. Though his title "General" leads one to suspect that what significance his career might hold was in his military exploits, such is hardly the case. To study his conduct as an officer gives insight into the frustrations and rewards experienced by the American forces, but it was his role as a political figure that reveals, in a clarity seldom found elsewhere, the nature of that internal revolution in which Georgians struggled to determine "who would rule at home." However, despite his political importance, McIntosh seemed to have a genuine dislike for politics. He avoided offices above the county level with a studied regularity that left him, by the eve of the Revolution, a Whig without personal political ambitions. It was that stance, all too rare in a colony where the rebellion against royal authority often masked deeper motives, that catapulted Lachlan McIntosh into the center of the storm, never to emerge again.

Thus McIntosh was called on to tread between warring Whig factions, each grappling for power and spouting ideologies to justify its quest. Finding himself with little experience upon which to draw, he briefly floundered, until loyalties to old friends and old principles combined with his love for order to set him on course. Embracing the conservative cause with the ease of a man who already shared such convictions, he cautiously took his stand, and in time left students of the era some of the best statements of that faction's position. It seems, despite his obvious dislike for radicals who he felt insulted his and his family's honor, that McIntosh may well have been one of the few in Georgia for whom ideology was a motivation rather than a justification. His Whiggish opposition to arbitrary rule, be it under the crown, the state, the Confederation, or the Constitution, and his firm belief in the legitimacy of locally controlled governments, directed by the "better sort," were at the core of his actions, and despite the shifting winds of Georgia politics, he remained true to those convictions. Personally and privately they served him well, but in the public arena, such sentiments did much to keep him in the center of the strife—and outside the circles of power.

This emphasis on McIntosh's political importance should not be taken to mean that he was not a capable military commander. Despite conditions that would have tried anyone's ability, his efforts won praise from superior officers as well as from men in the ranks. Still, wherever he went, controversy seemed to follow—usually the result of his unwillingness or inability to deal with political matters. Twice in Georgia and once in Pennsylvania, he became the subject of personal and political plots and counterplots not entirely of his own making. The final insult came when the state that should have rewarded him for his services found the general an uncomfortable reminder of past conflicts and slowly, but effectively, pushed him aside. As if he were a figure in a Greek tragedy, fate seemed determined to bring him down.

But through it all, Lachlan McIntosh never gave up. Although his fortunes declined as those of the United States were rising, any bitterness he may have felt soon disappeared. He continued to serve Georgia as he saw fit, to plant his crops, and to live—as best as limited means permitted—a life quite reminiscent of the Altamaha planter he once was. Today his efforts on behalf of the state and nation he helped create, and his frequent disappointments at the directions they took, reveal much of the nature of each, and stand as a lasting testament to the essence and impact of the American Revolution.

Notes

Preface

1. Most of the information relating to these Highland Scots was lost in the rebellion of 1745 (in Scotland), but much of what survived was collected for the Georgia Historical Society in the early 1840s by Dr. William Mackenzie of the University of Edinburgh. It has since been published in the *Georgia Historical Quarterly* (hereafter *GHQ*) under the editorship of Lilla M. Hawes and Albert S. Britt Jr. See William Mackenzie to William B. Hodgson, September 28 and November 1, 1844, in Hawes and Britt, "The Mackenzie Papers," *GHQ* 56 (Winter 1972): 545, 547. For an analysis of the roots of the close ties between Oglethorpe and the Scots see Harvey H. Jackson, "The Darien Antislavery Petition of 1739 and the Georgia Plan," *William and Mary Quarterly* (3d series) 34 (October 1977): 618–31. See also Robert G. McPherson, ed., *The Journal of the Earl of Egmont*, p. 117.

2. The location selected was near the site of Fort King George, built by the British in 1721 and abandoned a few years later. For a brief period the Scottish settlement was called New Inverness, and the district was called Darien, but soon the former was dropped. The choice of the name Darien was indicative of the Scots' attitude toward the English who ruled their homeland, for the original Darien was a Scottish commercial settlement on the Panama Isthmus which failed in 1700, largely because of a lack of English cooperation. See Bessie Mary Lewis, "Darien, a Symbol of Defiance and Achievement," *GHQ* 20 (September 1936): 186. The "Mohr" in John McIntosh's name indicates "large" or "greatest" and was a designation of rank as well as a means of distinguishing him from others of the same name. He was not the only leader at the outset, nor for that matter was his rank "captain," but soon he assumed full control of the community and was promoted. In addition, John McIntosh Mohr always spelled the family name "Mackintosh," but for uniformity the spelling adopted by his son, Lachlan, will be used throughout. For more on the role Captain McIntosh played in the growth of the settlement see Jackson, "The Darien Antislavery Petition."

3. Genealogical information on the McIntosh family is often contradictory and confusing. The best general explanation is in Lilla M. Hawes, ed., *Lachlan McIntosh Papers in the University of Georgia Libraries* (pp. 1–2), but one problem that neither it nor any other source settles is the date of McIntosh's birth. A family Bible, cited in J. G. B. Bulloch, *A History and Genealogy of the Family of Baillie of Dunain* (pp. 85–86), sets the date as March 5, 1725, but records in the "Mackenzie Papers" (*GHQ* 57 [Spring 1973]: 110–14) indicate

that he had to have been born in 1727. The confusion compounds when one realizes that it is unclear if the cited dates are Julian (Old Style) or Gregorian (New Style) (all dates in this study are in the latter). To make matters worse, on February 14, 1789 McIntosh wrote George Washington (Washington Papers, Library of Congress; microfilm copy in University of Georgia Library) and in that letter indicated that he was "past sixty-two," which, if taken literally, meant he was sixty-three and thus was born in 1726. However, it is more likely that McIntosh meant he had passed his sixty-second birthday but had not reached his sixty-third, which would occur on March 5 next, meaning he was born in 1727. Therefore, the date March 5, 1727, will be used here.

Besides Lachlan, the McIntosh children who came to America were William (the eldest), John, Phineas, and the twins Lewis and Janet. Two other children, Anne and George, were born in Georgia. Not all survived to adulthood.

Chapter One

1. James Oglethorpe to the Trustees, February 27, 1736, in Allen D. Candler and Lucian L. Knight, eds., *The Colonial Records of the State of Georgia*, 26 vols. (Atlanta: various state printers, 1904–1916), 21:76. Volume 27 and volume 28, part 1, have been edited by Kenneth Coleman and Milton Ready and published by the University of Georgia Press. The other volumes (28, part 2, through 39) are in manuscript at the Georgia Department of Archives and History, Atlanta (hereafter *CRG* or Ms. CRG).

For insight into the background and development of colonial Georgia see Kenneth Coleman, *Colonial Georgia;* Harold E. Davis, *The Fledgling Province;* Paul S. Taylor, *Georgia Plan;* Clarence L. Ver Steeg, *Origins of a Southern Mosaic;* Phinizy Spalding, *Oglethorpe in America;* and Milton L. Ready, *The Castle Builders.*

2. Oglethorpe to Trustees, February 27, 1736, *CRG*, 21:76.

3. Robert G. McPherson, ed., *The Journal of the Earl of Egmont*, p. 217; Elisah Dobree to Trustees, December 17, 1736, *CRG*, 21:285.

4. "The Journal of William Stephens," *CRG*, 4:165.

5. For a full explanation of this episode see Jackson, "The Darien Anti-slavery Petition of 1739 and the Georgia Plan."

6. Ms. CRG, 35:311; "The Journal of the Earl of Egmont," *CRG*, 5:241.

7. John Tate Lanning, ed., *The St. Augustine Expedition of 1740*, pp. xi,33–38; "Stephens' Journal," *CRG*, 4:621–22; Oglethorpe to Stephens, February 1, 1740, in *CRG*, 22, pt. 2: 312–15; Larry E. Ivers, *British Drums on the Southern Frontier*, pp. 113–24.

8. George White, *Historical Collections of Georgia*, pp. 334–35; E. Merton Coulter, ed., *The Journal of William Stephens, 1741–1743*, p. 117; Ivers, *British Drums*, p. 122.

9. Sarah B. Gober Temple and Kenneth Coleman, *Georgia Journeys*, p. 231; White, *Historical Collections*, p. 334.

10. John Calwell to Trustees, August 1, 1774, in *CRG*, 24:286; Lilla M. Hawes, ed., "Proceedings of President and Assistants in Council of Georgia, 1749–1751," *GHQ* 35 (December 1951): 346.

11. *CRG*, 6:233.

12. Hawes, *Lachlan McIntosh Papers*, pp. 81–82.

13. Ibid.

14. The story that McIntosh worked for Laurens has been repeated in almost all McIntosh's biographical sketches, but never documented. The first to relate the episode was Thomas Spalding in "Lachlan McIntosh," *National Portrait Gallery of Distinguished Americans*, ed. James B. Longacre and James Herring III. Spalding was McIntosh's grandnephew and his account has been accepted as reliable. See also Charles C. Jones Jr., "Lachlan McIntosh," in *Biographical Sketches of Delegates from Georgia to the Continental Congress*, pp. 141, 154.

Most of the papers of Henry Laurens are at the South Carolina Historical Society, Charleston, but as of this writing five volumes (through July 31, 1768), have been published under the editorship of George C. Rogers Jr., David R. Chesnutt, Peggy J. Clark, and Philip M. Hamer. Minor collections are in other repositories. See Henry Laurens to Lachlan McIntosh, November 23, 1773, pp. 133–36, in Letterbook, Henry Laurens Papers (microfilm copy at University of Georgia Library, Athens).

15. Hawes, *Lachlan McIntosh Papers*, p. 9.

16. Lachlan McIntosh's account with John Cuthbert, drawn up on April 11, 1778, in Miscellaneous Papers, New York Historical Society, New York.

17. W. W. Abbot, *The Royal Governors of Georgia, 1754–1775*, pp. 16, 23–24; Percy Scott Flippin, "Royal Government in Georgia, 1752–1776: The Land System," *GHQ* 10 (March 1926): 1–25.

18. Abbot, *Royal Governors of Georgia*, pp. 23–24.

19. Hawes, *Lachlan McIntosh Papers*, pp. 6, 82; Ms. CRG, 28, pt. 1: 67–68; *CRG*, 7:702.

20. *CRG*, 7:702.

21. *CRG*, 7:720.

22. Lachlan and William McIntosh to Jonathan Bryan, July 6, 1758, p. 632, in Conveyance Book, Georgia Department of Archives and History, Atlanta (hereafter GDAH).

23. In 1758 Georgia was divided into "parishes" and the home parish of the McIntoshes was designated as St. Andrew's.

Chapter Two

1. The best discussion of politics in colonial Georgia is in Abbot, *Royal Governors of Georgia*. Politics, for men like the McIntoshes, meant service in the lower house, the Commons House of Assembly, which was elected by

the colonists. The upper house, the Governor's Council, was appointed from the most prominent men in the colony. Though these men had much in common with the members of the lower house, they generally (but not always) sided with the executive on matters of power and privilege.

2. *CRG*, 18:399, 413.

3. *CRG*, 13:419–20, 431, 449.

4. Hawes, *Lachlan McIntosh Papers*, p. 2.

5. Abbot, *Royal Governors of Georgia*, pp. 82–88; Kenneth Coleman, "James Wright," in *Georgians in Profile*, ed. Horace Montgomery, pp. 40–60; Jack P. Greene, *The Quest for Power*, pp. 45–47, 68–71, 84–86, 119–20, 166–68, 202–4, 424–37. Wright was actually Lt. Governor when he arrived and later elevated to Governor.

6. List of executors, dated November 4, 1763, in McIntosh Papers, Perkins Library, Duke University, Durham, N.C.

7. Laurens to McIntosh, March 7, 1763, p. 108; September 13, 1763, p. 221; September 20, 1763, p. 230; September 27, 1763, p. 231; in Letterbook, Laurens Papers.

8. Abbot, *Royal Governors of Georgia*, pp. 100–102; David R. Chesnutt, "South Carolina's Penetration of Georgia in the 1760's: Henry Laurens as a Case Study," *South Carolina Historical Magazine* 73 (October 1972): 194–208.

9. Laurens to McIntosh, May 4, 1763, in *The Papers of Henry Laurens*, 3:436–37.

10. McIntosh to Laurens, December 7, 1763, Conveyance Book, GDAH. There may have been a swap here.

11. Georgia's crown grants have been compiled and published by the Surveyor General Department under the direction of Pat Bryant and Marion R. Hemperley. Especially helpful is Pat Bryant, ed., *English Crown Grants in St. Andrew Parish in Georgia, 1755–1775*. See also Silas Emmett Lucas Jr., *Index to the Headright and Bounty Grants in Georgia, 1756–1909*, pp. 435–36; McIntosh to John Jamison, November 30, 1772, Conveyance Book, GDAH; Laurens to McIntosh, May 10, 1769, p. 389; December 26, 1771, pp. 125–27; in Letterbook, Laurens Papers.

12. *CRG*, 10:46; Laurens to McIntosh, October 26, 1767, p. 62; December 4, 1767, p. 85; February 9, 1768, pp. 141–42; in Letterbook, Laurens Papers.

13. Lucas, *Index to the Headright and Bounty Grants*, pp. 436–37.

14. Ibid.; pp. 434–35; *CRG*, 8:270, 9:313, 640.

15. *CRG*, 9:241–42, 460, 10:431, 18:585, 641, and 19, pt. 1: 169; Hawes, *Lachlan McIntosh Papers*, p. 3.

16. *CRG*, 10:429.

17. *CRG* 10:647, 14:594, 629–30, 15:21; Coleman, *Revolution in Georgia*, pp. 28–29.

18. *CRG*, 10:913, 15:21; Edith Duncan Johnson, *The Houstouns of Georgia*, pp. 113–18.

19. *CRG*, 15:281; Coleman, *Revolution in Georgia*, pp. 33–34.

20. Coleman, *Revolution in Georgia*, pp. 33–34.

21. Ibid.; *CRG*, 11:333.

22. Hemperley, *English Crown Grants for Parishes of St. David, St. Patrick, St. Thomas, and St. Mary in Georgia, 1755–1775*, p. 85. What role, if any, McIntosh played in the protests is unknown. It is even possible that Wright dissolved the Assembly before he could attend. Still, based on his future actions, these conflicts between Governor and Commons House made a lasting impression.

23. Johnson, *Houstouns of Georgia*, pp. 345–46.

24. *CRG*, 12:314.

25. Laurens to McIntosh, October 26, 1767, p. 62; July 8, 1768, p. 232; September 28, 1768, p. 282; May 10, 1769, p. 389; in Letterbook, Laurens Papers.

26. Laurens to McIntosh, September 28, 1768, p. 282; February 9, 1768, pp. 141–42; December 5, 1768, pp. 317–18; in Letterbook, Laurens Papers.

27. Laurens to McIntosh, December 5, 1768, pp. 317–18, in Letterbook, Laurens Papers.

28. An example of the extent of their friendship, and the status to which McIntosh had risen, is seen in the fact that the eldest McIntosh son, John, was sent to Charleston to be educated and it was Laurens who took charge of him. Laurens to McIntosh, October 20, 1767, pp. 58–59; February 18, 1769, p. 351; in Letterbook, Laurens Papers.

29. Laurens to McIntosh, September 28, 1768, p. 282, in Letterbook, Laurens Papers; Mark Van Doren, ed., *The Travels of William Bartram*, pp. 39–40.

30. There were moments when the two disagreed on business matters, sometimes strongly (Laurens to McIntosh, December 5, 1768, pp. 317–18, in Letterbook, Laurens Papers), but never to the point that their friendship was in danger.

Chapter Three

1. Laurens to McIntosh, October 15, 1768, pp. 286–87; March 3, 1769, p. 362; September 27, 1774, pp. 370–71; in Letterbook, Laurens Papers.

2. Much of what follows is based on Harvey H. Jackson, "Consensus and Conflict: Factional Politics in Revolutionary Georgia, 1774–1777," *GHQ* 59 (Winter 1975): 388–401. See also Ms. CRG, 38, pt. 1: 308–9.

3. Greene, in *Quest for Power* (pp. 493–95), reveals the extent to which the Christ Church coalition dominated the Commons House, while Abbot, *Royal Governors of Georgia*, is the best detailed evaluation of politics during that period. Additional insight into this era and the relationship between status and power may be found in Jack P. Greene, "An Uneasy Connection: An Analysis of the Preconditions of the American Revolution," in *Essays on the American Revolution*, ed. Stephen G. Kurtz and James H. Hutson (pp.

32–80). See also James M. Grant, "Legislative Factions in Georgia, 1754–1798: A Socio-Political Study" (Ph.D. dissertation, University of Georgia, 1975).

4. Greene, in *Quest for Power*, analyzes this development in the southern royal colonies.

5. Abbot, *Royal Governors of Georgia*, pp. 103–83. The effect of Wright's action upon many of the colony's leaders has been pointed out in Harold E. Davis, "The Scissors Thesis, or Frustrated Expectations as a Cause of the Revolution in Georgia," *GHQ* 61 (Fall 1977): 246–57.

6. This coalition led by Christ Church has often been called the "city" or the "merchant" party, but these designations, though they have some validity, can be misleading since the influence of Savannah merchants was no greater than that of large planters, and because there were artisans and mechanics in the city who did not support the faction's goals. Therefore, as we use the Christ Church coalition's general aims as a guide and rely heavily upon the terminology and justification supplied by Merrill Jensen in *The Articles of Confederation* (p. 10n), the label "conservative" was decided upon.

7. Most noted among the members of the coalition whose relatives remained loyal to Wright and the King were Noble W. Jones and the Habersham brothers. Their fathers, Noble Jones and James Habersham, supported the crown until their deaths in 1775. Coleman, *Revolution in Georgia*, pp. 73–74.

8. For background information on St. John's Parish see Charles C. Jones, *The Dead Towns of Georgia*, pp. 141–223. James Wright to the Earl of Dartmouth, April 24, 1775, in White, *Historical Collections*, p. 523.

9. Jones, *Dead Towns*, p. 155. Additional insight into the people who made up the St. John's population may be found in James Stacy, *History and Records of Midway Church*.

10. The extent of St. John's dilemma can be seen in the fact that as the Revolution neared, conservatives were tightening their grip on leadership in the Commons House. Between 1765 and 1775, Greene (*Quest for Power*, pp. 493–95) points out, eight of the thirteen leading legislators were from Christ Church Parish. Only one of the thirteen was from St. John's.

11. This faction has often been designated the "country" or "popular" party, labels which are accurate up to a point. At the outset the St. John's group was indeed rural based, and throughout the war its strength was always in the "country." But in 1777 this faction expanded its base to include elements in the "city" as well. It was at that point, as we shall see, that the St. John's faction became the "popular" party. However, in an effort to find a designation which could be used throughout the struggle the term "radical" was selected, for it was evident, in looking at the goals of both factions, that the St. John's coalition wanted sweeping alterations in the system, rather than the less disruptive changes sought by Christ Church. See Jackson, "Consensus and Conflict," for examples of how radicals and conservatives sought to accomplish their ends.

12. White, *Historical Collections*, pp. 44–46, 48–49; *Georgia Gazette*, August 17, 1774; letter from St. John's Parish (author unidentified), Sept. 2, 1774, in Peter Force, ed., *American Archives*, 4th series, 6 vols. (Washington, 1837–46), 1:766–67.

13. Letter from St. John's in *American Archives*, 4th series, 1:766–67; *Georgia Gazette*, August 24, September 7, 1774; Coleman, *Revolution in Georgia*, p. 43.

14. Hawes, *Lachlan McIntosh Papers*, pp. 10–14. A good insight into the logic of McIntosh's thought is found in this petition, for after denouncing British efforts to "enslave" Georgians he turned to the condition of blacks in the colony and called for their manumission when circumstances permitted. As will be seen, this pledge would not be carried out after the war.

15. Laurens to McIntosh, September 27, 1774, pp. 370–71, in Letterbook, Laurens Papers.

16. Hawes, *Lachlan McIntosh Papers*, p. 12. Further evidence of the McIntoshes' nonallegiance to the crown is the family tradition that when news of the Pretender's landing in Scotland ("the Forty-five") reached Georgia, Lachlan McIntosh and his brother William stowed away on a vessel bound for England, determined to aid the Stuart cause. Oglethorpe found them out and, the story goes, persuaded them not to go. See Spalding, "Lachlan McIntosh."

17. Hawes, *Lachlan McIntosh Papers*, pp. 10–14; White, *Historical Collections*, pp. 58–61; Coleman, *Revolution in Georgia*, pp. 45–46.

18. White, *Historical Collections*, pp. 58–61. For a general discussion of the First Provincial Congress and the issues involved see Coleman, *Revolution in Georgia*, pp. 45–50.

19. Noble W. Jones, Archibald Bulloch, and John Houstoun to President of the Continental Congress, April 6, 1775, in Charles C. Jones, *The History of Georgia*, 2:172–74; Council Minutes, February 10, 1775, in *Collections of the Georgia Historical Society*, 10:11–12 (hereafter *Collections*, GHS); Jackson, "Consensus and Conflict," pp. 391–93. It is difficult to believe that conservatives expected Wright to do otherwise, but they may have hoped that the Governor, considering his alternatives, would compromise to keep the protests in more moderate hands. Obviously, they were wrong.

20. Jones, Bulloch, and Houstoun to President of the Continental Congress, April 6, 1775, in Jones, *History of Georgia*, 2:172–74; Worthington Chauncey Ford and Gaillard Hunt, eds., *Journals of the Continental Congress*, 34 vols. (Washington, 1904–1939), 2:45–48 (hereafter *JCC*); Coleman, *Revolution in Georgia*, pp. 49–50.

21. Jackson, "Consensus and Conflict," p. 393; Coleman, *Revolution in Georgia*, pp. 50–52.

22. Hawes, *Papers of Lachlan McIntosh*, pp. 50–51.

23. The journal of the Second Provincial Congress is in Allen D. Candler, ed., *The Revolutionary Records of the State of Georgia*, 3 vols. (Altanta, 1908), 1:229–59 (hereafter *RRG*).

24. Coleman, *Revolution in Georgia*, pp. 56–61; Jackson, "Consensus and Conflict," 394–95. Just how firmly committed many were to their respective causes is questionable, for later in the conflict some changed loyalties as the situation demanded.

25. Coleman, *Revolution in Georgia*, pp. 62–63; *RRG*, 1:122, 125, 127.

26. Coleman, *Revolution in Georgia*, pp. 62–68; John Houstoun to George McIntosh, June 10, 1775, in Johnson, *Houstouns of Georgia*, p. 347.

27. Part of what follows is from Harvey H. Jackson, "The Battle of the Riceboats: Georgia Joins the Revolution," *GHQ* 58 (Summer 1974): 229–43. See also *RRG*, 1:84–98.

28. *RRG*, 1:101; *American Archives*, 4th series, 4:799.

29. *RRG*, 1:102–3.

30. *JCC*, 3:324–27; *RRG*, 1:269.

31. Charles F. Jenkins, *Button Gwinnett*, p. 72; Joseph Habersham to William Henry Drayton, February 1776, in Robert Wilson Gibbes, *Documentary History of the Revolution, 1764–1776*, p. 259; Joseph Clay to Henry Laurens, October 16, 1777, in *Letters of Joseph Clay, Merchant of Savannah, 1776–1793*, p. 50. *RRG* (1:229–30, 254–55) reveals how representation was reallocated to the advantage of those outside Christ Church.

32. Jenkins's *Button Gwinnett* is the only full biography of this signer. Though uncritical, it is nevertheless sound in most of its factual material and contains a number of letters relative to Gwinnett's career. See p. 183 and also Lyman Hall to Roger Sherman, May 16, 1777 (p. 228). In addition see Charles C. Jones, *Biographical Sketches of the Delegates from Georgia to the Continental Congress*, pp. 48–67.

33. Jenkins, *Button Gwinnett* (pp. 21–69), covers Gwinnett's prewar career. The interpretation presented here, however, differs markedly from Jenkins's.

34. Ibid., pp. 55–68. Apparently, the two did not serve together, for by the time of McIntosh's election Gwinnett had ceased to attend. See below, note 35.

35. Ibid., pp. 44–54.

36. No interpretation is developed in a vacuum, and this view of Gwinnett's career and its impact is no exception. Particularly influential were the writings of Jack P. Greene, Bernard Bailyn, and Staughton Lynd, but many of the ideas came together after reading Joyce Appleby, "Liberalism and the American Revolution," *New England Quarterly* 49 (March 1976): 3–26.

37. "Remarks on a Pamphlet, Entitled 'Strictures on a Pamphlet, entitled The Case of George McIntosh' . . . " (Savannah, 1777), p. 15 (Hazard Pamphlets, Library of Congress). This highly partisan attack on Gwinnett gives the only indication of what he was doing during the critical year 1775.

38. Habersham to Drayton, February 1776, in Gibbes, *Documentary History*, p. 259; Clay to Laurens, October 16, 1777, in *Letters of Joseph Clay*, p. 50; *RRG*, 1:273. For an analysis of how Americans perceived qualifications for military command see Don Higginbotham, "Military Leadership in the

American Revolution," in *Leadership in the American Revolution*, pp. 91–111.

39. White, *Historical Collections*, p. 94; Habersham to Drayton, February 1776, in Gibbes, *Documentary History*, p. 259; Henry Laurens to John Laurens, August 14, 1776, in *Collections*, New York Historical Society (1872), p. 217 (hereafter *Collections*, NYHS).

40. Habersham to Drayton, February 1776, in Gibbes, *Documentary History*, p. 259; Clay to Laurens, October 16, 1777, in *Letters of Joseph Clay*, p. 50; Ann Gwinnett to President of the Continental Congress, August 1, 1777, in Jenkins, *Button Gwinnett*, p. 238.

41. White, *Historical Collections*, p. 94.

42. "Remarks on a Pamphlet . . . ," p. 17; John Adam Treutlen to John Hancock, June 19, 1777, in Jenkins, *Button Gwinnett*, p. 245.

43. For examples of McIntosh's friendship with Gwinnett see McIntosh to Gwinnett, May 1 [1776], pp. 5–6, and McIntosh to George Walton, July 11, 1776, pp. 8–9, in Hawes, *Papers of Lachlan McIntosh*.

44. McIntosh to Washington, February 16, 1776, in White, *Historical Collections*, p. 93. The question of civil versus military authority was not new to Washington. See Dave Richard Palmer, *The Way of the Fox*, pp. 50–75.

Chapter Four

1. *RRG*, 1:106–7, 269–72; Coleman, *Revolution in Georgia*, p. 68.

2. McIntosh to Washington, February 16, 1776, in White, *Historical Collections*, p. 93; McIntosh to Washington, March 8, 1776, in Hawes, *Papers of Lachlan McIntosh*, p. 1.

3. McIntosh to Washington, March 8, 1776, in Hawes, *Papers of Lachlan McIntosh*, p. 1.

4. Ibid.; McIntosh to General Charles Lee, August 26, 1776, in Force Transcripts, Library of Congress.

5. McIntosh to Washington, March 8, 1776, in Hawes, *Papers of Lachlan McIntosh*, p. 2.

6. Ibid.; *RRG*, 1:111–12.

7. *RRG*, 1:110–11, 272–73.

8. McIntosh to Washington, March 8, 1776, in Hawes, *Papers of Lachlan McIntosh*, pp. 2–3; William Ewen to South Carolina Council of Safety, March 4, 1776, in White, *Historical Collections*, pp. 88–89. These two letters give the clearest account of the engagement, and though somewhat different in emphasis, the wording is very similar, indicating the two discussed the battle prior to writing.

9. Ibid.

10. Ibid.

11. Ibid.

12. Ibid.

13. Ibid.

14. Ibid.

15. Ibid.

16. McIntosh to Washington, March 8, 1776, in Hawes, *Papers of Lachlan McIntosh*, p. 3.

17. Coleman, *Revolution in Georgia*, pp. 96, 100.

18. *JCC*, 4:15.

19. C. Shirreff to Major William Shirreff, September 25, 1775, in *American Archives*, 4th series, 3:788–89. For a thorough account of the war along the Georgia-Florida frontier, as seen from the Florida side, see J. Leitch Wright Jr., *Florida in the American Revolution*. See also James H. O'Donnell III, *Southern Indians in the American Revolution*.

20. Chesley Bostick to McIntosh, February 28, 1776, in Dreer Collection, Historical Society of Pennsylvania; Arthur Carny to McIntosh, March 24, 1776, in McIntosh Papers, Georgia Historical Society; McIntosh to Washington, April 28, 1776, in Hawes, *Papers of Lachlan McIntosh*, pp. 4–5.

21. McIntosh to Washington, April 28, 1776, in Hawes, *Papers of Lachlan McIntosh*, p. 4; White, *Historical Collections*, p. 96.

22. White, *Historical Collections*, p. 95–96.

23. Ibid.; *JCC*, 4:174, 180–81.

24. *RRG*, 1:139, 150–54; *JCC*, 5:521–22, 528.

25. McIntosh to George Walton, July 11, 1776, in Hawes, *Papers of Lachlan McIntosh*, p. 8.

26. Extract from a letter from Charleston, S.C., July 27, 1776, in *American Archives*, 4th series, 6:1230. This letter says the raids were led by Colonel McIntosh, but the dates show that it must have been his brother. This is supported by *RRG*, 1:123–24; Ms. CRG, 39:263–88.

27. McIntosh to Lee, July 7, 1776, p. 125; Lee to John Rutledge, President of South Carolina, July 19, 1776, p. 149; July 22, 1776, p. 156; July 23, 1776, pp. 157–60; July 24, 1776, p. 163; in *Collections* NYHS, 1872.

28. Lachlan McIntosh Jr. to McIntosh, July 22, 1776, pp. 52–53; McIntosh to Lee, July 29, 1776, pp. 10–11; in Hawes, *Papers of Lachlan McIntosh*.

29. McIntosh to Lee, July 29, 1776, in Hawes, *Papers of Lachlan McIntosh*, pp. 10–11; Lee to Rutledge, August 1, 1776, pp. 186–87; Lee's report to the Council of Safety, August 19, 1776, pp. 233–34, 240–241; in *Collections*, NYHS, 1872; *RRG*, 1:168.

30. Ms. CRG, 39:264; extract of a letter from St. Augustine to a gentleman in London, August 20, 1776, in *American Archives*, 5th series, 1:1076.

31. Ibid. There is a good deal of confusion in the accounts of this campaign, but it is clear that McIntosh's immediate goals, the disruption of Loyalist territory and protection of the Altamaha frontier, were accomplished. See Wright, *Florida in the American Revolution* (pp. 38–39), for another view of these events.

32. White, *Historical Collections*, pp. 200–201; Lee to Rutledge, August 6, 1776, in *Collections*, NYHS, 1872, pp. 200–202; extract of a letter from Charleston, August 7, 1776, in *American Archives*, 5th series, 1:805.

33. Lee's report to the Council of Safety and the Council's reply, August 19, 1776, in *Collections*, NYHS, 1872, pp. 233–36.

34. Lee to Board of War and Ordnance, August 27, 1776, pp. 242–43; Lee to President and Council of Georgia, August 23, 1776, p. 238, and August 24, 1776, pp. 240–41, in *Collections*, NYHS, 1872; *RRG*, 1:183–84.

35. Lee to Armstrong, August 17, 1776, in *Collections*, NYHS, 1872, p. 246.

36. William Moultrie, *Memoirs of the American Revolution*, 1:186; William Ellery to Governor Cooke, October 11, 1776, in *American Archives*, 5th series, 2:990; Coleman, *Revolution in Georgia*, p. 102.

37. Hawes, *Lachlan McIntosh Papers*, pp. 68–69.

38. McIntosh to Robert Howe, October 1, 1776, pp. 11–12, and October 2, 1776, pp. 12–13, in Hawes, *Papers of Lachlan McIntosh*.

39. McIntosh to Lt. Col. William McIntosh, October 22, 1776, in Hawes, *Papers of Lachlan McIntosh*, pp. 15–16. Elements of this plan had been advanced before, in part by General Lee, but never so completely as in this proposal.

40. Orders to William McIntosh, October 24, 1776, pp. 16–17; McIntosh to Howe, October 22, 1776, pp. 14–15; McIntosh to Col. Peter Muhlenburg, October 8, 1776, p. 14; in Hawes, *Papers of Lachlan McIntosh*. Fort Barrington was renamed Fort Howe later in the war, but to avoid confusion the initial name will be used.

41. Recruiting orders to Captain Walton, December 21, 1776, pp. 26–27; McIntosh to Howe, October 22, 1776, pp. 14–15; in Hawes, *Papers of Lachlan McIntosh*.

42. *JCC*, 5:761–63.

43. Laurens to McIntosh, October 28, 1776, p. 54, in Letterbook, Laurens Papers.

44. McIntosh to Howe, October 29, 1776, pp. 9, 17–18 (2 letters); [McIntosh] to Bulloch, November 1, 1776; in Hawes, *Papers of Lachlan McIntosh*, pp. 57–59.

45. [McIntosh] to Bulloch, November 1, 1776, in ibid., pp. 57–59.

46. [McIntosh] to Bulloch, November 1, 1776, pp. 57–59; McIntosh to Howe, November 19, 1776, pp. 18–19; McIntosh to Marbury, November 25, 1776, pp. 19–20; in ibid.

47. McIntosh to Lt. Col. William McIntosh or Major Marbury, December 12, 1776, pp. 21–22; McIntosh to Howe, December 13, 1776, p. 23; ibid.

48. McIntosh to George Walton, Lyman Hall, and Nathan Brownson, December 17, 1776, ibid., pp. 24–25.

49. Hawes, *Papers of Lachlan McIntosh* (pp. 25–36, 59–60), contains a number of letters relating to problems described here, as well as McIntosh's "talk" to the Indians.

50. McIntosh to William McIntosh or Marbury, January 8, 1776, in Hawes, *Papers of Lachlan McIntosh*, pp. 33–34.

51. McIntosh to Samuel Elbert, [January] 17, 17[77], p. 36; McIntosh to Howe, January 24, 1777, p. 38; McIntosh to Noble W. Jones, February 15, 1777, p. 41; McIntosh to Hall, Brownson, and Walton, January 23, 1777,

pp. 37–38; McIntosh to William Kennon, January 26, 1777, p. 39; ibid.

52. Captain Richard Winn to Col. Francis Harris, February 17, 1777, and Captain Bostick to McIntosh, February 18, 1777, in Miscellaneous Papers, New York Historical Society; McIntosh to Howe, February 19, 1777, p. 41; McIntosh to James Screven, February 19, 1777, pp. 41–42; McIntosh to Bostick, February 20, 1777, p. 42; McIntosh to Washington, April 13, 1777, p. 46; in Hawes, *Papers of Lachlan McIntosh*. McIntosh's wound was "a ball in the heel." See pension application of Jesse Hooper, July 28, 1832, National Archives.

Chapter Five

1. White, *Historical Collections*, pp. 96–98; Jackson, "Consensus and Conflict," pp. 395–96.

2. McIntosh to Walton, July 11, 1776, p. 8, and December 15, 1776, p. 23, in Hawes, *Papers of Lachlan McIntosh*.

3. Walton to McIntosh, April 18, 1777, pp. 225–26; McIntosh to Laurens, May 30, 1777, p. 254; in Jenkins, *Button Gwinnett*. Elbert to McIntosh, September 23, 1776, in "Letters Colonial and Revolutionary," *Pennsylvania Magazine of History and Biography* 42 (1918): 78 (hereafter *PMHB*).

4. Jackson, "Consensus and Conflict," pp. 396–98.

5. Elbert to McIntosh, September 23, 1776, in *PMHB* 42:77–78; Jenkins, *Button Gwinnett*, pp. 98–100.

6. This interpretation is indebted to Bernard Bailyn, "The Central Themes of the American Revolution: An Interpretation," in *Essays on the American Revolution*, ed. Kurtz and Hutson, pp. 15–19. Though Bailyn was addressing himself to the case of the Loyalists, his insight into the action of groups that lost power to popular movements applies to the conservatives as well.

7. Jenkins, *Button Gwinnett* (pp. 108–10), has a partial copy of the minutes of the convention.

8. The constitution is found in *RRG*, 1:282–97. See also Coleman, *Revolution in Georgia*, pp. 79–85. Former parishes were rearranged into counties in the following manner: Liberty County—St. John's, St. Andrew's, St. James's parishes; Chatham County—Christ Church and lower St. Philip's; Effingham County—St. Matthew's and upper St. Philip's; Burks County—St. George's; Richmond County—St. Paul's; Wilkes County—Indian Cession of 1773; Glynn County—St. David's and St. Patrick's; Camden County—St. Thomas's and St. Mary's.

9. McIntosh to Walton, December 15, 1776, in Hawes, *Papers of Lachlan McIntosh*, p. 24.

10. Note on William McIntosh in Force Transcripts, Library of Congress.

11. Ibid.; McIntosh to Walton, December 15, 1776, p. 23, and McIntosh to Elbert, January 8, 1777, p. 34, in Hawes, *Papers of Lachlan McIntosh*.

12. McIntosh to Walton, December 15, 1776, p. 23, ibid.; Walton to McIntosh, April 18, 1777, in Jenkins, *Button Gwinnett*, p. 225.

13. *RRG*, 1:305; Jenkins, *Button Gwinnett*, pp. 121–24, 135–36; "The Case of George McIntosh, Esquire," Hazard Pamphlets, p. 5.

14. McIntosh to Screven, February 19, 1777, in Hawes, *Papers of Lachlan McIntosh*, pp. 41–42; Gwinnett to John Hancock, March 28, 1777, in Jenkins, *Button Gwinnett*, pp. 217–18.

15. Gwinnett to Hancock, March 28, 1777, in Jenkins, *Button Gwinnett*, pp. 218–19; Howe to ———, May 29, 1777, in McIntosh Papers, Perkins Library; Coleman, *Revolution in Georgia*, p. 103.

16. Tonyn to Lord George Germain, July 19, 1776, in Papers of the Continental Congress, no. 73, pp. 35–38 (microfilm copy in University of Georgia Library) (hereafter PCC): *JCC*, 7:8–9; Hancock to Archibald Bulloch, January 8, 1777, in Edmund C. Burnett, ed., *Letters of Members of the Continental Congress*, 8 vols. (Washington, 1921–36), 2:208–9; Gwinnett to Hancock, March 28, 1777, in Jenkins, *Button Gwinnett*, p. 215.

17. Coleman, *Revolution in Georgia*, pp. 88–89. Most of the information relating to the case can be found in a series of pamphlets, written by Lachlan McIntosh and John Wereat and titled "The Case of George McIntosh, Esquire . . . ," "Remarks on a Pamphlet, Entitled 'Strictures on a Pamphlet, entitled the Case of George McIntosh' . . . ," and "An Addition to the Case of George McIntosh, Esquire . . . " Gwinnett supporters responded with "Strictures On a Pamphlet, entitled, The Case of George McIntosh, Esq. . . . ," published by William Belcher and the Liberty Society. All may be found in the Hazard Pamphlets, Rare Book Room, Library of Congress, and are also available in Clifford K. Shipton, ed., *Early American Imprints, 1689–1800*.

18. Tonyn to Germain, July 19, 1776, in PCC, 73:35–36.

19. "The Case of George McIntosh," pp. 7–8, 23–24.

20. Gwinnett to Hancock, March 28, 1777, in Jenkins, *Button Gwinnett*, pp. 219–20.

21. Lee to Board of War and Ordnance, August 27, 1776, in *Collections*, NYHS, 1872, pp. 242–43.

22. "The Case of George McIntosh," p. 23; Walton to McIntosh, April 18, 1777, pp. 225–26; Gwinnett to Hancock, March 28, 1777, pp. 219–20; in Jenkins, *Button Gwinnett*.

23. Gwinnett to Hancock, March 28, 1777, p. 216; John Adam Treutlen to Hancock, June 19, 1777, p. 243; Ann Gwinnett's Petition to the Continental Congress, August 1, 1777, pp. 236–37; in Jenkins, *Button Gwinnett*. Bail bond for George McIntosh, in Force Transcripts, Library of Congress.

24. Ann Gwinnett's Petition, p. 237; Bail bond for George McIntosh.

25. Gwinnett to Hancock, March 28, 1777, in Jenkins, *Button Gwinnett*, pp. 216–17.

26. Ibid., pp. 219–21; Howe to ———, May 29, 1777, in McIntosh Papers, Perkins Library.

27. Gwinnett to Hancock, March 28, 1777, in Jenkins, *Button Gwinnett*, pp. 220–21.

Chapter Six

1. Gwinnett to Hancock, March 28, 1777, in Jenkins, *Button Gwinnett*, p. 219.

2. Ibid., pp. 220–21. General Howe was equally suspicious of Gwinnett's motives. See Howe to ———, May 29, 1777, in McIntosh Papers, Perkins Library.

3. McIntosh to Lt. Col. Harris, March 23, 1777, pp. 42–43; McIntosh to Col. Sumpter, March [24, 1777], p. 43, in Hawes, *Papers of Lachlan McIntosh*.

4. Hall to Roger Sherman, June 1, 1777, in Jenkins, *Button Gwinnett*, pp. 228–29; McIntosh to Gwinnett, March 28, 1777, in Hawes, *Papers of Lachlan McIntosh*, p. 44.

5. McIntosh to Gwinnett, March 28, 1777, in Hawes, *Papers of Lachlan McIntosh*, p. 44.

6. McIntosh to Howe, April 2, 1777, ibid., pp. 44–45.

7. McIntosh to Gwinnett, April 11, 1777, p. 45; McIntosh to Washington, April 13, 1777, pp. 45–47; ibid.

8. McIntosh to Laurens, April 13, 1777, in Force Transcripts, Library of Congress.

9. Hall to Sherman, June 1, 1777, in Jenkins, *Button Gwinnett*, p. 229; McIntosh to Georgia Assembly, May, 1777, in Hawes, *Papers of Lachlan McIntosh*, pp. 61–62.

10. McIntosh to Assembly, May, 1777, in Hawes, *Papers of Lachlan McIntosh*, p. 62.

11. McIntosh to Gwinnett, April 17, 1777, ibid., p. 47.

12. McIntosh to Assembly, May, 1777, ibid., pp. 62–63; Coleman, *Revolution in Georgia*, p. 104.

13. Elbert to McIntosh, April 24, 1777, in "Order Book of Samuel Elbert, Colonel and Brigadier General in the Continental Army, October 1777 to November 1778," vol. 5, pt. 2, of *Collections*, GHS, p. 19.

14. McIntosh to Elbert, April 26, 1777, in Hawes, *Papers of Lachlan McIntosh*, pp. 47–48.

15. Elbert to McIntosh, May 25, 1777, ibid., pp. 64–66; Robert Howe to ———, May 29, 1777, in McIntosh Papers, Perkins Library; John Baker to McIntosh, May 22, 1777, in Force Transcripts, Library of Congress.

16. Walton to McIntosh, April 18, 1777, in Jenkins, *Button Gwinnett*, pp. 225–26; Walton to McIntosh, May 1, 1777, in Force Transcripts, Library of Congress.

17. Jenkins, *Button Gwinnett*, pp. 150–51.

18. Hall to Sherman, May 16, 1777, ibid., p. 227.

19. Ibid., June 1, 1777, p. 229.

20. "George Wells' Statement," in Edward G. Williams, ed., "A Revolutionary Journal and Orderly Book of General Lachlan McIntosh's Expedition, 1778," *Western Pennsylvania Historical Magazine* 43 (March 1960): 3–4 (hereafter *WPHM*); McIntosh to Laurens, May 30, 1777, in Jenkins, *Button Gwinnett*, p. 255.

21. "Wells' Statement," *WPHM* 43:3–4.

22. Ibid.; Hall to Sherman, June 1, 1777, in Jenkins, *Button Gwinnett*, pp. 229–30.

23. Hall to Sherman, June 1, 1777, p. 229; McIntosh to Laurens, May 30, 1777, pp. 253–55, in Jenkins, *Button Gwinnett*.

24. McIntosh to Laurens, May 30, 1777, ibid., pp. 253.

25. Ibid., pp. 253–55; McIntosh to Walton, July 14, 1777, ibid., pp. 256–60.

26. McIntosh to Laurens, May 30, 1777, ibid., p. 254; Treutlen to Hancock, June 19, 1777, ibid., pp. 244–45.

27. These petitions may be found in PCC, 73:51–58, 67–95, 112–14; Jenkins, *Button Gwinnett*, p. 169; McIntosh to Laurens, June 3, 1777, in Jenkins, pp. 253–56.

28. Clay to Messrs. Bright and Pechin, July 2, 1777, in *Letters of Joseph Clay*, p. 35; Col. John Coleman to McIntosh, July 31, 1777, in Force Transcripts, Library of Congress; Laurens to Wereat, August 30, 1777, in Letterbook, Laurens Papers, pp. 142–43.

29. General orders, July 12, 1777, in "Order Book of Samuel Elbert," p. 44; letter circulated by the Liberty Society, in Hawes, *Papers of Lachlan McIntosh*, pp. 73–74.

30. Ann Gwinnett's letters and petition to Congress, August 1777, in Jenkins, *Button Gwinnett*, pp. 233–40; Treutlen to Hancock, July 19, 1777, ibid., p. 246, note on the petitions, in Force Transcripts, Library of Congress.

31. Wereat to Walton, August 30, 1777, in Hawes, *Papers of Lachlan McIntosh*, pp. 66–73; McIntosh to Walton, July 14, 1777, pp. 256–61, Treutlen to Hancock, August 6, 1777, pp. 246–50, in Jenkins, *Button Gwinnett*. The pamphlets are in the Hazard Pamphlets, Library of Congress. See chap. 5, note 17 above.

32. Ibid. Jenkins, *Button Gwinnett*, p. 169. The Georgia delegation consisted of Hall, Langworthy, Wood, Walton, and Dr. Nathan Brownson. The first three men were clearly in the radical camp, while Brownson, from Liberty County, had ties with both sides. Only Walton could be considered a supporter of the McIntoshes, but he could do little against these odds.

33. Walton to Washington, August 5, 1777, p. 439; Laurens to McIntosh, August 11, 1777, pp. 443–44; in Burnett, *Letters*, vol. 2; Washington to Walton, August 6, 1777, in John C. Fitzpatrick, ed., *The Writings of George Washington from the Original Manuscript Sources, 1745–1789*, 37 vols. (Washington, 1931–1940), 9:25; *JCC*, 8:616.

34. McIntosh to N. W. Jones, September 11, 1777, in Force Transcripts, Library of Congress.

35. Elbert to Jones, September 11, 1777, in "Order Book of Samuel Elbert," p. 55.

36. Petition of the Georgia Assembly, September 13, 1777, in Jenkins, *Button Gwinnett*, pp. 265–66.

37. George McIntosh's memorial to Congress, October 8, 1777, in PCC, 41:vi, 33–37; *JCC*, 9:764–65, 787–90.

38. Laurens to Wereat, August 30, 1777, in Letterbook, Laurens Papers, pp. 142–43.

39. Laurens to McIntosh, September 1, 1777, ibid., pp. 144–45.

40. Reply to a Bill in Equity, September 10, 1793, in Hawes, *Lachlan McIntosh Papers*, p. 83; McIntosh to General Benjamin Lincoln, December 20, 1779, in Benjamin Lincoln Papers, Massachusetts Historical Society (microfilm copy in University of Georgia Library).

Chapter Seven

1. Secondary studies which describe Valley Forge abound, but the one that touches on McIntosh's role in the ordeal is Hugh F. Rankin, *The North Carolina Continentals*.

2. Ibid., p. 139.

3. Fitzpatrick, *Writings of George Washington*, 10:180; "Return of the North Carolina Brigade," in William L. Saunders, Walter Clark, and Stephen B. Weeks, eds., *State Records of North Carolina*, 20 vols., numbered 11–30 (1895–1914), 11:824 (hereafter *SRNC*).

4. "Return of the North Carolina Brigade," *SRNC*, 11:700, 13:336, 365, 366, 377.

5. McIntosh to Governor Richard Caswell, March 20, 1778, in *SRNC*, 13:67–68.

6. Caswell to Thomas Burke, February 15, 1778, pp. 42–43; Caswell to Clothier General, March 14, 1778, p. 66; in *SRNC*, vol. 13.

7. Rankin, *North Carolina Continentals*, pp. 140–45. Not all of McIntosh's officers were North Carolinians. Lachlan Jr. ("Lackie") and Major Berrien also accompanied him to Valley Forge, probably as a result of the political situation in Georgia. McIntosh's affidavit on John Berrien in John M. Berrien Papers, University of North Carolina (microfilm copy in University of Georgia Library).

8. Washington to McIntosh, January 5, 1778, in Fitzpatrick, *Writings of George Washington*, 10:268–69.

9. Washington to McIntosh, March 21, 1778, and March 24, 1778, in ibid., 11:120–21, 135–36; McIntosh to Washington, March 23, 1778, and March 26, 1778, in George Washington Papers (microfilm copy in University of Georgia Library).

10. Washington to Dr. Benjamin Rush, January 12, 1778, 10:296; Washington to McIntosh, April 4, 1778, 11:206; Washington to Commanders of Hospitals, April 4, 1778, 11:209; in Fitzpatrick, *Writings of George Washington.*

11. James Thomas Flexner, *George Washington in the American Revolution*, pp. 289–91.

12. David T. Bushnell, "The Virginia Frontier in History, 1778," *Virginia Magazine of History and Biography* 23 (July 1915): 256 (hereafter *VMHB*); *JCC*, 11:416–17. Congress authorized "operations" in the Western Department; this was later defined as an expedition against Detroit. *JCC*, 11:587–89.

13. Thomas Perkins Abernethy, *Western Lands and the American Revolution*, pp. 8–9. Palmer, *The Way of the Fox* (pp. 85–86, 156–57), touches on the general effect that Washington's interests in Ohio had on war strategy.

14. Louise Phelps Kellogg, ed., *Frontier Advance on the Upper Ohio, 1778–1779*, vol. 23 of *Collections of the State Historical Society of Wisconsin*, vol. 4 of *Draper Series* (Madison, 1916), p. 14; Abernethy, *Western Lands*, pp. 200–201; Washington to McIntosh, May 26, 1778, in Fitzpatrick, *Writings of George Washington*, 11:460; *JCC*, 11:416–17. For a background survey of the situation McIntosh faced see Edward G. Williams, "Fort Pitt and the Revolution on the Western Frontier," *WPHM* 59 (January–April 1976): 1–37, 129–52.

15. Washington to President of Congress, May 12, 1778, 11:379; Washington to Col. William Russell, May 19, 1778, 11:422; Washington to Gouverneur Morris, March 20, 1779, 14:262; in Fitzpatrick, *Writings of George Washington.*

16. The best explanation of the conflicting claims is Abernethy, *Western Lands* (pp. 192–242). See also Max Savelle, *George Morgan, Colony Builder*, pp. 76–110, 130–82.

17. Washington to Morris, March 20, 1779, in Fitzpatrick, *Writings of George Washington*, 14:262.

18. Washington to Captain Lachlan McIntosh, May 27, 1778, pp. 60–61; McIntosh to Washington, June 7, 1778, pp. 78–79; in Kellogg, *Frontier Advance*. Edgar W. Hassler, *Old Westmoreland*, p. 67.

19. Washington to McIntosh, June 10, 1778, in Kellogg, *Frontier Advance*, pp. 87–88; ibid., p. 15.

20. Washington to Russell, May 28, 1778, in Kellogg, *Frontier Advance*, p. 61.

21. Col. George Morgan to Board of War, July 17, 1778, ibid., pp. 112–13. Morgan's interests in the Ohio Valley, through his involvement in the Indiana Company, are discussed in Savelle, *Morgan*, pp. 76–110.

22. *JCC*, 11:587–89.

23. McIntosh to Daniel Brodhead, June 25, 1778, in Hawes, *Lachlan McIntosh Papers*, p. 30; Bushnell, "Virginia Frontier," *VMHB* 23:257–58.

24. Board of War to Pennsylvania Vice President George Bryan, July 16, 1778, in Samuel Hazard, ed., *Pennsylvania Archives*, 1st series, 12 vols. (Philadelphia, 1852–56), 6:646; Savelle, *Morgan*, pp. 156–60.

25. Kellogg, *Frontier Advance*, p. 121; Morgan to Board of War, July 17, 1778, in Kellogg, pp. 112–13.

26. Ibid., p. 19; McIntosh to the Officers and Inhabitants of Westmoreland, August 15, 1778, in Gratz Collection, Historical Society of Pennsylvania.

27. McIntosh to Officers of Westmoreland, ibid.; Hawes, *Lachlan McIntosh Papers*, pp. 31–32.

28. Bushnell, "Virginia Frontier," *VMHB* 23:339–41; note on McIntosh, August 19, 1778, in Force Transcripts, Library of Congress.

29. Savelle, *Morgan*, pp. 156–60; Kellogg, *Frontier Advance*, pp. 20–21; General Andrew Lewis to Col. William Fleming, August 14, 1778, in Kellogg, pp. 127–28.

30. *JCC*, 11:565; Bushnell, "Virginia Frontier," *VMHB* 24:55; Kellogg, *Frontier Advance*, pp. 138–42; Charles J. Kappler, ed., *Indian Affairs, Laws, and Treaties* (Washington, 1903), 1:1–3.

31. Kappler, ibid.; Savelle, *Morgan*, pp. 157–59.

32. Savelle, *Morgan*, pp. 158–59. Morgan's excuse for being away from Fort Pitt was the need to buy supplies, but he spent much of his time dealing with the conflict between the Indiana Company, in which he had invested heavily, and the state of Virginia. This argument concerned part of the territory that McIntosh's expedition would secure.

33. Kellogg, *Frontier Advance*, pp. 144, 433.

34. McIntosh to Washington, April 27, 1779, in Jared Sparks, ed., *Correspondence of the American Revolution Being Letters of Eminent Men to George Washington from the Time of His Taking Command to the End of His Presidency*, 4 vols. (Boston, 1853), 1:284–86.

35. Washington referred to Detroit throughout the campaign. See Washington to Andrew Lewis, October 15, 1778, 13:79–80; Washington to James Duane, January 12, 1779, 13:251–52; in Fitzpatrick, *Writings of George Washington*.

36. Bushnell, "Virginia Frontier," *VMHB* 24:168.

37. Ibid., pp. 341–42; Captain Patrick Lockhart to Fleming, September 13, 1778, in Kellogg, *Frontier Advance*, p. 138.

38. Kellogg, *Frontier Advance*, pp. 148, 433–34; Joseph H. Bausman, *History of Beaver County Pennsylvania and Its Centennial Celebration*, 2 vols. (New York, 1904), 1:86, 93. Williams, "Fort Pitt," *WPHM* (October 1976), p. 388. McIntosh and Brodhead did not follow the same route. The latter's road, south of the Ohio River, was better located and became the major route to Fort McIntosh.

39. Bausman, *Beaver County*, 1:86; "Recollections of John Cuppy," in Kellogg, *Frontier Advance*, p. 158.

40. McIntosh to Col. John Campbell, October 25, 1778, pp. 148–49;

McIntosh to Col. Archibald Steel, October 19, 1778, pp. 145–46; McIntosh to Lockhart, November 4, 1778, p. 166; in Kellogg, *Frontier Advance*.

41. McIntosh to Steel, October 19, 1778, pp. 145–46; McIntosh to Magistrates of Westmoreland County, October 21, 1778, pp. 147–48; Westmoreland Magistrates to McIntosh, October 26, 1778, pp. 149–50; in Kellogg, *Frontier Advance*.

42. McIntosh to Steel, October 19, 1778, pp. 145–46; McIntosh to Fleming, October 30, 1778, p. 154; in Kellogg, *Frontier Advance*.

43. McIntosh to Campbell, November 3, 1778, p. 164; McIntosh to Lockhart, November 4, 1778, p. 166; in Kellogg, *Frontier Advance*.

44. Ibid.

45. John Irwin to McIntosh, November 8, 1778, in Hawes, *Lachlan McIntosh Papers*, pp. 32–33.

Chapter Eight

1. Kellogg, *Frontier Advance*, pp. 23, 439–40; Edward G. Williams, ed., "A Revolutionary Journal and Orderly Book of General Lachlan McIntosh's Expedition," *WPHM* 53 (March–September 1960): 11. See also Thomas I. Pieper and James B. Gidney, *Fort Laurens, 1778–1779*.

2. Kellogg, *Frontier Advance*, pp. 23, 434, 444–45; McIntosh to Campbell, November 7, 1778, in Kellogg, pp. 167–68.

3. Williams, "Revolutionary Journal," pp. 12, 271; Kellogg, *Frontier Advance*, pp. 443–46.

4. Campbell to McIntosh, November 10, 1778, pp. 169–70; McIntosh to Campbell, November 13, 1778, pp. 172–73; Campbell to McIntosh, November 18, 1778, pp. 174–75; Steel to Campbell, November 16–17, 1778, p. 173; in Kellogg, *Frontier Advance*.

5. Williams, "Revolutionary Journal," pp. 14–16; "Recollections of Capt. Jacob White," in Kellogg, *Frontier Advance*, p. 163.

6. McIntosh's speech to the Delaware, in Kellogg, *Frontier Advance*, pp. 178–80. Detroit also was on the mind of General Washington, for in two letters written later, advising McIntosh on how to conduct the spring offensive, the Virginian made it clear that despite the action taken by Congress, he saw the British headquarters as the ultimate objective. Washington to McIntosh, January 31 and February 15, 1779, in Fitzpatrick, *Writings of George Washington*, 14:58–62, 114–18.

7. McIntosh's speech to the Delaware, in Kellogg, *Frontier Advance*, pp. 178–80.

8. Kellogg, *Frontier Advance*, pp. 24, 446–49; McIntosh to Fleming, December 7, 1778, in Kellogg, pp. 183–84.

9. "Recollections of Stephen Burkam," p. 157; "Recollections of Captain Jacob White," p. 163; "Recollections of Henry Jolley," pp. 184–85; in Kellogg, *Frontier Advance*. See also John C. Appel, "Colonel Brodhead and the Lure of Detroit," *Pennsylvania History* 38 (July 1971): 265–82.

10. Washington to Duane, January 12, 1779, 13:250–52; Washington to McIntosh, January 31, 1779, 14:58–62, and February 15, 1779, 14:114–18; in Fitzpatrick, *Writings of George Washington*.

11. David Zeisberger to Gibson, January 19, 1779, in *Illinois Historical Collections*, 32 vols. (Springfield, 1907–1945), 1:381–82. McIntosh to Lochry, January 29, 1779, in Kellogg, *Frontier Advance*, p. 210. The intercepted letters are found in Kellogg, pp. 205–6.

12. McIntosh to Taylor, February 8, 1779, p. 221; McIntosh to Col. David Shepherd, February 21, 1779, pp. 233–34; McIntosh to Capt. John Killbuck, February 25, 1779, pp. 236–38; in Kellogg, *Frontier Advance*. McIntosh to Lochry, February 20, 1779, in Miscellaneous Papers, New York Historical Society.

13. Gibson to McIntosh, February 13, 1779, and McIntosh to Lochry, March 3, 1779, in Gratz Collection, Historical Society of Pennsylvania. McIntosh to Laurens, March 13, 1778, pp. 249–51; McIntosh to Washington, March 12, 1779, pp. 241–42; in Kellogg, *Frontier Advance*.

14. McIntosh to Washington, March 19, 1779, p. 256; "Recollections of Benjamin Biggs," pp. 256–57; in Kellogg, *Frontier Advance*.

15. Kellogg, *Frontier Advance*, pp. 25–26; John D. Barnhart, *Henry Hamilton and George Rogers Clark in the American Revolution with the Unpublished Journal of Lieutenant Governor Henry Hamilton*, p. 72.

16. Court-martial of Mr. A. Steel on orders of McIntosh, January 1, 1779, in Fitzpatrick, *Writings of George Washington*, 14:423; Morgan to Court of Inquiry sitting at Fort Pitt, January 25, 1779, in Bausman, *Beaver County*, 1:92.

17. Brodhead to Washington, January 16, 1779, in Kellogg, *Frontier Advance*, pp. 200–201.

18. McIntosh to Bryan, December 29, 1778, Kellogg, in *Frontier Advance*, pp. 188–90.

19. Zeisberger to Morgan, January 20, 1779, pp. 201–2; John Dodge to Congress, January 25, 1779, pp. 206–8; in Kellogg, *Frontier Advance*. Both Morgan and McIntosh have their supporters and critics—there is enough blame to go around. The Treaty of Fort Pitt (also called the Treaty of Pittsburgh) was never lived up to, and there is little to indicate that McIntosh believed it would be. However, White Eyes was an intelligent, perceptive man, and it is hard to believe that he did not understand what was expected of the Delaware. It is possible that the Indians were playing the same game by promising more than they intended to deliver. See Randolph C. Downs, *Council Fires on the Upper Ohio*, pp. 217–22; Savelle, *Morgan*, pp. 159–60; and Kellogg, *Frontier Advance*, pp. 22–23, 26–27, 39, 215.

20. Morgan to Brodhead, January 31, 1779, in Kellogg, *Frontier Advance*, p. 216.

21. Washington to Brodhead, February 15, 1779, in Kellogg, *Frontier Advance*, pp. 230–31; Brodhead to General Armstrong, April 16, 1779, in *Pennsylvania Archives*, 1st series, 10:109–10.

22. Washington to McIntosh, March 5, 1779, in Fitzpatrick, *Writings of George Washington*, 14:193–94. Up to the time he left, McIntosh was still thinking of Detroit. See McIntosh to Washington, April 3, 1779, in Kellogg, *Frontier Advance*, pp. 269–70.

23. *JCC*, 13:213; Washington to Morris, March 20, 1779, in Fitzpatrick, *Writings of George Washington*, 14:262.

24. Joseph Reed to Washington, April 24, 1779, in *Pennsylvania Archives*, 1st series, 7:342; McIntosh to Washington, May 14, 1779, p. 327; Alexander Hamilton to McIntosh, May 14, 1779, p. 328; McIntosh to Hamilton, May 14, 1779, pp. 329–30; in Kellogg, *Frontier Advance*.

25. Kellogg, *Frontier Advance*, pp. 22, 27–28.

26. William Crawford to McIntosh, July 19, 1779, in Emmet Collection, New York Public Library; Appel, "Lure of Detroit," pp. 265–66.

Chapter Nine

1. "Muster Roll of the First Continental Georgia Battalion," *GHQ* 11 (December 1927): 342–43; "Muster Roll of the Third Continental Georgia Battalion," *GHQ* 12 (March 1928): 103–4; "Muster Roll of the Fourth Continental Georgia Battalion," *GHQ* 12 (September 1928): 197–98; McIntosh to Lincoln, August 4, 1779, in Miscellaneous Collection, Clements Library, University of Michigan, Ann Arbor.

2. McIntosh to Lincoln, August 4, 1779, in Miscellaneous Collection, Clements Library; McIntosh to Lincoln, August 10, 1779, in Hawes, *Papers of Lachlan McIntosh*, pp. 77–78.

3. McIntosh to Lincoln, August 4, 1779, in Miscellaneous Collection, Clements Library.

4. See Edward J. Cashin Jr., "Augusta's Revolution of 1779," *Richmond County History* 7 (Summer 1975): 5–13. Understanding of the period has been greatly hampered by a lack of records, and therefore this is one of the more controversial episodes in Georgia's revolution. For further information see chapter 11 below.

5. Cashin, "Augusta's Revolution" pp. 5–13; *RRG*, 2:144, 151, 154–55. In addition to Wereat, the Supreme Executive Council included Seth John Cuthbert, William Gibbons, Joseph Habersham, Humphrey Wells, William Few, Myrick Davis, John Dooly, and Joseph Clay.

6. *RRG*, 2:153, 160, 168, 171–72; Supreme Executive Council to Lincoln, August 18, 1779, in *RRG*, 2:155–57; Lincoln to McIntosh, August 14, 1799, in Force Transcripts, Library of Congress; O'Donnell, *Southern Indians in the Revolution*, pp. 80–94; Coleman, *Revolution in Georgia*, p. 127.

7. The best study of the siege of Savannah is Alexander A. Lawrence, *Storm Over Savannah*. See also Coleman, *Revolution in Georgia*, pp. 127–28.

8. Coleman, *Revolution in Georgia*, p. 128; Journal of General Lincoln, September 3–4, 1779, in Force Transcripts, Library of Congress; Marbury to McIntosh, January 21, 1782, in Gratz Collection, Historical Society of

Pennsylvania; affidavit of William Glascock, in Hawes, *Papers of Lachlan McIntosh*, pp. 123–25. This amazement at the militia's enthusiasm was no doubt greater because it was known that some in the state's troops resented McIntosh's assumption of command but, at the time, were able to do little about it.

9. Journal of General Lincoln, September 5, 1779, in Force Transcripts, Library of Congress; Lawrence, *Storm Over Savannah*, pp. 26–30; Coleman, *Revolution in Georgia*, p. 128.

10. McIntosh to Lincoln, September 11, 1779, in Lincoln Papers, Massachusetts Historical Society; Journal of General Lincoln, September 13, 1779, in Force Transcripts, Library of Congress; Lawrence, *Storm Over Savannah*, p. 59.

11. Lawrence, *Storm Over Savannah*, pp. 24–25. No doubt most of the militia who did not march to Savannah remained behind to guard the frontier.

12. Ibid., pp. 157–58; McIntosh to John Twiggs, September 17, 1779, in Hawes, *Lachlan McIntosh Papers*, p. 37.

13. Lawrence, *Storm Over Savannah*, pp. 158–59.

14. Ibid., pp. 76, 80; Joseph Habersham to "Bella" (Mrs. Habersham), October 5, 1779, in Habersham Papers, Perkins Library; John Jones to Mrs. Jones, October 7, 1779, in White, *Historical Collections*, p. 536.

15. Lawrence, *Storm Over Savannah*, pp. 80, 159; Habersham to "Bella," October 5, 1779, in Habersham Papers, Perkins Library.

16. Lawrence, *Storm Over Savannah*, pp. 89–97.

17. Ibid., pp. 96–97; "Major Thomas Pinckney's Account of the Siege of Savannah," in *The Siege of Savannah by the Combined American and French Forces, Under the Command of General Lincoln and the Count d'Estaing in the Autumn of 1779*, pp. 164–66.

18. Lawrence, *Storm Over Savannah*, pp. 97–98, 103–8; "Pinckney's Account," pp. 165–66.

19. Lawrence, *Storm Over Savannah*, 104–8; "Pinckney's Account," pp. 165–66.

20. "Pinckney's Account," pp. 167–69.

21. Lawrence, *Storm Over Savannah*, pp. 109–14, 160.

22. McIntosh to Lincoln, October 16, 1779, in Miscellaneous Papers, New York Public Library; McIntosh to Lincoln, October 18, 1779, in Miscellaneous Papers, New York Historical Society.

23. Lawrence, *Storm Over Savannah*, pp. 160–61.

Chapter Ten

1. For a perceptive look at the conditions in back-country Georgia during this period see Cashin, "Augusta's Revolution," pp. 5–13.

2. Ibid., pp. 7–8. For a more detailed description of these events and their effect on McIntosh see chapter 11 below.

3. McIntosh to Lincoln, December 11, 1779, in McIntosh Papers, Perkins Library; Wereat to McIntosh, January 19, 1780, in Force Transcripts, Library of Congress.

4. McIntosh to Lincoln, December 11, 1779, in McIntosh Papers, Perkins Library; McIntosh to Lachlan McIntosh Jr., December 26, 1779, in Force Transcripts, Library of Congress.

5. McIntosh to Lachlan McIntosh Jr., December 26, 1779, in Force Transcripts, Library of Congress.

6. Ibid. His fears may not have been as well grounded as some have claimed, for groups of outlaws were operating in the area. See Walton to Lincoln, December 25, 1779, in Lincoln Papers, Massachusetts Historical Society.

7. McIntosh to Lachlan McIntosh Jr., December 26, 1779, in Force Transcripts, Library of Congress; McIntosh to Lincoln, January 10, 1780, in Hargrett Collection, University of Georgia Library; Hawes, *Lachlan McIntosh Papers*, p. 83.

8. John R. Alden, *The American Revolution*, p. 231.

9. McIntosh's journal of the siege of Charleston, February 13, 14, 29 and March 8, 9, 1780, in Hawes, *Lachlan McIntosh Papers*, pp. 96–97. The siege of Charleston produced a number of contemporary journals and other works. Hawes, *Lachlan McIntosh Papers*, contains journals by McIntosh (February 12–May 4, 1780; pp. 96–112), by Major John Habersham (March 28–April 13; pp. 113–15), by an unidentified subaltern (April 20–May 16; pp. 115–22), and a series of notes taken by Col. Bernard Beakman, 4th South Carolina Artillery (p. 112). Lincoln's journal and his orderbook, which cover the siege, are in the DeRenne Collection, University of Georgia Library. William Moultrie, *Memoirs of the American Revolution* (2:65–68), covers the siege but quotes extensively from the above journals without citing them. Relating the British side are the diaries and letters of four Hessian officers who took part in the battle. See Bernard Uhlendorf, ed. and trans., *The Siege of Charleston*.

10. McIntosh's journal, March 11, 1780, in Hawes, *Lachlan McIntosh Papers*, p. 98.

11. Ibid., March 12–16, pp. 98–99.

12. Samuel Huntington to McIntosh, February 15, 1780, in PCC, no. 162, p. 313; McIntosh to Huntington, May 21, 1780, in PCC, no. 162, p. 297.

13. McIntosh's journal, March 14–22, April 9–10, 1780, pp. 98–99; Major John Habersham's journal of the siege of Charleston, April 5, 1780, p. 114; in Hawes, *Lachlan McIntosh Papers*.

14. McIntosh's journal, April 10, in ibid., p. 99.

15. Ward, *The War of the Revolution*, 2:698–700.

16. McIntosh's journal, April 12–13, 1780, in Hawes, *Lachlan McIntosh Papers*, p. 100.

17. McIntosh's journal, April 13, 1780, in ibid., pp. 100–101.

18. Ibid., p. 101.

19. Ibid., April 14, 18, 1780, pp. 101, 102–3.

20. Ibid., April 15–19, 1780, pp. 101–4.

21. Ibid., April 19, 1780, p. 104.

22. Ibid.

23. Ibid.

24. Ibid., pp. 104–5.

25. Ibid., p. 105.

26. Ibid., April 20, 1780, p. 105; minutes of the council of war, April 20–21, in Miscellaneous Collection, Clements Library.

27. McIntosh's journal, April 21–26, 1780, pp. 106–8; subaltern's journal, April 25, 1780, p. 118; in Hawes, *Lachlan McIntosh Papers*.

28. McIntosh's journal, April 27–29, 1780, in ibid., pp. 108–10.

29. McIntosh's journal, May 1–4, 1780, pp. 111–12; subaltern's journal, May 5, 1780, p. 118; ibid.

30. Subaltern's journal, May 8–11, 1780, ibid., pp. 119–21.

31. Ibid., May 12, 1780, p. 121.

Chapter Eleven

1. For the general circumstances surrounding these events see Cashin, "Augusta's Revolution," pp. 5–11.

2. *RRG*, 2:129, 136; affidavit of William Glascock, in Hawes, *Papers of Lachlan McIntosh*, p. 123; Glascock to Congress, July 10, 1779, in PCC, no. 73, pp. 240–44; Coleman, *Revolution in Georgia*, pp. 155–56.

3. Glascock to Congress, July 10, 1779, in PCC, no. 73, pp. 240–44; *RRG*, 2:140–44.

4. *RRG*, 2:140–44; Supreme Executive Council to Lincoln, August 18, 1779, ibid., pp. 154–56; affidavit of William Glascock, in Hawes, *Papers of Lachlan McIntosh*, p. 123.

5. *RRG*, 2:144; McIntosh to Lincoln, August 6, 1779, in Miscellaneous Collection, Clements Library; McIntosh to Wereat, January 8, 1780, in Hargrett Collection, University of Georgia; Coleman, *Revolution in Georgia*, p. 156. Though accounts conflict, McIntosh may have attended the meeting that selected the Supreme Executive Council.

6. *RRG*, 2:171–72; Walton to William Gibbons, January 21, 1783, in Hawes, *Papers of Lachlan McIntosh*, pp. 113–14. McIntosh's call for a general pardon may have been a better idea than most were willing to admit. Many in Georgia were neither Loyalist nor Whig, but rather rallied to the side which seemed best able to protect them. A general pardon at this time might have welded them to the American cause and in the long-run prevented much of the bloody civil strife which occurred later in the war. For more on this problem see Ronald Hoffman, "The 'Disaffected' in the Revolutionary South," in *The American Revolution: Explorations in the History of American Radicalism*, ed., Alfred F. Young, pp. 290–98.

7. Supreme Executive Council to Lincoln, August 18, 1779, in *RRG*, 2:155–59; Edward J. Cashin, "'The Famous Colonel Wells': Factionalism in Revolutionary Georgia," *GHQ* 58 (Supplement, 1974): 145–47.

8. Glascock's affidavit, in Hawes, *Papers of Lachlan McIntosh*, pp. 124–25. In recent years the events in the fall of 1779 have been subjected to careful analysis, often with markedly different results. Walton finds support for his action in Edward J. Cashin, "George Walton and the Forged Letter," *GHQ* 62 (Summer 1978): 133–45, while Wereat is defended in George R. Lamplugh, "'To Check & Discourage the Wicked & Designing': John Wereat and the Revolution in Georgia," *GHQ* (Winter 1977): 295–307. I would like to thank Professor Cashin for kindly allowing me to see his essay prior to publication.

All who have studied the period agree that a congressional appropriation of $500,000, to be given to the legitimate government, weighed on the minds of both factions. See *JCC*, 14:990–91.

9. As yet, no full treatment of Walton has been published. C. C. Jones, *Biographical Sketches of the Delegates from Georgia to the Continental Congress* (pp. 183–86), contains one of the longest essays on his life but fails to resolve the question of his motives in this matter. See also Alexander Lawrence, "General Lachlan McIntosh and His Suspension from Continental Command during the Revolution," *GHQ* 38 (June 1954): 101–41. Mr. Edwin Bridges of the Georgia Department of Archives and History is working on a Walton biography and I am indebted to him for sharing with me his insight and information on this period.

10. Lincoln to Walton, October 14 and 17, 1779, in Lincoln Papers, Boston Public Library; Walton to Lincoln, October 28, 1779, in Sang Collection (private), Chicago. Photocopies of these letters are in the possession of Mr. Bridges, who kindly allowed me to use them. See also note on Walton re October 1779, in Force Transcripts, Library of Congress.

11. Walton to Lincoln, October 28, 1779, in Sang Collection; Cashin, "The Forged Letter." For examples of Walton's dislike for the Gwinnett faction and support for McIntosh see Walton to McIntosh, April 18, 1777, in Jenkins, *Button Gwinnett*, pp. 225–26, and Walton to McIntosh, May 1, 1777, in Force Transcripts, Library of Congress.

12. Coleman, *Revolution in Georgia*, p. 158; Cashin, "The Forged Letter."

13. McIntosh to Lincoln, December 11, 1779, in McIntosh Papers, Perkins Library, Duke University.

14. McIntosh to Parker, December 13, 1779, in Force Transcripts, Library of Congress; McIntosh to Wereat, January 8, 1780, in Hargrett Collection, University of Georgia.

15. McIntosh to Lincoln, December 11, 1779, in McIntosh Papers, Perkins Library, Duke University.

16. Ibid.; McIntosh to Parker, December 13, 1779, in Force Transcripts, Library of Congress, and McIntosh to Lachlan McIntosh Jr., December 26, 1779, ibid.

17. McIntosh to Wereat, January 8, 1780, in Hargrett Collection, University of Georgia. The papers Walton sent are in PCC, no. 73, pp. 250–65. McIntosh's copies are in Hawes, *Papers of Lachlan McIntosh*, pp. 78–85, 115–17.

18. Council resolution, in Hawes, *Papers of Lachlan McIntosh*, p. 83; McIntosh to Wereat, January 8, 1780, in Hargrett Collection, University of Georgia.

19. Letter from William Glascock, November 30, 1779, in Hawes, *Papers of Lachlan McIntosh*, pp. 79–80.

20. Walton to President of Congress, December 15, 1779, ibid., pp. 115–16.

21. This interpretation of Walton's action has been advanced by Mr. Edwin Bridges, Georgia Department of Archives and History, and by Prof. Edward J. Cashin in "The Forged Letter."

22. McIntosh arrived in Augusta sometime between December 1 and 10. He left the town on either December 12 or 13. See Hawes, *Papers of Lachlan McIntosh*, p. 81; McIntosh to Lincoln, December 11, 1779, in McIntosh Papers, Perkins Library, Duke University; McIntosh to Parker, December 13, 1779, in Force Transcripts, Library of Congress.

23. Wereat to McIntosh, January 19, 1780, in Force Transcripts, Library of Congress. For the full impact of the popular victory see Grand Jury Presentment with McIntosh Notes, March 1780, in Hawes, *Papers of Lachlan McIntosh*, pp. 86–91; Cashin, "Augusta's Revolution," pp. 9–11, and Coleman, *Revolution in Georgia*, p. 159.

24. Wereat to McIntosh, January 19, 1780, in Force Transcripts, Library of Congress.

25. McIntosh journal, March 17, 1780, in Hawes, *Lachlan McIntosh Papers*, p. 99; Huntington to McIntosh, February 15, 1780, in PCC, no. 162, p. 313; McIntosh to Huntington, May 21, 1780, in PCC, no. 162, p. 297; *JCC*, 16:169–70.

26. Glascock's affidavit, in Hawes, *Papers of Lachlan McIntosh*, pp. 124–25; Glascock to President of Congress, May 12, 1780, in ibid., pp. 91–92; McIntosh evidence, September 20, 1781, in PCC, no. 162, p. 314.

27. Glascock to President of Congress, May 12, 1780, in Hawes, *Papers of Lachlan McIntosh*, pp. 91–92. The testimony is so contradictory that the question of whom the people of Georgia supported may never be fully determined. Walton and his faction seem to have been strong in the back country, while McIntosh and his allies had firm backing in the coastal areas, which of course were occupied. There are exceptions to this, but the geographic division that is seen in this struggle is an indication of at least one of the lines along which future political factions will form. Nevertheless, it is apparent from the testimony that General McIntosh had more support than his critics acknowledged, but neither geographically nor politically was this support in a position to do him much good.

28. Glascock's affidavit, in Hawes, *Papers of Lachlan McIntosh*, pp. 124–25.

29. Glascock to President of Congress, ibid., pp. 91–92.

30. McIntosh to Huntington, May 21, 1780, in PCC, no. 162, p. 297. The bulk of the evidence that McIntosh sent to Congress is in PCC, no. 162, pp. 297, 314–20. See also McIntosh to Mrs. McIntosh, August 7, 1780, in Hawes, *Lachlan McIntosh Papers*, pp. 41–42.

31. Lawrence, "McIntosh and His Suspension" (pp. 126–30), relates these events. Supporting papers are found in PCC, no. 73, pp. 270–80. See memorial of George Walton, September 7, 1780, in PCC, no. 73, pp. 270–72.

32. Lamplugh, "To Check & Discourage" (pp. 302–3), covers their cooperative efforts. Though McIntosh was the central figure in this controversy, Wereat had no love for Walton at this point, and one should not overlook his contribution to McIntosh's defense.

33. Lawrence, "McIntosh and His Suspension," pp. 131–32; McIntosh to Thomas McKean, July 16, 1781, in PCC, no. 162, pp. 301–2; *JCC*, 20:752–53.

34. McIntosh to McKean, July 18, 1781, in PCC, no. 162, pp. 305–6 and September 20, 1781, ibid., p. 309. Evidence for a new investigation is found in PCC, no. 162, pp. 313–28.

35. McIntosh to Congress, [February] 1782, in Hawes, *Papers of Lachlan McIntosh*, pp. 106–7; Aedanus Burke to McIntosh, October 28, 1781, in Dreer Collection, Historical Society of Pennsylvania.

Chapter Twelve

1. Wereat to McIntosh, March 12, 1782, in Hargrett Collection, University of Georgia Library. For a full analysis of Georgia's postwar political and economic conditions see Coleman, *Revolution in Georgia*, pp. 189–220, and Abbot, "The Structure of Politics in Georgia: 1782–1789," *William and Mary Quarterly* (3d series) 14 (1957): 47–65.

2. Col. James Jackson to Wereat, November 31, 1782, pp. 104–5; Wereat to Jackson, December 2, 1782, pp. 105–6; in Hawes, *Papers of Lachlan McIntosh*. Jackson was also concerned about his upcoming trial for killing George Wells in a duel. See William Omer Foster, *James Jackson*, p. 6; *RRG*, 3:300. The Assembly clerk recorded the name "Pinkney."

3. Lawrence, "McIntosh and His Suspension," pp. 134–36; testimony of Col. Robert Middleton, January 18, 1783, in Hawes, *Papers of Lachlan McIntosh*, p. 110. The whole body of evidence may be found in Hawes, pp. 108–118; *RRG*, 3:227. The clerk, still having problems, confused Gibbons with John Gibbson.

4. Testimony of Samuel Stirk, [January 20, 1783], pp. 112–13; Walton

to the Committee, January 21, 1783, pp. 113–14; note on Howley, p. 114; in Hawes, *Papers of Lachlan McIntosh*.

5. Hawes, *Papers of Lachlan McIntosh*, pp. 117–18; *RRG*, 3:248.

6. See George R. Lamplugh, "Politics on the Periphery: Factions and Parties in Georgia, 1776–1806" (Ph.D. dissertation, Emory University, 1973), pp. 117–253, and Abbot, "Structure of Politics in Georgia," pp. 47–65, for an analysis of the changes in political alliances.

7. *RRG*, 3:245. To balance things, the Assembly also appointed McIntosh to a state office (Indian Treaty Commission) before ruling on his case. *RRG*, 3:231.

8. Lamplugh, "Politics on the Periphery" (pp. 203–5), ably covers this exchange. The authors are unknown, but probably Wereat, the general, and his son William wrote most of it.

9. Hawes, *Lachlan McIntosh Papers*, p. 58.

10. Ibid., p. 63.

11. Ibid., p. 60.

12. *Gazette of the State of Georgia*, March 13, 1783; Lamplugh, "Politics on the Periphery," pp. 204–7. *RRG*, 2:471–72.

13. *RRG*, 2:471–72; Lamplugh, "Politics on the Periphery," 204–7; Hawes, *Papers of Lachlan McIntosh*, p. 120; *Gazette of the State of Georgia*, October 14, 1784.

14. PCC, no. 19, 4:25–28.

15. Lawrence, "McIntosh and His Suspension," p. 138.

16. McIntosh to Anthony Wayne, September 24, 1791, in Anthony Wayne Papers, Clements Library, University of Michigan.

17. McIntosh's memorial to the Georgia Assembly, June 27, 1783, in Ford Collection, New York Public Library.

18. Coleman, *Revolution in Georgia*, pp. 201–2; *CRG*, 19, pt. 2: 216–42, 263–79; *RRG*, 2:511–12.

19. Account of Lachlan McIntosh against the public, July 1783, in Force Transcripts, Library of Congress; *Gazette of the State of Georgia*, November 20, 1783, *RRG*, 3:346–47.

20. *Gazette of the State of Georgia*, November 20, 1783.

21. McIntosh's memorial to the Georgia Assembly, June 27, 1783, in Ford Collection, New York Public Library; McIntosh's instructions to his brother John and his son John, October 15, 1783, in Charles F. Jenkins Collection, Historical Society of Pennsylvania; *RRG*, 3:336.

22. Lamplugh, "Politics on the Periphery," p. 115; McIntosh's petition to the Georgia Assembly (December 31, 1788), in Force Transcripts, Library of Congress, clearly describes his plight.

23. *CRG*, 19, pt. 2: 229, 234.

24. Lamplugh, "Politics on the Periphery" (pp. 117–41), covers the problems of Georgia "Tories" and those who wished to temper justice with mercy.

25. *RRG* (3:21, 107–9, 115–16, 117, 165–66, 228, 438–39, 524–25, 545) contains the special grants given after the war.

26. *Gazette of the State of Georgia*, February 5, 1784.

27. Ibid., May 15, 1783, and February 19, 1784; McIntosh to John McIntosh, March 6, 1784, in McIntosh Papers, New York Historical Society; McIntosh's affidavit, January 15, 1784, in McIntosh Papers, Perkins Library.

28. Coleman, *Revolution in Georgia*, p. 235.

29. McIntosh to Muhlenburg, September 4, 1783, in Dreer Collection, Historical Society of Pennsylvania; McIntosh's instructions to the delegates to Cincinnati, April 20, 1784, in Hawes, *Papers of Lachlan McIntosh*, pp. 131–32.

30. Coleman, *Revolution in Georgia*, p. 186; McIntosh to Speaker of Georgia House, January 1783, in Force Transcripts, Library of Congress; letter from committee of officers, February 8, 1783, in Hawes, *Papers of Lachlan McIntosh*, p. 118; *RRG*, 2:587, 605; Alex M. Hitz, "Georgia Bounty Land Grants," *GHQ* 38 (December 1954): 340.

31. *CRG*, 19, pt. 2: 292–304; *RRG*, 2:606; Coleman, *Revolution in Georgia*, pp. 218, 240.

32. *RRG*, 2:606.

33. Address of officers of the Georgia line, March 19, 1784, in Hawes, *Papers of Lachlan McIntosh*, pp. 129–30; McIntosh to Governor of Georgia, March 18, 1784, in Gratz Collection, Historical Society of Pennsylvania; *RRG*, 2:624.

34. Hitz, "Georgia Bounty Land Grants," pp. 337–38; McIntosh to Col. Joseph Pannill, August 25, 1784, in Hawes, *Papers of Lachlan McIntosh*, pp. 135–36; David Rees to John Houstoun, June 2, 1784, in Houstoun Papers, Georgia Historical Society.

35. McIntosh to Governor of Georgia, September 1, 1784, pp. 136–38; McIntosh to Major John Milton, September 3, 1784, p. 138; in Hawes, *Papers of Lachlan McIntosh*.

36. *RRG*, 3:540.

37. [McIntosh's] Account with the Public as Stated & Settled by the Auditor, April 22, 1784, in Hawes, *Papers of Lachlan McIntosh*, pp. 133–34; *RRG*, 2:629; *Gazette of the State of Georgia*, January 6, 1785; McIntosh Account of What the Public Owes Him, December 1784, in Hawes, *Lachlan McIntosh Papers*, pp. 68–70. From these records it is impossible to tell just what amount was paid and how much of that was specie, which was what McIntosh needed to retire his debts. The house apparently was never sold, for McIntosh still owned it when he died.

38. John Mackintosh to McIntosh, August 30, 1784, pp. 65–67; John Mackintosh to McIntosh, November 30, 1785, pp. 71–72; in Hawes, *Lachlan McIntosh Papers*; William McIntosh to McIntosh, December 8, 1785, in Ford Collection, New York Public Library; McIntosh to Governor in

Council, August 15, 1785, transcript in McIntosh file, GDAH; McIntosh to John McIntosh Jr., July 4, 1785, in McIntosh Papers, Perkins Library; Laurens to McIntosh, August 3, 1785, p. 112; Laurens to John McIntosh, September 10, 1785, pp. 120–21; Laurens to McIntosh, September 10, 1785, pp. 121–22; in Letterbook, Laurens Papers.

Chapter Thirteen

1. The best treatment of the background of Georgia's Indian problem is found in Kenneth Coleman, "Federal Indian Relations in the South, 1781–1789," *Chronicles of Oklahoma* 35 (Winter 1957/1958): 440–43, and Coleman, *Revolution in Georgia*, pp. 238–40.

2. *RRG*, 2:544–45; 3:231; Randolph C. Downs, "Creek-American Relations, 1782–1790," *GHQ* 22 (June 1937): 145–46; Coleman, *Revolution in Georgia*, p. 242.

3. Coleman, "Federal Indian Relations," p. 438; *JCC*, 27:453–64; Richard Henry Lee to James Madison, December 27, 1784, Burnett, *Letters*, 7:638; Walter H. Mohr, *Federal Indian Relations*, p. 146.

4. *JCC*, 28:118–20, 159–62, 183–84; Coleman, "Federal Indian Relations," p. 439.

5. *JCC*, 28:183–84; Coleman, "Federal Indian Relations," p. 439; Joseph Habersham to John Habersham, Summer 1785, U. B. Phillips, ed., "Some Letters of Joseph Habersham, 1775–1790," *GHQ* 10 (June 1926): 152; Rufus King to Elbridge Gerry, March 24, 1785, p. 72, and Richard Dobbs Spaight to William Blount, March 27, 1785, p. 75, Burnett, *Letters*, 8.

6. Coleman, *Revolution in Georgia*, p. 242; G. Handley to McIntosh, April 18, 1785, Force Transcripts, Library of Congress; Elbert to Benjamin Hawkins, June 3, 1785, "Letter Book of Samuel Elbert," *Collections*, GHS, vol. 5, pt. 2, p. 206; Merritt B. Pound, *Benjamin Hawkins*, pp. 42–43.

7. *JCC*, 28:362.

8. Elbert to Col. Elijah Clark, June 9, 1785, p. 207. Elbert to Hawkins, Pickens, Martin, July 20, 1785, p. 212, "Letter Book of Samuel Elbert," *Collections*, GHS, vol. 5, pt. 2; Pound, *Benjamin Hawkins*, p. 40; Coleman, *Revolution in Georgia*, pp. 242–43; Hawkins to McIntosh, June 25, 1785, Etting Collection, Historical Society of Pennsylvania.

9. Elbert to McIntosh, September 28, 1785, "Letter Book of Samuel Elbert," *Collections*, GHS, vol. 5, pt. 2, pp. 219–20. There is no actual record of the resignation, but from this point McIntosh is always identified as a federal agent. See also Pound, *Benjamin Hawkins*, p. 42–43.

10. Pound, *Benjamin Hawkins*, p. 44; Ms. Executive Council minutes, 1785, p. 192, GDAH, typescript copy in the University of Georgia Library; Alexander McGillivray to Pickens, September 5, 1785, *American State Papers, Indian Affairs*, 1:17–18 (hereafter *ASP, IA*); *JCC*, 29:690–91; Elbert to William Houstoun, John Habersham, Abraham Baldwin, September 14, 1785, "Letter Book of Samuel Elbert," *Collections*, GHS, vol. 5, pt. 2, pp. 220–21.

11. Coleman, *Revolution in Georgia*, pp. 242–43, "Federal Indian Relations," pp. 440–41.

12. Coleman, "Federal Indian Affairs," pp. 441–42; Ms. CRG, 39: 509–13; *ASP,IA*, 1:40–43; Hawkins and Pickens to Charles Thompson, December 30, 1785, ibid. p. 49.

13. *ASP, IA*, 1:17; "My Acct. against the Public for Indian Treaty," Hawes, *Lachlan McIntosh Papers*, p. 72; Ms. Assembly journal, 1786, pt. 2: 368; McGillivray to Hawkins, July 30, 1786, in Hawes, *Papers of Lachlan McIntosh*, pp. 140–42.

14. Coleman, *Revolution in Georgia*, pp. 257–58.

15. *RRG*, 3:282–85; Ms. Assembly Journal, 1785, pt. 1: 225, 257–59; Elbert to the Governor of South Carolina, February 12, 1785, "Letter Book of Samuel Elbert," *Collections*, GHS, vol. 5, pt. 2, p. 200; Coleman, *Revolution in Georgia*, pp. 257–58.

16. *JCC*, 28:408–10; Secretary of Congress to Judges appointed in the case of *South Carolina* vs. *Georgia*, in Burnett, *Letters*, 8:468; Ms. Executive Council minutes, August 10, 1785, p. 146; Elbert to William Houstoun, John Habersham, and Abraham Baldwin, September 14, 1785, in "Letter Book of Samuel Elbert," *Collections*, GHS, vol. 5, pt. 2, p. 220; George Mathews to McIntosh, John Houstoun, and John Habersham, February 15, 1787, in Governor's Letterbook, pp. 29–31, GDAH, typescript copy in the University of Georgia Library.

17. Mathews to McIntosh, Houstoun, and Habersham, April 18, 1787, in Governor's Letterbook, pp. 49–51; Ms. Assembly journal, 1786, pt. 3: 540.

18. Mathews to McIntosh, Habersham and Houstoun, April 18, 1787, in Governor's Letterbook, pp. 49–51.

19. Coleman, *Revolution in Georgia*, pp. 258–60; *JCC*, 33:467–76. The negotiations for the Convention of Beaufort are found in Ms. "Journal of the Commissioners for the Treaty of Beaufort," GDAH.

20. Coleman, *Revolution in Georgia*, pp. 259–60; *JCC*, 33:467–76.

21. *Gazette of the State of Georgia*, June 21, 1787.

22. McIntosh to John McIntosh, May 20, 1786, Emmet Collection, New York Public Library; McIntosh to John McIntosh, September 23, 1786, in Hawes, *Papers of Lachlan McIntosh*, pp. 143–44.

23. See Harvey H. Jackson, "The Road to the Constitution, 1783–1787: Georgia's First Secession," *Atlanta Historical Bulletin* 20 (Spring 1976): 43–52.

Chapter Fourteen

1. John P. Kaminski, "Controversy amid Consensus: The Adoption of the Federal Constitution in Georgia," *GHQ* 58 (Summer 1974): 244–61; Jackson, "Road to the Constitution," pp. 43–52.

2. McIntosh to Wereat, December 17, 1787, in Hawes, *Papers of Lachlan McIntosh*, pp. 144–46.

3. Ibid., p. 145.

4. Ibid., pp. 145–46.

5. Ibid., p. 146

6. Ibid. Much had changed since 1775, when, flushed with revolutionary ardor, he and the Darien committee had reasoned that if it was wrong for Britain to enslave them, it was equally wrong for Georgians to enslave blacks. But faced with postwar economic difficulties, McIntosh, like so many who earlier felt the tension between ideology and practice, postponed the thought of manumission until prosperity returned. The problem would be left for later generations. See Hawes, *Lachlan McIntosh Papers*, pp. 12–14.

7. *Gazette of the State of Georgia*, February 7, 1788. Journals of the ratifying convention and subsequent state constitutional conventions are in GDAH.

8. McIntosh to John McIntosh, January 9, 1788, in Hawes, *Papers of Lachlan McIntosh*, p. 147; McIntosh to John McIntosh, January 26, 1788, in Emmet Collection, New York Public Library; McIntosh to John McIntosh, September 28, 1788, in McIntosh Papers, Perkins Library; McIntosh's petition to the Assembly, December 31, 1788, in Force Transcripts, Library of Congress.

9. McIntosh to Washington, February 14, 1789, in Washington Papers, Library of Congress.

10. *Georgia Gazette*, August 27, 1789.

11. McIntosh to Samuel Osgood, October 23, 1789, in Etting Collection, Historical Society of Pennsylvania.

12. McIntosh to Washington, February 14, 1789, in Washington Papers, Library of Congress.

13. *Georgia Gazette*, January 28, 1790.

14. Johnston, *Houstouns of Georgia*, p. 154; mayor of Savannah's invitation, May 12, 1791, in Hawes, *Papers of Lachlan McIntosh*, p. 148; *Georgia Gazette*, May 19, 1791, and September 5, 1793.

15. McIntosh to Wereat, June 23, 1791, p. 150, and August 13, 1791, pp. 153–54; Wereat to McIntosh, July 11, 1791, pp. 151–53; in Hawes, *Papers of Lachlan McIntosh*.

16. McIntosh to John McIntosh, January 29, 1788, in Emmet Collection, New York Public Library; *Georgia Gazette*, April 17, 1788, and June 16, 1791.

17. *Georgia Gazette*, May 17, 1792; March 28, 1793; May 9, 1793; November 28, 1793; August 20, 1795.

18. Tax digest for 1793, Chatham County, in GDAH.

19. Ibid.; McIntosh to Francis Courvoisie, May 23, 1791, in Hawes, *Lachlan McIntosh Papers*, p. 77.

20. *Georgia Gazette*, April 10 and 17, 1794; August 5, 1795.

21. McIntosh to Elisha B. Hopkins, February 6, 1797, in Hawes, *Papers of Lachlan McIntosh*, pp. 161–62; John Steele to McIntosh, March 13, 1800, in Hawes, *Lachlan McIntosh Papers*, p. 91.

22. William Bartram to McIntosh, May 31, 1796, in Bartram Papers,

New York Historical Society; *Columbia Museum and Savannah Advertiser*, May 10, 1796; April 25, 1797; March 12, 1799; *Georgia Gazette*, August 30, 1798.

23. *Georgia Gazette*, December 5, 1799; Mary Bondurant Warren, *Marriages and Deaths, 1763–1820*, pp. 41, 54, 64, 71, 123.

24. Warren, *Marriages and Deaths*, p. 120.

25. Ibid., p. 71.

26. McIntosh's will (microfilm copy, GDAH).

Chapter Fifteen

1. American Library Service to Georgia Department of Archives, November 18, 1947, McIntosh file, GDAH.

Bibliography

The following makes no pretense at being a complete bibliography of Georgia's colonial, revolutionary, confederation, and federalist eras. It is simply a compilation of the material that was utilized in this study. Included in the list of secondary works are a few books and articles not cited in the footnotes. Though they were not used directly, they helped explain and clarify certain aspects of the period and their value should be acknowledged.

I. PRIMARY SOURCES

A. *Manuscripts*

Boston Public Library, Boston, Massachusetts
  Benjamin Lincoln Papers
Duke University, Perkins Library, Durham, N.C.
  Habersham Family Papers
  Lachlan McIntosh Papers
  George Walton Papers
  John Wereat Papers
Georgia Department of Archives and History, Atlanta
  Claims books
  Conveyance books
  File of miscellaneous material relating to Lachlan McIntosh
  Journal of the Commissioners for the Convention of Beaufort
  Journal of the Georgia Federal Constitutional Convention
  Journals of the Georgia State Constitutional Conventions, 1788–1789
  Military commissions
  Miscellaneous bonds
  Tax Digest for Chatham County, 1793
  Will of Lachlan McIntosh, microfilm copy
Georgia Historical Society, Savannah
  Joseph Clay Papers
  Joseph Habersham Papers
  John Houstoun Papers
  Noble W. Jones Papers
  Lachlan McIntosh Papers

Historical Society of Pennsylvania, Philadelphia
    Dreer Collection
    Etting Collection
    Gratz Collection
    James Hamilton Papers
    Charles F. Jenkins Collection
    Henry Laurens Papers
Library of Congress, Washington, D.C.
    Peter Force Transcripts of Georgia Records
    George Washington Papers
Massachusetts Historical Society, Boston
    Benjamin Lincoln Papers
National Archives, Washington, D.C.
    Papers of the Continental Congress
    Pension applications
New York Historical Society, New York
    Miscellaneous papers relating to Lachlan McIntosh
New York Public Library, New York
    Emmet Collection
    Ford Collection
    Miscellaneous papers relating to Lachlan McIntosh
Sang Collection (private), Chicago
    George Walton Letter
South Carolina Historical Society, Charleston
    Henry Laurens Papers
Surveyor General Department, State of Georgia, Atlanta
    Colonial Land Grant Records
    Maps relating to colonial, revolutionary, and postwar Georgia
University of Georgia Library, Athens
    Assembly Journals, typescript copy
    Colonial Records of the State of Georgia, 12 vols. (numbered 27
        through 39, edited by Allen D. Candler and Lucian Lamar Knight),
        typescript copy
    Cuyler Collection
    DeRenne Collection
    Executive Council Minutes, typescript copy
    Hargrett Collection
    Letterbooks of Governor George Mathews, typescript copy
    Phillips Collection of the Egmont Manuscripts, 13 vols. (with supple-
        ment), typescript copy
    Read Collection

University of Michigan, Clements Library, Ann Arbor
    Thomas Gage Papers
    Nathanael Green Papers
    Miscellaneous papers relating to Lachlan McIntosh
    Presidential Collection
    Anthony Wayne Papers
University of North Carolina, Chapel Hill
    John M. Berrien Papers

B. Published Primary Sources

Alford, Clarence Walworth, ed. *Illinois Historical Collections*. 32 vols. Springfield: Illinois State Historical Library, 1907–1945.
American State Papers, Indian Affairs. 2 vols. Washington: Gales and Seaton, 1832.
Bryant, Pat, ed. *English Crown Grants for Islands in Georgia, 1755–1775.* Atlanta: The State of Georgia, 1972
––––––. *English Crown Grants in St. Andrew Parish in Georgia, 1755–1775.* Atlanta: The State of Georgia, 1972.
––––––. *English Crown Grants in St. George Parish in Georgia, 1755–1775.* Atlanta: The State of Georgia, 1974.
Burnett, Edmund C., ed. *Letters of Members of the Continental Congress*. 8 vols. Washington: The Carnegie Institute of Washington, 1921–1936.
Candler, Allen D., ed. *The Revolutionary Records of the State of Georgia*. 3 vols. Atlanta: Franklin-Turner Co., 1908.
Candler, Allen D., and Knight, Lucian Lamar, eds. *The Colonial Records of the State of Georgia*. 26 vols. Atlanta: various state printers, 1904–1916.
Coleman, Kenneth, and Ready, Milton L., eds. *The Colonial Records of the State of Georgia*. Vol. 28, pt. 1. Athens: University of Georgia Press, 1976.
––––––.The Colonial Records of the State of Georgia. Vol. 27. Athens: University of Georgia Press, 1978.
Collections of the New York Historical Society. *Charles Lee Papers*. New York Historical Society, 1872.
Coulter, E. Merton, ed. *The Journal of William Stephens, 1741–1743.* Wormsloe Foundation Publications, no. 2. Athens: University of Georgia Press, 1958.
––––––. *The Journal of William Stephens. 1743–1745.* Wormsloe Foundation Publications, no. 3. Athens: University of Georgia Press, 1959.
––––––, and Saye, Albert B., eds. *A List of the Early Settlers of Georgia*. Athens: University of Georgia Press, 1949.

Darlington, Mary Carson. *Fort Pitt and Letters from the Frontier*. Pittsburgh: J. R. Welden and Co., 1892.

Fitzpatrick, John C., ed. *The Writings of George Washington from the Original Manuscript Sources, 1745–1789*. 37 vols. Washington: U.S. Government Printing Office, 1931–1940.

Force, Peter, ed. *American Archives*. 4th series. 6 vols. Washington: M. St. Clair and Peter Force, 1837–1846.

Gibbes, Robert Wilson. *Documentary History of the Revolution, 1764–1776*. New York: D. Appleton and Co., 1856.

Hawes, Lilla M., *Lachlan McIntosh Papers in the University of Georgia Libraries*. University of Georgia Libraries Miscellanea Publications, no. 7. Athens: University of Georgia Press, 1968.

————. *The Papers of Lachlan McIntosh*. Collections of the Georgia Historical Society, vol. 12. Savannah: Georgia Historical Society, 1957.

————. "Proceedings of the President and Assistants in Council of Georgia, 1749–1751," *Georgia Historical Quarterly* 35 (December 1951): 323–50.

Hawes, Lilla M., and Britt, Albert S., Jr. "The Mackenzie Papers," *Georgia Historical Quarterly* 56 (Winter 1972): 535–83, and 57 (Spring 1973): 85–144.

Hazard, Samuel, ed. *Pennsylvania Archives*. 1st series. 12 vols. Philadelphia: Joseph Stephens and Company, 1852–1856.

Hemperley, Marion R. *English Crown Grants in Christ Church Parish in Georgia, 1755–1775*. Atlanta: The State of Georgia, 1973.

————. *English Crown Grants in the Parishes of St. David, St. Patrick, St. Thomas and St. Mary in Georgia, 1755–1775*. Atlanta: The State of Georgia, 1973.

————. *English Crown Grants in St. John Parish in Georgia, 1755–1775*. Atlanta: The State of Georgia, 1972.

————. *English Crown Grants in St. Matthew Parish in Georgia, 1755–1775*. Atlanta: The State of Georgia, 1974.

————. *English Crown Grants in St. Paul Parish in Georgia, 1755–1775*. Atlanta: The State of Georgia, 1974.

————. *English Crown Grants in St. Philip Parish in Georgia, 1755–1775*. Atlanta: The State of Georgia, 1972.

Jones, Charles C., ed. *The Siege of Savannah in 1779 as Described by Two Contemporaneous Journals of French Officers in the Fleet of Count d'Estaing*. Albany, N.Y.: Joel Munsell, 1874.

Kappler, Charles J., ed. *Indian Affairs, Laws and Treaties*. 2 vols. Washington: U.S. Government Printing Office, 1903.

Kellogg, Louise Phelps, ed. *Frontier Advance on the Upper Ohio, 1778–1779*.

Collections of the State Historical Society of Wisconsin, vol. 23. Draper Series, vol. 4. Madison: State Historical Society of Wisconsin, 1916.

Kennedy, Benjamin, ed. and trans. *Muskets, Cannon Balls and Bombs: Nine Narratives of the Siege of Savannah in 1779.* Savannah: Beehive Press, 1974.

[Langworthy, Edward]. *Strictures on a Pamphlet, entitled, The Case of George McIntosh, Esq., Published by Order of the Liberty Society.* Savannah: Lancaster and Mumford, 1777. Clifford K. Shipton, ed. *Early American Imprints, 1639–1800.* New York: Readex Microprint, 1967–1968.

Lanning, John Tate, ed. *The St. Augustine Expedition of 1740: A Report to the South Carolina General Assembly.* Columbia: South Carolina Archives Department, 1954.

"Letter Book of Governor Samuel Elbert, from January, 1785 to November, 1785." *Collections of the Georgia Historical Society,* vol. 5, pt. 2. Savannah: Georgia Historical Society, 1902.

"Letters, Colonial and Revolutionary," *Pennsylvania Magazine of History and Biography* 42 (1918): 77–78.

Letters of Joseph Clay, Merchant of Savannah, 1776–1793. Collections of the Georgia Historical Society, vol. 8. Savannah: Georgia Historical Society, 1913.

McIntosh, Lachlan, and Wereat, John. *An Addition to the Case of George McIntosh, Esquire, Earnestly recommended to the serious Attention of every Reader, particularly those of the State of Georgia* [Savannah]: 1777. Clifford K. Shipton, ed. *Early American Imprints, 1639–1800.* New York: Readex Microprint, 1967–1968.

[McIntosh, Lachlan, and Wereat, John]. *The Case of George McIntosh, Esquire, a Member of the late Council and Convention of the State of Georgia; With the Proceedings thereon in the Hon. the Assembly and Council of that State.* [Savannah]: 1777. Clifford K. Shipton, ed. *Early American Imprints, 1639–1800.* New York: Readex Microprint, 1967–1968

———. *Remarks on a Pamphlet, Entitled "Strictures on a Pamphlet, entitled the Case of George McIntosh . . . " To Which is added, A concise account of the Justice of the Executive and Legislative Bodies of the State of Georgia: Together with Some Account of the Lives and upright Principles of the Leaders of the Nocturnal Junto.* [Savannah]: 1777. Clifford K. Shipton, ed. *Early American Imprints, 1639–1880.* New York: Readex Microprint, 1967–1968.

McPherson, Robert G., ed. *The Journal of the Earl of Egmont.* Athens: University of Georgia Press, 1962.

Moultrie, William. *Memoirs of the American Revolution.* 2 vols. New York: D. Longworth, 1902.

"Muster Roll of the First Continental Georgia Battalion," *Georgia Historical Quarterly* 11 (December 1927): 342–43.

"Muster Roll of the Third Continental Georgia Battalion," *Georgia Historical Quarterly* 12 (March 1928): 103–4.

"Muster Roll of the Fourth Continental Georgia Battalion," *Georgia Historical Quarterly* 12 (September 1928): 197–98.

"Official Letters of Governor Telfair," *Georgia Historical Quarterly* 1 (June 1917): 141–54.

"Order Book of Samuel Elbert, Colonel and Brigadier General in the Continental Army, October, 1776 to November, 1778." *Collections of the Georgia Historical Society*, vol. 5, pt. 2. Savannah: Georgia Historical Society, 1902.

Phillips, Ulrich Bonnell, ed. "Some Letters of Joseph Habersham, 1775 to 1790," *Georgia Historical Quarterly* 10 (June 1926): 145–63.

Reese, Treavor Richard, ed. *The Clamorous Malcontents: Criticism and Defenses of the Colony of Georgia, 1741–1743*. Savannah: Beehive Press, 1973.

Rogers, George C., Hamer, Philip, and Chesnutt, David R., eds. *The Papers of Henry Laurens*. 5 vols. Columbia: University of South Carolina Press, 1968–1976.

Saunders, William L., Clark, Walter, and Weeks, Stephen B., eds. *The State Records of North Carolina*. 20 vols. (vols. 11–30). Raleigh: various state printers, 1895–1914.

The Siege of Savannah by the Combined American and French Forces, under the Command of General Lincoln and the Count d'Estaing in the Autumn of 1779. Albany, N.Y.: J. Munsell, 1866.

Simpson, John Eddins, ed. *The Jones Family Papers: 1760–1810. Collections of the Georgia Historical Society*, vol. 17. Savannah: Georgia Historical Society, 1957.

Sparks, Jared, ed. *Correspondence of the American Revolution Being Letters of Eminent Men to George Washington From the Time of His Taking Command to the End of His Presidency*. 4 vols. Boston: Little, Brown and Co., 1853.

Stacy, James. *History of Midway Congregational Church, Liberty County, Georgia*. Newnan, Ga.: S. W. Murry, 1903.

Uhlendorf, Bernard, ed. and trans. *The Siege of Charleston*. Ann Arbor: University of Michigan Press, 1938.

Van Doren, Mark, ed. *The Travels of William Bartram*. New York: Barnes and Noble, 1940.

Ver Steeg, Clarence L., ed. *A True and Historical Narrative of the Colony of Georgia by Patrick Telfair and Others, with Comments by the Earl of Egmont*. Wormsloe Foundation Publications, no. 4. Athens: University of Georgia Press, 1960.

White, George. *Historical Collections of Georgia*. New York: Pudney and Russel, 1854.

Williams, Edward G., ed. "A Revolutionary Journal and Orderly Book of General Lachlan McIntosh's Expedition, 1778," *Western Pennsylvania Historical Magazine* 44 (March–September 1960): 1–18, 157–84.

C. Newspapers

Columbia Museum and Savannah Advertiser (Savannah)
Georgia Gazette (Savannah)
Gazette of the State of Georgia (Savannah)

II. SECONDARY SOURCES

A. Books

Abbot, W. W. *The Royal Governors of Georgia, 1754–1775.* Chapel Hill: University of North Carolina Press, 1959.

Abernethy, Thomas Perkins. *Western Lands and the American Revolution.* New York: D. Appleton-Century Co., 1937.

Alden, John Richard. *The American Revolution.* New York: Harper and Row, 1954.

Barnhart, John D. *Henry Hamilton and George Rogers Clark in the American Revolution wth the Unpublished Journal of Lieutenant Governor Henry Hamilton.* Crawfordsville, Ind.: R. E. Banta, 1951.

Bausman, Joseph H. *History of Beaver County Pennsylvania and Its Centennial Celebration.* 2 vols. New York: Knickerbocker Press, 1904.

Bill, Alfred Hoyt. *Valley Forge, the Making of an Army.* New York: Harper and Brothers, 1952.

Boorstin, Daniel. *The Americans: The Colonial Experience.* New York: Random House, 1958.

Bulloch, J. G. B. *A History and Geneaology of the Family of Baillie of Dunain, Dochfour, and Lamington. With a Short Sketch of the Family of McIntosh, Bulloch and Other Families.* Green Bay, Wis.: Gazette Print, 1898.

Butterfield, Consul W. *History of the Girtys.* Columbus, O.: Long's College Book Co., 1950.

Cashin, Edward J., Jr., and Robertson, Heard. *Augusta and the American Revolution: Events in the Georgia Back Country, 1773–1783.* Darien, Ga.: Ashantilly Press, 1975.

Caughey, John Walton. *McGillivray of the Creeks.* Norman: University of Oklahoma Press, 1958.

198   BIBLIOGRAPHY

Coleman, Kenneth. *The American Revolution in Georgia*. Athens: University of Georgia Press, 1958.

———. *Colonial Georgia: A History*. New York: Scribners, 1976.

———, ed. *A History of Georgia*. Athens: University of Georgia Press, 1977.

Coulter, E. Merton. *Georgia, a Short History*. Chapel Hill: University of North Carolina Press, 1960.

Davis, Harold E. *The Fledgling Province: Social and Cultural Life in Colonial Georgia, 1733–1776*. Chapel Hill: University of North Carolina Press, 1976.

Downes, Randolph C. *Council Fires on the Upper Ohio*. Pittsburgh: University of Pittsburgh Press, 1940.

Ettinger, Amos Aschbach, *James Edward Oglethorpe, Imperial Idealist*. New York: Clarendon Press, 1936.

Flexner, James Thomas. *George Washington in the American Revolution*. Boston: Little, Brown and Co., 1968.

Foster, William Omer. *James Jackson, Duelist and Militant Stateman, 1757–1806*. Athens: University of Georgia Press, 1960.

Gamble, Thomas. *Savannah Duels and Duellists, 1733–1877*. Savannah: Review Publishing Company, 1923.

Greene, Jack P. *The Quest for Power: The Lower Houses of Assembly in the Southern Royal Colonies, 1689–1776*. Chapel Hill: University of North Carolina Press, 1963.

Hassler, Edgar W. *Old Westmoreland: A History of Western Pennsylvania during the Revolution*. Pittsburgh: J. R. Welden and Co., 1900.

Ivers, Larry E. *British Drums on the Southern Frontier: The Military Colonization of Georgia, 1733–1749*. Chapel Hill: University of North Carolina Press, 1974.

Jenkins, Charles F. *Button Gwinnett*. New York: Doubleday, Page and Co., 1926.

Jensen, Merrill. *The Articles of Confederation: An Interpretation of the Social-Constitutional History of the American Revolution, 1774–1781*. Madison: University of Wisconsin Press, 1940.

Johnston, Edith Duncan. *The Houstouns of Georgia*. Athens: University of Georgia Press, 1950.

Jones, Charles C. *Biographical Sketches of the Delegates from Georgia to the Continental Congress*. Boston: Houghton Mifflin, 1891.

———. *The History of Georgia*. 2 vols. Boston: Houghton Mifflin, 1883.

Lanning, John Tate. *The Diplomatic History of Georgia: A Study of the Epoch of Jenkins' Ear*. Chapel Hill: University of North Carolina Press, 1936.

Lawrence, Alexander A. *Storm Over Savannah*. Athens: University of Georgia Press, 1951.

Lucas, Silas Emmitt. *Index to the Headright and Bounty Grants in Georgia,* *1756–1909.* Vidalia, Ga.: Georgia Genealogical Reprints, 1970.

McCain, James Ross. *Georgia as a Proprietary Province.* Boston: Richard G. Badger, 1917.

Mohr, Walter H. *Federal Indian Relations.* New York: AMS Press, 1933.

Mowat, Charles L. *East Florida as a British Province, 1763–1784.* Berkeley: University of California Press, 1943.

O'Donnell, James H., III. *Southern Indians in the American Revolution.* Knoxville: University of Tennessee Press, 1973.

Palmer, Dave Richard. *The Way of the Fox: American Strategy in the War for America, 1775–1783.* Wesport, Conn.: Greenwood Press, 1975.

Phillipps, Ulrich Bonnell. *Georgia and States Rights.* Washington: American Historical Society, 1902.

Pieper, Thomas I., and Gidney, James B. *Fort Laurens, 1778–1779: The Revolutionary War in Ohio.* Kent, O.: Kent State University Press, 1976.

Pound, Merritt B. *Benjamin Hawkins: Indian Agent.* Athens: University of Georgia Press, 1951.

Rankin, Hugh F. *The North Carolina Continentals.* Chapel Hill: University of North Carolina Press, 1971.

Ready, Milton. *The Castle Builders: Georgia's Economy under the Trustees, 1732–1754.* New York: Arno Press, 1978

Reed, John Frederick. *Campaign to Valley Forge.* Philadelphia: University of Pennsylvania Press, 1965.

Reese, Trevor Richard. *Colonial Georgia: A Study in British Imperial Policy in the Eighteenth Century.* Athens: University of Georgia Press, 1963.

Savelle, Max. *George Morgan, Colony Builder.* New York: AMS Press, 1967.

Sosin, Jack M. *The Revolutionary Frontier, 1763–1783.* Albuquerque: University of New Mexico Press, 1961.

Spalding, Phinizy. *Oglethorpe in America.* Chicago: University of Chicago Press, 1977.

Taylor, Paul S. *The Georgia Plan.* Berkeley: The Regents of the University of California, 1972.

Temple, Sarah B. Gober, and Coleman, Kenneth. *Georgia Journeys.* Athens: University of Georgia Press, 1961.

Ver Steeg, Clarence L. *Origins of a Southern Mosaic: Studies of Early Carolina and Georgia.* Athens: University of Georgia Press, 1975.

Wallace, David Duncan. *The Life of Henry Laurens.* New York: G. P. Putnam's Sons, 1915.

Ward, Christopher. *The War of the Revolution.* 2 vols. New York: Macmillan, 1952.

Warren, Mary Bondurant. *Marriages and Deaths, 1763–1820, Abstracted from Extant Georgia Newspapers.* Danielsville, Ga.: Heritage Press, 1968.

Wood, Gorden S. *The Creation of the American Republic, 1776–1787.* Chapel Hill: University of North Carolina Press, 1969.

Wright, J. Leitch, Jr. *Florida in the American Revolution..* Gainesville: University Presses of Florida, 1975.

B. Articles and Periodicals

Abbot, W. W. "The Structure of Politics in Georgia, 1782–1789," *William and Mary Quarterly,* 3d series, 14 (1957): 47–65.

Appel, John C. "Colonel Brodhead and the Lure of Detroit," *Pennsylvania History* 38 (July 1971): 265–82.

Appleby, Joyce. "Liberalism and the American Revolution," *New England Quarterly* 49 (March 1976): 3–26.

Bailyn, Bernard. "The Central Themes of the American Revolution: An Interpretation," in *Essays on the American Revolution.* Edited by Stephen G. Kurtz and James H. Hutson. Chapel Hill: University of North Carolina Press, 1973.

Bushnell, David I. "The Virginia Frontier in History, 1778," *Virginia Magazine of History and Biography* 23 (1915): 113–23, 256–68, 337–51, and 24 (1916): 44–55, 168–79.

Cashin, Edward J. "Augusta's Revolution of 1779," *Richmond County History* 8 (Summer 1975): 5–13.

————. "'The Famous Colonel Wells': Factionalism in Revolutionary Georgia," *Georgia Historical Quarterly* 58 (Supplement, 1974): 137–56.

Chesnutt, David R. "South Carolina's Penetration of Georgia in the 1760's: Henry Laurens, A Case Study," *South Carolina Historical Magazine* 73 (October 1972): 194–208.

————. "George Walton and the Forged Letter," *Georgia Historical Quarterly* 62 (Summer 1978): 133–45.

Coleman, Kenneth. "Federal Indian Relations in the South, 1781–1789," *Chronicles of Oklahoma* 35 (Winter 1957–1958), 435–58.

————. "James Wright," in *Georgians in Profile: Historical Essays in Honor of Ellis Merton Coulter.* Edited by Horace Montgomery. Athens: University of Georgia Press, 1958. Pp. 40–60.

————. "Restored Colonial Georgia, 1779–1782," *Georgia Historical Quarterly* 40 (March 1956): 1–20.

————. "The Southern Frontier: Georgia's Founding and Expansion of South Carolina," *Georgia Historical Quarterly,* 56 (Summer 1972): 163–74.

Davis, Harold E. "The Scissors Thesis, or, Frustrated Expectations as a

Cause of the Revolution in Georgia," *Georgia Historical Quarterly* 61 (Fall 1977): 246–257.

Downes, Randolph C. "Creek–American Relations, 1782–1790," *Georgia Historical Quarterly* 21 (June 1937): 142–48.

Flippin, Percy Scott. "Royal Government in Georgia, 1752–1776: The Land System," *Georgia Historical Quarterly* 10 (March 1926): 1–25.

Gordon, William W. "Count Casimir Pulaski," *Georgia Historical Quarterly* 13 (October 1929): 171–227.

Greene, Jack P. "An Uneasy Connection: An Analysis of the Preconditions of the American Revolution," in *Essays on the American Revolution*. Edited by Stephen G. Kurtz and James H. Hutson. Chapel Hill: University of North Carolina Press, 1973.

Higginbotham, Don. "Military Leadership in the American Revolution," in *Leadership in the American Revolution*. Washington: Library of Congress, 1974.

Hitz, Alex M. "Georgia Bounty Land Grants," *Georgia Historical Quarterly*, 38 (December 1954): 337–48.

Hoffman, Ronald, "The 'Disaffected' in the Revolutionary South," in *The American Revolution: Explorations in the History of American Radicalism*. Edited by Alfred F. Young. DeKalb, Ill.: Northern Illinois University Press, 1976.

Jackson, Harvey H. "Consensus and Conflict: Factional Politics in Revolutionary Georgia, 1775–1777," *Georgia Historical Quarterly* 59 (Winter 1975): 338–401.

———. "The Battle of the Riceboats: Georgia Joins the Revolution," *Georgia Historical Quarterly* 58 (Summer 1974): 229–43.

———. "The Darien Antislavery Petition of 1739 and the Georgia Plan," *William and Mary Quarterly*, 3d series, 34 (1977); 618–31.

———. "The Road to the Constitution, 1783–1787: Georgia's First Secession," *Atlanta Historical Bulletin* 20 (Spring 1976): 43–52.

Jordan, John W. "Hospitals at Bethlehem and Letitz during the Revolution," *Pennsylvania Magazine of History and Biography* 20, no. 2 (1896): 137–57.

Kaminski, John P. "Controversy amid Consensus: Adoption of the Federal Constitution in Georgia," *Georgia Historical Quarterly* 58 (Summer 1974): 244–61.

Lambert, Robert S. "The Confiscation of Loyalist Property in Georgia, 1782–1786," *William and Mary Quarterly*, 3d series, 20 (1963): 80–94.

Lamplugh, George R. "Farewell to the Revolution," *Georgia Historical Quarterly* 56 (Fall 1972): 387–403.

————. "'To check and discourage the Wicked and Designing': John Wereat and the Revolution in Georgia," *Georgia Historical Quarterly* 61 (Winter 1977): 295–307.

Lawrence, Alexander A. "General Lachlan McIntosh and His Suspension from the Continental Command during the Revolution," *Georgia Historical Quarterly* 38 (June 1954): 101–41.

Lewis, Bessie Mary. "Darien, a Symbol of Defiance and Achievement," *Georgia Historical Quarterly* 20 (September 1936): 185–98.

Naiswald, L. Van Loon. "Major General Howe's Activities in South Carolina and Georgia, 1776–1779," *Georgia Historical Quarterly* 35 (March 1951): 23–30.

Spalding, Thomas. "Lachlan McIntosh," in vol. 3 of *The National Portrait Gallery of Distinguished Americans*. Edited by James B. Longacre and James Herring. Philadelphia: Henry Perkins, 1836.

Williams, Edward G. "Fort Pitt and the Revolution on the Western Frontier," *Western Pennsylvania Historical Magazine* 59 (January, April, July, October 1976): 1–37, 129–52, 251–87, 379–444.

C. Unpublished Material

Grant, James M. "Legislative Factions in Georgia, 1754–1798: A Socio-Political Study" (Ph.D. dissertation, University of Georgia, 1975).

Lamplugh, George R. "Politics on the Periphery: Factions and Parties in Georgia, 1776–1806" (Ph.D. dissertation, Emory University, 1973).

Index

also Popular party; Whigs, radical

Whig factionalism, 21–22, 102–3

Whigs, 21, 25, 26, 27, 35, 36, 95–96

Whigs, conservative: defined, 21–22; block delegates to Congress, 24; call Provincial Congress, 25; in Provincial Congress and Assembly, 26; join with radicals, 26; in 2nd Provincial Congress, 27; nominate Elbert, 29; officers in battalion 33; reestablish leadership, 51–52; in election of *1776*, 52–53; McIntosh joins, 53–55; unable to defend McIntosh, 67; comeback in *1779*, 113. *See also* Christ Church parish, Christ Church coalition

Whigs, radical: defined, 23; propose delegates to Congress, 23–24; oppose Provincial Congress, 25–26; join conservatives, 26; nominate

Gwinnett, 29; in Georgia battalion, 33; oppose Rules and Regulations of *1776*, 51–52; election of *1776*, 52–53; attempt to take over military, 54–55, 61; attack McIntosh, 58, 66–67; in Walton's Assembly, 103, 115–17; role in creation of popular party, 112. *See also* Popular party, St. John's parish, Western members

White Eyes, Delaware Chief, 79, 80

Wood, Joseph, 66, 67

Wright, Gov. Sir James, 16, 21–22; attitude toward his office, 11–12, prorogues Commons, 26; arrest and parole, 29, 35; leaves Georgia, 39; returns, 97

Wright, Jermyn, 42–43

Wright's fort, 43

Wyoming Valley, 77

York, Pa., 76, 77

THE AUTHOR

Harvey H. Jackson is associate professor of history and chair-
man of the social sciences division at Clayton Junior College.
His articles have appeared in the *William and Mary Quarterly*,
Georgia Historical Quarterly, and *Atlanta Historical Journal*.